T0345851

Islam, Ethnicity, and Power Politics

Islam, Ethnicity, and Power Politics

Constructing Pakistan's National Identity

Rasul Bakhsh Rais

OXFORD
UNIVERSITY PRESS

OXFORD
UNIVERSITY PRESS

Oxford University Press is a department of the University of Oxford.
It furthers the University's objective of excellence in research, scholarship,
and education by publishing worldwide. Oxford is a registered trade mark of
Oxford University Press in the UK and in certain other countries

Published in Pakistan by
Ameena Saiyid, Oxford University Press
No.38, Sector 15, Korangi Industrial Area,
PO Box 8214, Karachi-74900, Pakistan

ISBN 978-0-19-940759-0

Typeset in Adobe Garamond Pro
Printed on 70gsm Offset Paper

Printed by Le Topical Pvt. Ltd, Lahore

Contents

v

Dedicated to my father, Haji Gaman,
who taught me self-reliance, resilience, and
the value of hard work.

Preface

Pakistan is a society of multiple identities which have been shaped by family lineage, caste, tribe, language, region, sect, religion, and a variety of conflictive nationalisms. A Pakistani individual comfortably navigates his/her identity in everyday life at a local, regional, or national level, depending on the context of his/her interaction with other members of society. Historically, well before the birth of modern day political nationalism—the Pakistan Movement and winning freedom on the basis of the two-nation theory—people had been defining themselves in terms of local, social structures of caste, tribe, and village. The question of multiple identities therefore stems from narrow, geographically-bounded, social structures. Even in communities where people have lived together for hundreds of years, they continue to identify themselves as members of a particular caste or tribe. The reason for slow changes in parochial, primordial identities is a segmentary family structure, pride in one's caste, and a reluctance to accept other castes as social equals. The forces of modernity, urbanization, and expansion of education have softened the rigid caste and tribal boundaries through intermarriages. We are witnessing social integration among castes and tribes but without a change in essential social character as the marker of primary identity.

The diverse linguistic and ethnic regions that comprise Pakistan present a rich cultural and social mosaic. The people belonging to these regions have a strong sense of ownership with regards to their cultures, histories, and heritage. The question of identity then becomes one of the fundamental precepts of social inquiry—who you are, where you come from, and the caste or tribe you belong to. In the traditional sense, identity is a social and cultural issue: about belonging to a social category, and about social differentiation as a member of a clan. The clannish affiliations are exclusionary and run deep due to the rigid nature of the caste system.

The social and political movements in the subcontinent introduced Muslim nationalism, ethnicity, and ideology as the new markers of identity. The Islamic revivalist movements as one of the responses to the decline of Muslim rule and the advent of British colonialism, pulled Islam out of the private to the public, collective, and political sphere, competing with other ideas about Muslim empowerment, national liberation, and post-independence political reconstruction. The issue of political identity acquired primary significance in the context of the demand for a separate homeland, the idea of Muslim nationalism becoming the driving rationale behind this movement. The leaders of the Pakistan movement found in Islam a powerful and emotive political tool to express Muslim aspirations for a separate homeland. While India had the advantage of its historically rooted identity as 'Bharat', 'Hindustan', and 'India', the new state of Pakistan had to reconstruct its identity. It had become a structural necessity in the new Muslim state's old geographical zones, and one which had to simultaneously maintain the integrity of their essential historical character. Since the idea of separatism thrived on the rhetoric of Muslim nationalism in Muslim majority areas, the two-nation theory emerged as a convenient tool of identity-making of the new state. I have argued that while the two-nation theory served its objective of achieving an independent Pakistan, its utility in forging national integration, unity, and solidarity among diverse regions of the country could merely be symbolic.

The management of ethnic diversity required its recognition

and accommodation through representation and autonomy, not its rejection as a problem labelled 'provincialism'. The idealistic nature of the concept of Pakistan left the central authorities oblivious to the ground realities of ethnic diversity. They regarded diversity as a threat, and demands resting on it as hostile to their idea of Muslim nationalism. As opposed to the cohesiveness of Islamic identity, ethnicity was seen as divisive, and one that would run counter to their idea of constructing an Islamic nation-state. Our view is that postcolonial states are primarily political constructions, inclusive of diverse communities with particular identities and political interests. Therefore, seeking homogeneity by replicating the European framework of cultural nationalism would be a futile exercise, because indigenous cultures have evolved over hundreds of years and they are woven into the social fabric of the society. The alternative lies in acclaiming diversity as a collective heritage of the nation and in recognizing regional social groups, their languages, cultures, and identities. Contrarily, those responsible for state and nation-building in Pakistan used Islam, a common religion of the majority, and Urdu language as the basis of developing a national culture, national identity, and nationhood. As a result of such policies, minority ethnic groups have found themselves ignored and marginalized. With cultural policies and the identity frame-of-reference being imposed by the centre, they have felt more subjects than equal participants in the making of state and nation.

I have taken a constructivist view of identity formation. Our argument is that national identity is constructed by the dominant elites in multiple spheres of culture, politics, economy, literature, and education. Not all of them, in any case, can, or would, exercise equal influence in shaping national identity, as they have varying capacities, constituencies, and instrumentalities. Nor can they have unanimity on the identity of a nation. The elite contestation in Pakistan has made the issue of identity one of the most contested ones. Four powerful forces continue to influence identity construction: political Islam; liberal, moderate sections of the society; the military; and ethnic groups. Each template of identity is linked to their ideal of Pakistan—an Islamic state; a republican, democratic state; a praetorian, security state; and new federalism, favouring devolution of greater power and resources to the units. As a result of power struggles among these actors, the last seventy years of Pakistan's identity, state, and nation-building processes reflect contradictory tendencies.

Contrary to the conventional view, my opinion is that multiple identities do not inherently clash with the idea of a nation-state if we give space and recognition to each identity—ethnic, regional, national, religious, and secular. These identities represent and correspond with the cultural and ethnic pluralism that prevails in Pakistan. The fact is that all of these identities have co-existed for centuries and cannot be easily eliminated to create a national identity. We question the very concept of singular national identity as politically desirable or a doable project. Rather I take the view that identities, though constructed through the agency of politics, must have some historical reference and must manifest the cultural ethos and political interests of the people. Since cultures and politics, the two powerful forces that shape identity are dynamic processes, dependent on modernization, economic development, and social change, the identity issue should remain fluid and somewhat unsettled. Identities, like cultures, have path-dependency, and will change with the emergence of new economies, social change, technology, and industrialization.

Pakistan is witnessing major transformations, like democratic politics, urbanization, the rise of media, and an emerging, large, middle-class with social and economic mobility. The society, diverse as it is, is experiencing evolutionary pluralism, which is the acceptance of diversity as a social, political, and historical fact. The societal forces at large feel more comfortable with multiculturalism than state-sponsored attempts to change it through imposed policies and ideological templates—the traditional instruments that have failed. Will that end national identity as a central issue or the contestation over it? Perhaps not. The forces and actors that have remained engaged in this struggle will continue to do so because of the diverse political constituencies and power centres that they represent. This work is a modest effort to explain the question of identity and the role political Islam and state, and ethnic and political groups have played in shaping it. I hope this effort will contribute to the quality of academic as well as policy discourse on national identity.

Acknowledgements

In writing this book, I have greatly benefitted from the Lahore University of Management Sciences (LUMS) that provided me true freedom, openness, and an academic environment conducive for writing and research. My colleagues and students, striving for excellence, have been a source of inspiration and encouragement for me. I have found their brilliance and enthusiasm for learning motivating. I am immensely indebted to all of them. I want to particularly acknowledge the Humanities and Social Sciences Department for providing me the research grant for hiring a research assistant. I wish to express my deep gratitude to the Higher Education Commission of Pakistan for providing me research funds as a Distinguished National Professor over the past two years that I have used for hiring research assistants. I would like to thank my research assistants, Anam Husain, Rabiyya Kamal, and Anam Fatima for helping with the research and writing of this book. Amber F. Riaz has done a great job on copyediting the book and cleaning the text page by page. I cannot thank her enough.

I have greatly benefitted from my discussions with Professor M. Rafique Afzal, my friend and colleague at the Quaid-i-Azam University. He has been very generous with his time and sharing his views. I cannot thank him enough. I owe a special thanks to the Oxford University Press, particularly to Ameena Saiyid, Nadia Ghani, and Soha Tanwir Khan for giving me the contract for this work and bringing it out to the public. It would have been impossible to write, let alone complete this book on time, without their encouragement, support, and polite reminders. I am very grateful to them.

Rasul Bakhsh Rais
Humanities and Social Sciences Department
Lahore University of Management Sciences, Lahore
3 April 2017

Chapter I

Introduction: The Politics of Identity

The objective of this chapter is to explore how social forces, ethnic groups, political elites, and religious factions have attempted to influence identity construction, and why identity has become a contested issue. The subject of identity in Pakistan and in other societies is instrumental primarily because it is directly associated with the question of power. Each identity group promotes a different vision of the state and nation in an attempt to establish its own claim to power in the structure of the state or in order to challenge the power of other dominant groups. Therefore, the search for national identity not only becomes conflict-ridden but also elusive if the elites representing different ethnicities, social groups, and political parties fail to negotiate and reach a compromise on a common vision of the nation-state, and the collective as well as individual selves. The problem can be further compounded when a secular idea of ethnic identities demanding recognition of regional cultures, languages, autonomy, and rights is interpreted by the dominant elites as conflicting with Islam. The history of Pakistan itself is a strong case to argue that using religion as a unifying factor or creating social solidarity around it is a convenient force yet not a sufficient one when it comes to the multi-ethnic society that is Pakistan.

Constructing Identities

Social groups throughout the world have used history, culture, language, geography, race, and/or religion to construct their ethnic, national, and identity narratives. First, identity formation as a political enterprise is a dynamic process, no matter which narrative and constitutive elements social or national groups and elites use. Being dynamic means that it is subject to change, transformation, passivity, and activism, depending on how satisfied or dissatisfied a particular group is with the national distribution of power. Here, we define national power in the broadest of terms, as socio-cultural, economic, and political. The process of modernization, particularly economic and social development, acts both as an integrative force as well as a factor in giving salience to identity and ethnicity of some groups. Much would depend on the outcome of modernization, whether or not its effects are equitably distributed and so understood and perceived by constituent groups. Much of the ethnic alienation in Pakistan and other countries is due to distributive effects, as marginalization and mainstreaming of various groups work as two parallel processes. The fact is that not all composite national groups have undertaken a national journey together; their trajectories have been at odds with an uneven endowment of resources and capabilities like education, skills, level of development, and presence in the power structure of the new state. The old and well-entrenched power groups attempted to retain power and those competing with them were left frustrated due to their high expectation(s) from a new political framework. The feeling of having been left out was then used as an instrument of promoting ethnic consciousness. The case of Baloch ethnicity is illustrative of this.

The privileged social groups that once dominated state power and contributed to the development of a national narrative of identity, like *Pakistaniat* and centralization, have fallen back upon ethnic particularism to prevent their decline and claim domination at a local level using the geographical density of their group.[1] We will address this point further when we examine the case of Mohajir identity in

Karachi, Sindh. The fear of losing power among the immigrants from India as other competing social groups climbed up the social and political ladder was one of the major factors behind Mohajir ethnicization. It shows how a social group, historically committed to the idea of Pakistan and Pakistani nationhood, used ethnicity for social and political mobilization of the group to stake a claim to power in Karachi and greater representation in the Sindh and national assemblies of Pakistan.[2] So identities can change across time and space, depending on the incentives or disincentives major social and political actors in the national politics may perceive for their reference group.

Second, identities are layered and contextualized. Individuals, as well as social groups, carry multiple identities. It is more so in countries like India and Pakistan. No single identity can explain any Pakistani group today. Even in the largest province, the Punjab, where people generally speak the Punjabi language and identify themselves with the land of the five rivers (Punjab), their Punjabi identity slices into religious sects, castes, sub-castes, tribes, and other linguistic groups like Baloch and Seraiki. Nor do we see any ethnic or even linguistic coherence in other provinces of Pakistan. Balochistan is not all Baloch. This vast province, rich in natural resources but sparsely populated, is home to Pashtuns, Baloch, Sindhi, and Brahavi social groups. These groups are further fragmented into tribes, sub-tribes, and clans. Sindh, Khyber Pakhtunkhwa, and Gilgit-Baltistan have ethnic mixes of their own. Narrow social solidarities and sub-group formation is so common that all provincial spaces have become competitive arenas in the face of scarce resources. With the weakening of political parties and their fragmentation by military regimes, social group solidarity has replaced political parties. Not that the political parties don't have a following; they do have loyal constituency and party identities, but these are weak, and are often negotiated and balanced against narrow social identities.

Third, the issue of layered identities raises an important question: which identity becomes salient, visible, and more defining than others and why? As we discussed briefly, identity is related to the question of power, particularly its mobilizing political effects. Therefore, access to power structures affect which identity strain takes precedence in identity formation. Moreover, social and economic incentives also serve as significant determinants of adoption or suppression of one or another layer of identity. Adoption of a new language, religious sect, or locality are usually driven less by ambiguous emotional content and more by material urges to improve one's condition, status, or the achievement of social and economic mobility. Almost in every geographical region of Pakistan, the new minority groups have, after migrating from adjacent regions, adopted local languages, if not as first, then as the second language. But this depends on the time factor as well as the incentive structure—how long it takes immigrant groups to become localized depends on the ease of the process and what they expect to gain by renouncing their ancestral language. All indigenous migrant groups have changed their language and identities. There are Baloch in many parts of Sindh; Sindhis in the Seraiki region of the Punjab; Baloch in the Punjab; and Pashtuns in the adjoining Punjab districts. Some tribes and sub-tribes among all these groups have retained their language, traditions, and identity, depending on their geographical location. The closer they are to their historical homeland, the greater the propensity to retain older identities; if they are deeper in the mix of new populations, they tend to adopt newer ones. Practical convenience of the language of the market, disincentives for being a small minority and positive gains of merging with the larger cultural whole are some of the reasons for these shifts.[3] But these shifts have taken centuries and they are largely confined to the language and geographical identities. Never have they erased altogether, the original ethnic base of the interprovincial migrant groups. For instance, the Baloch in Sindh and Punjab may have adopted Sindhi, Seraiki, or the Punjabi language but their Baloch identity remains a dense layer in their identity formation in more than one form—through customs, tribal affiliation, and heritage.

This shifting of language and identity, however, is problematic in the case of post-independence internal migrant groups as well as external migrants from India and Afghanistan. The Indian immigrants, now adopting the Mohajir (which literally translates to 'immigrant') identity, have a strong incentive to retain their language, culture, and traditions for two reasons. One, their language, Urdu, has been adopted as the national language of the country. The literary tradition of this language is spatial and historical and its influence on the construction of Muslim identity is so deep that the Urdu mother-tongue group, the Mohajir(s), have every incentive to retain it as their own because they had a stronger identification with the national language.[4] Second, they have used migration as a motif to construct the Mohajir identity such that it amalgamates a large variety of social groups coming from different regions of India but with a few common strands, including that of suffering through Partition and its violence, and carrying the dream of a new Muslim homeland.

Fourth, in ethnically pluralistic societies, the choice of one or more than one competing identities from a possible collection is an outcome of the social interaction between the carriers of these identities. How members of a group or many groups in one space and time relate to one another is a definitive factor in which identities are chosen from a competing pool. The process of identity formation, shifts, and the use of identity as a social and political marker is largely shaped by social interaction. In places where the ethnic groups compete for power, political space, and resources, the interaction can be violent in the absence of strong political institutions. The case of Karachi witnessing perpetual bloodshed for decades now demonstrates this.[5] Political violence in Karachi is not confined to the linguistic identities of the social groups anymore. Religious and sectarian identities have provided some of the groups with a powerful tool to organize themselves and link up with similar groups in other parts of the country.[6] In a socially fragmented society like Pakistan, narrow identities become an instrument of empowerment and security. There is fierce competition over resources, social spaces, and politics here, and in some other places in Pakistan. Competition forces social groups to seek security from narrow social solidarities because the state fails to provide it. In the previous decades, even the mainstream political parties failed to transcend these narrow social boundaries in their choices of candidates for the electoral contests. Nothing reflects the narrow social identities more than the electoral behaviour in the rural and tribal constituencies of the country. Some of the national political parties like the PML-N, PTI, and PPP have nationwide constituencies and have made some progress towards creating political communities based on larger, inclusive, and common political programmes. Positive as some of these developments in recent decades have been, they haven't blurred narrow-based social identities of caste and tribe that remain the essential social moorings of individuals and groups.

Depending on the political climate of the time, the kind of regime, and the character of politics, interactions among diverse social groups can be positive for society as well the polity. When social groups cooperate, while promoting their own interests, they create common political channels of communication and then begin to subscribe to values of progress and positive social change around shared interests. Most of the nation-building process rests on this positive aspect of interaction among groups. Overall, the Pakistani political landscape presents a mixed picture of social interaction. There is differentiation and disagreement among social groups but there is also the emergence of social and political movements on a national scale, with a common vision for the nation and the state. Several democratic movements, mostly against the military regimes, and for the independence of judiciary, emancipation of media, and development of national civil society, represent a different kind of interaction that has often transcended narrower social identities. The democratic process itself has necessitated inter-elite consociation, electoral alliances, and coalition building. This has created common stakes in a parliamentary, federal, and democratic Pakistan.

Fifth, the actors and forces that shape both ethnic as well national identities, possess means and capacities that are disproportionately distributed among them. Political entrepreneurs, civil society activists, media persons, and notably public intellectuals, all contribute to the identity formation process through ideas, arguments, and the selective use of symbols and discourses. But not all of them have the same influence. Some occupy a more privileged position in the social and political order, while others find themselves struggling on the margins. Some actors have more access to the population; others have greater credibility or more effective channels of transmitting ideas. If we rank them roughly in terms of the strengths, capacities, and effectiveness, those perched in the upper echelons of state power—the military, and political elites of mainstream political parties—have contributed to a sense of *Pakistaniat*, or Pakistani nationalism. They have greater incentives for doing so, and have hugely benefitted from discourse, ideas, and policy choices that promote Pakistani nationalism. We turn to them later in the chapter. The challenge to this mainstream national identity has come from ethnic groups and religious political parties. Though dialectically opposite, these two groups do challenge the mainstream vision of national identity. One does so on the grounds of ethnic particularism, and the other on a religious basis. But their challenge is not the negation of Pakistani nationhood, but about how it should be structured, what it should look like, and how they can contribute towards its shaping and understanding.

One of the failures of Pakistan in its early years was coming to grips with the idea of accommodating multiple and diverse ethnic identities, and giving fair representation and an equitable distribution of resources to its federating units, which in turn became a major failure in building a pluralistic, democratic Pakistan. A misconceived and over-emphasized notion of Islam as a common bond during Partition blinded the rulers from ethnic particularities of different regions, which caused a major conflict between the two wings of the country in the years that followed. East Pakistan became Bangladesh following a military crackdown, civil war, and Indian military intervention in 1971.[7]

Historically speaking, Islamic identity and its usage in Pakistan is important both as an animated, core idea in the independence movement, as well as a widely contested subject in the post-independence decades. As we go along, we will explore the reasons why identity politics is one of the most complex and a continuing issue in Pakistan. At the outset, identity construction must be viewed as a means of securing a claim to power or empowerment. As a process, it is about choosing a trajectory of social, political reconstruction in accordance with a group's view of history, heritage, culture, ideas, and ideals woven into the fabric of the society. Identity construction involves all shades of socio-political activity and instruments of politics. It seeks to shape a nation and define its constitutive elements—a process of self-recognition, self-reorganization, and self-definition that many post-colonial states have gone through after gaining independence.[8] A nation's search for identity places the total colonial experience, from ideas to institutions, in sharp relief against a pre-colonial (real or imagined) past and the new ideals and beliefs held by the postcolonial power groups. These groups are entrenched within the structure of the state or state elites, political party factions, and ethnic and religious groups. In Pakistan, as in many other countries, there is also a serious questioning of some of the colonial heritage, particularly, law, educational design, and general outlook of the state formed under the British influence.[9]

There is no easy way to approach the identity issue of Pakistan or the political strategies of different social and political groups in Pakistan with regards to this particular issue. The reason why these issues are so contested and complex is that the idea of Pakistan seems to be wrapped in many social and historical layers. Among these layers are thousands of years of ethnic, religious, and linguistic pluralism within a broader Indian subcontinental context. In this mix, we must include, a strong overlay of colonial heritage that includes political institutions, democratic ideas and traditions, and the shaping of Muslim national identity in contrast to Indian nationalism.[10] An independent Pakistan inherited many of these pluralistic, multicultural communities—a reflection of the grand civilizational mix of the subcontinent. The nation and state builders in Pakistan have tragically ignored the composite character of the Pakistan's populace where multiple ethnicities are present and that entails the presence of strong pluralistic sub-identities. Because of ignorance or wilful deviation, the leaders of Pakistan, generation after generation, have placed the idea of Islam as the basis of Pakistani nationhood above the facts of history and social realities of constituent regions of the country. The quest for Islamic identity has overshadowed these pluralistic social and ethnic communal identities that had existed long before the Muslim reformers stumbled on the idea of a separate Muslim state with a common Muslim interest in mind. In this context therefore it was quite natural that the dream and ideal of Pakistan became a contested issue after these multiple ethnic groups procured the country.[11]

The issue of identity became intertwined with the larger question of political power. In this respect, most of the debates in Pakistan about the constitution, distribution of power, structure of the state, law, Islam, and secularism reflect conflictive visions of identity that many contestants in the power matrix of Pakistan have presented. At least three groupings of social and political contestants that have wanted to draw their own meanings about the purposes of Pakistan and shape its identity and future development have attempted to influence the nation-building process.

For the sake of analytical convenience, these groups can be categorized broadly as Pakistani nationalists, regionalists, and Islamists. The regionalist parties and their ideologies essentially have a secular character. On the question of neutrality of the state in religious matters, they are closer to the independence-era Pakistani nationalists. They, however, differ from them on the issue of identity construction essentially on the basis of religion, which many regionalists believe is a ruse for denying them true empowerment and rights over their resources.[12] The regionalists emphasize linguistic and ethnic particularism and partake in the idea of Pakistani nationhood but with a big qualifier: they maintain that a nationhood that is ethnically composite must respect the cultural rights of the composite regions and structure the constitution and national polity according to true federalist principles.

The Centralist Elite

Creating a nation out of diverse ethnic pluralities that have strong regional identities is, and has been, a difficult political enterprise mainly because the centralist political elites of Pakistani nationalists misunderstood or misinterpreted the social basis of allegiance of provincial people to Pakistan. For the centralists, it was Islam and its common cultural and civilizational foundations that bound the diverse ethnic groups to Pakistan. This is a theme that has been so dangerously overplayed over the past six decades that it has resulted in the alienation of some ethnic groups, like the Baloch and Sindhis, who have found themselves on the margins of power and privilege, both perceptually and objectively.[13]

For the regionalists—the social and political activists who use ethnicity for demanding regional rights—there could be no Pakistan without them being in its fold, and they insist they did so in their own interest for a better future, hoping for a fair distribution of power and resources, and an equitable role in defining and executing the idea of Pakistan. Since the composite territorial units have their own identities, histories, and regional aspirations, they wanted a comfortable balance between their regional interests and the construction of the Pakistani state—a state consisting of old historical regions but with a new name, title, and place in the postcolonial geopolitical setting of South Asia. Religion, from their standpoint, could only be one of the layers, though thin, that could bind them together. In the end, in any form of politics, the issue of power will be central, with a major question being what the stakeholders will get out of it. What was, and still is, important is the favorable balance of provincial interests that the regionalists have been striving to negotiate, even launching political movements, both peaceful and violent, to get the point across in Islamabad. Their reference point is the Pakistan Resolution of 1940 that set the idea of Pakistan rolling. Their interpretation of this landmark event in the history of Muslim India is not unitary but that of a federated vision with greater rights for the provinces. In discussing these conflictive visions of ethnicity, cultural streams, and Islam shaping a layered identity of Pakistan, we will use some of the literature on nationalism and identity and pull evidence from the history of Pakistan.

Let us first discuss the national identity choices and approaches of the Pakistani nationalists. In this respect, we wish to examine the factors that really contribute towards progress in nation-building, the identity choices the Pakistan ruling groups have made, and what their relative success is.

As mentioned above, the nation-state is a Western political form, the result of a 'competitive enterprise of war and politics'.[14] Thousands of rival authorities were eliminated or subordinated before the emerging state succeeded in expanding the boundaries of its centralization.[15] The evolution of the Western state went much further than establishing control, order, and conditions of internal peace. In time, it developed a host of autonomous, differentiated institutions that, though propelled by the dynamics of its own needs, promoted the growth of civil society as a core social value.[16] It was this creation and strengthening of civil society that redefined the bond between the individual and the state in terms of rights, social contract, and corresponding obligations, giving rise to the idea of a constitutive and legitimate political authority. As the twin processes of state and nation-building coincided, a sense of national identity evolved which further reinforced the social and cultural bases of national integration. The academic and political discourses on nation-building in developing countries have fixated on some of these essential characteristics of the Western nations.[17] But what these discourses tend to ignore is the Industrial Revolution, urbanization, and the entire process of modernization that has transformed their societies. Modernization also cultivated standardization of life patterns through common work patterns, law, education, and styles of consumption and entertainment. All these factors produced a national culture that gradually overshadowed, and replaced sub-cultures. Thus a national culture based on a common national identity emerged over successive generations.

The centralist elites in Pakistan, and elsewhere among developing countries, against the objective social realities of their national environment, have uncritically accepted the Western notions of nation-state and centralization in structuring the state and promoting national integration. This idealization is predicated on two interrelated postulates: that (1) the nation is a unitary idea, largely defined by bonds of language, culture, ideology, and common history, and that (2) the objective of such nationhood can be promoted by the centralization of power and authority. The ruling groups in Pakistan, for well over six decades, have applied the familiar strategy of creating a centralized political order in which the balance of power would remain with the military and the bureaucracy, with the political elites either on the margins or as junior partners. With the appropriation of the state and power, the military regimes and their subordinate political class wrote the script for state and nation-building and determined the cultural path of national identity.

Let us state from the outset that universalizing the European pattern of nation-state or even fashioning a uniform model of nation-building for ethnically-plural developing countries would be dangerous, and might result in the alienation of composite social groups. There are many reasons for this cautionary note, but it will suffice to explain the pitfalls of pursuing the policies of nation-building through a strong central government alone. Centralization in divided societies is necessary for order and even development, provided an elite consensus exists on the distribution of power between the centre and federating units. Another condition for centralization to work is the adequate representation of all constituent social groups into state organs, like the bureaucracy and military. In reality, it is a hazardous approach because historical legacies of uneven development and resource constraints in a political climate of rising expectations give rise to issues of neglect and political discrimination. The neglected social groups fall back upon their ethnic identities to claim a greater share in power and resources. Thus ethnicization of social groups in Pakistan and the robustness of local identities is one of the consequences of centralization.

It is a historical accident that most of the postcolonial states like Pakistan have inherited a mosaic of ethnic, religious, and linguistic groups that have a proud past, a strong sense of ethnic or communal identity and rich cultural traditions. Needless to say, these groups had a semiautonomous existence, if not self-rule, for centuries before the British amalgamated the present day constituent regions of Pakistan into their Indian Empire. Only empires and empire builders—local, regional, and from distant lands like Europe—brought these diverse, territorialized, social elements together. The British in India, however, made a big qualitative difference; they introduced and developed infrastructure, the kind that was to be found in modern nation-states. India and Pakistan inherited both the diversities as well as the apparatus of the centralizing state machinery, the relatively modern economy, communications, and institutional development. In varying degrees, both the states adopted centralizing instruments while subscribing to federalism tempered by greater power for the central state. In a comparative sense, both the cohesive elements and institutional endowment of Pakistan—a new state struggling for a new identity and physical survival—were weaker than that of India. The leaders of Pakistan, for several decades, were not alive to the dangers of over-centralizing power and subsequently risking the estrangement of ethnic regions. The construction of a cohesive national identity by the central state, primarily through 'primitive accumulation of power',[18] and without political legitimacy, provoked resistance, alienated important sectors of the society, and undermined even the legitimacy of the Pakistani state itself in some of the disillusioned parts of the country, like the erstwhile East Pakistan.

Let us not forget that becoming a nation-state is an evolutionary, historical process that takes a long time—even centuries—to complete, depending on each case. This is not to suggest that Pakistan or other developing countries have to pass through the same sequences of state making as the European nation-states did, or that they have to have the same template and model of the nation defined largely in terms of cultural coherence and one-nationality, one-state model.[19] Each state is different in terms of its constituent ethnic groups and their bonding with different set of cultures, and so is Pakistan.

The ethnic pluralism of Pakistan must be highlighted in understanding the limits and constraints that history, geography, and the contestation over what could be a shared vision of a political future, placed on it, once the common spirit of the movement for Pakistan faded. While the internal obstacles to national integration like ethnic diversity are well known, one must also consider the geopolitical pressures that emanated from regional and international environments i.e. the security climate within which Pakistan had to build itself.[20] The Pakistani elites resorted to quick-fix solutions of diversity, like the bureaucratic appropriation of power and the subjugation of representative politics to military-bureaucratic authoritarianism. By capturing the state, the military-bureaucratic elites created their own visions of Pakistan and its identity that were removed from the ground-realities and popular sentiments. In imposing their will on every important national issue, including identity, they ignored some of the fundamental lessons of history: that identities form through a long process and must align with the historical paths they have established, and that identities can't be engineered or artificially imposed, but only aided by policies that are sensitive to the cultures and contemporary needs of the constituent groups and that integrate their multiple interests.

What are the policies that various Pakistani regimes have undertaken to strengthen the idea of Pakistani nationhood? What are the cultural, historical, and religious referents of these policies? How have various ethnic, linguistic, and religious groups responded to them? Which elements of the state and society influence the politics of national identity? In answering these questions, we will focus on the following two propositions:

1. Accommodation of economic or cultural interests of ethnic groups alone does not guarantee their integration, until and unless they are allowed to participate in the political process, share power,

and develop stakes in the state they must belong to—not only in the physical sense but also in terms of real interest in the political union.

2. Devolution of power, regional autonomy, and recognition of multiple linguistic and cultural identities within a pluralistic, democratic framework would contribute to national solidarity and lay the foundations for the development of a nation-state. Absence of interest-integrating politics would only result in disaffection, division, and movements toward separation. In the light of these propositions, let us try to answer the questions we have raised above.

Islam, Nationalism, and Identity

The problem of Islam and Pakistani nationhood goes back to the economic and political conditions of the Muslim populated areas of the subcontinent in the nineteenth century. Largely secular factors of practical politics and questions like access to power, and representation in the colonial bureaucracy, state, and economy shaped a sense of community and generated a political consciousness, but largely among Muslims where they were in minority like Bihar, Utter Pradesh, and around Delhi. How the economic interests among a section of the Muslim population greatly interested in government jobs led them to participate in the movement for a separate country, an argument that Hamza Alavi makes—is neither understood nor given any weight in the mainstream discourses on identity and nationalism in Pakistan.[21] An ambitious Muslim middle class with the benefit of modern education and its material interests shaped the undercurrents of Muslim identity. However, in the decisive phase of the Pakistan Movement (1940–7), the leaders popularizing the idea of an independent state for the Muslims found the use of Islam as a mobilizing tool for Muslim communities that were spread over the vast Indian landmass to be an attractive idea as well as a convenient political slogan. Once the dream of Pakistan was realized in the regions of Muslim majority concentrations on the fringes of old and imperial India, Islam as a basis of Pakistani nationhood began to produce conflicting interpretations of its relevance to the construction of a Pakistani nation. At the root of this controversy, that refuses to die down in Pakistan, are three ideas of the state: Pakistani state, Muslim state, and Islamic state. We will be referring to some elements of this conflict in other sections of the book as well. Partly, this controversy stems from the fact that the leaders of the movement, including Quaid-i-Azam Mohammed Ali Jinnah, rested the claim for Pakistan on the idea of a 'Muslim nation' and a more generalized construct of the 'two-nation' theory—that Hindus and Muslims comprise two separate nations. This binary view of nations blinded the founders of Pakistan to ethnic and social diversity that existed within the Muslim majority areas that formed Pakistan and Bangladesh. Jinnah argued that Islam was not just a religion, but represented a separate social order, culture, and a civilization that gave the Muslims a distinctive character as a political community.[22] Diverse ethnic groups and different social strata of Muslims in the subcontinent supported the concept of Muslim nationalism, although for different reasons, except some of the religious factions.[23] Most of the supporters of Pakistan rejected the notion of territorial nationalism, claiming that Islam transcended narrow ethnic and linguistic differences. Mohammad Iqbal, the poet and philosopher, who proposed the idea of Pakistan in the 1930s, said, 'It is not the unity of language or country or the identity of economic interests that constitutes the basic principle of our nationality...we are members of the society founded by the Prophet.'[24] However, Jinnah did not conceive Pakistan in purely pan-Islamic terms. His conceptualization of Muslim nationalism was territorial as it was confined to the Muslim majority regions of the subcontinent, based on the protection of minority rights, and defined in relation to the Hindu majority.[25]

After the creation of the country, the Pakistani leaders, political parties, and intelligentsia avoided confronting one of the most fundamental issues: how could Islam serve as a unifying force as effectively as it did during the struggle for the creation of Pakistan? The post-independence social, cultural, and political realities shaped a different political environment than the movement for Pakistan. With a new dawn of freedom, the Pakistanis found themselves divided along political parties pursuing different, and often conflicting, programs, with constituent ethnic groups voicing concerns about fair share in power and economic resources. The politics of conflicting interests and multiple polarizations replaced the common agenda of creating an independent homeland, Pakistan. The point to note is that the consensus on Islam as a glue of national solidarity broke down, which was quite natural, as politics of conflicting interests began to generate different demands. Ethnic pluralism and regional diversity, along with Islam and conventional politics of the Muslim League, the founding party, vied for finding and interpreting the meanings of Pakistan. These streams have more or less, though in different forms, continued striving for the rationale and thus the identity of the state. Let us characterize these roughly as Islamist, modernist, and sub-nationalist. The Islamist position on nation needs a little explanation. The Islamists believe that Islam is a complete code of life, has answers to all modern problems, and it must be relied upon as a source of guidance in personal conduct and public affairs. They define Islam essentially as a political ideology, and set the mission of the faithful, at least in areas where they have formed an independent state, to create an Islamic state. Although ideals and ideas of an Islamic state vary greatly from region to region, the dominant view of an Islamic state in Pakistan is that of establishing supremacy of the shariah (Islamic law or way of life).[26] The Islamists doctrinally refuse to consider the territorial definition of a nation as relevant to the Muslims. Their conception of an Islamic *millat* (nation) would embrace all believers irrespective of their race, language, or domicile. Faith in Allah, Qur'an, and the

Prophet gives them a far greater sense of togetherness than any other factor.[27] Using this phraseology, or, symbolism, the Islamists stress the role of religion in achieving national unity.

By deconstructing the history of the Pakistan movement, they claim that the country's independence was won in the name of Islam, and that the driving force behind the idea of Pakistan was the creation of an Islamic state.[28] This seems to be a total reversal of the position that they took during the political struggle for Pakistan. The ulema (Islamic scholars) from Ahrar, Jamiat-e-Ulema-e-Hind, and even Jamaat-e-Islami had refused to support the creation of Pakistan because they believed that a nationalist movement could not be Islamic. Nor did they trust the leadership of Westernized Muslims like Jinnah.[29] The Jamiat-i-Ulema-i-Hind and the famous Deoband Islamic seminary, in fact, associated themselves with Indian nationalism.[30] The position of Maulana Abul A'la Maududi, the most articulate and celebrated exponent of Islamic state, on the creation of Pakistan was no different from the orthodox ulema.[31] The only difference is that he was equally opposed to Indian nationalism.[32] But their opposition to Pakistan in no way could exclude them from participating in the political process, or prevent them from migrating to the new country, as many of them did. After the creation of Pakistan, the Islamists have contended that Pakistan is an ideological state, meaning that the sole purpose of making Pakistan was to create conditions for the protection and advancement of Islamic values and way of life. Maulana Maududi went to the extreme of characterizing any failure in implementing Islam in state affairs as 'a form of national apostasy'.[33]

A more complex construction among the Islamist stream of thinking is the 'ideology of Pakistan' that was thrown into public debate for the first time in the 1970s, during the second military regime (1969–71), and that got official support during the third military regime of Zia ul-Haq (1977–88). Its advocates have yet to define exactly what it means, but by implication, the 'ideology of Pakistan' refers to two things: that Islam is the basis of nationhood in Pakistan, and that Islam must be accepted as the supreme guiding principle of the state.[34] Even the most professed secular leaders have frequently brought the 'ideology of Pakistan' into political debate, not realizing that it would strengthen the politics of Islamization, and further lead to religious intolerance and extremism. It is partly this ambivalence and political use of Islam by the secular elites that has allowed the Islamists to set the agenda of Islamic politics.[35]

Before we go any further, let us examine some of the contradictions of the Islamist position on nation-building. First, it is historically incorrect to state that the demand for Pakistan rested on the promise of creating an Islamic state in the vision of the present-day Islamic fundamentalists. There is a big difference between claiming a state for Muslims, which was the case, and Islamizing a state once it has been created. It was the consistent failure to reach an acceptable agreement on the constitutional guarantees to the rights of the Muslims in British India that strengthened the demand for Pakistan. The objective was the preservation of cultural identity and the protection of the economic and political interests of Muslims by creating a state in the Muslim majority areas. As indicated earlier, Islamic symbolism was regarded as necessary for the political mobilization of the Muslim masses, and it served that purpose well. Second, the founders of Pakistan, particularly Iqbal and Jinnah, have been grossly misinterpreted by the Islamists to support their views on the relation between Islam and the state. Jinnah was a 'liberal', and 'modernist' Muslim and 'in short, Jinnah aspired to establish a liberal, democratic Muslim welfare state in Pakistan'.[36] Neither of them were even remotely associated with the idea of an authoritarian, hegemonic, or theocratic state, which the Islamists pursued with so much dedication. There is no doubt that, on occasions, Jinnah made brief references to Islam in seeking support for Pakistan, but dragging him closer to the Islamist position is an ingenious intellectual political strategy to change the identity of Jinnah and his political mission of creating a new country. An objective reading of history would reveal that the creator of Pakistan was a constitutionalist democrat to the core, and a secular Muslim.[37] His presidential address to the Constituent Assembly of Pakistan on 11 August 1947 stands as testimonial to this: 'You are free, you are free to go to your temples, you are free to go to your mosques or to any other places of worship in this state of Pakistan. You may belong to any religion or caste or creed—that has nothing to do with the business of the state.'[38] Unfortunately, Jinnah's real personality and ideological outlook fell victim to the political exigencies of the military-dominated authoritarian state and obscurantist ulema. These two forces have often collaborated on the common ground of national security, essentially directed against India.

Third, once Pakistan was achieved, Islam alone could not foster solidarity. As the political environment changed, the central dynamics of politics also changed, requiring a utilitarian approach to strengthen the bonds of political community. After separation from the Hindu majority, new polarization along centre-province lines emerged. The contention was over rights and fair share of power in the new state. And in the struggle for rights, Islamic sloganeering was no substitute for participatory politics. Ibn-e-Khaldun (1332–1406), a North African Muslim scholar recognized this dilemma long ago by asserting that religion was a weak force compared to *asabiya* (ethnic solidarity) in promoting common identity or preserving a state.[39] The separation of former East Pakistan, now Bangladesh, amply demonstrated the fact that faith and political interests are two different matters. This episode must have put an end to the wishful thinking that the material interests of diverse regional groups are insignificant, or can be superseded by the holy politics of Islam.

The message of the East Pakistan tragedy was loud and clear: economic disparity, denial of political power, and the superimposition of new forms of cultural or ideological identity foment ethnic nationalism. This should have ended the reliance on Islam as the sole basis of nation formation. Unfortunately, it has not. The Islamists have continued their rhetoric, paying little or no attention to pragmatic issues that might involve the genuine and concrete interests of the people of different regions. What I am suggesting is that basing national solidarity on religion obscures real issues pertaining to the distribution of political power and participation, eroding trust and confidence in the political union. And thus not only is it a poor, but also a dangerous political tool that causes fragmentation rather than achieving the intended cohesion.

State Elites, Modernization, and National Solidarity

The Pakistan Army and the civil bureaucracy that have formed the core of the country's ruling establishment for well over thirty-two years have approached the issue of national solidarity from the angle of modernization. Ayub Khan, who imposed the first martial law in 1958, was the most forceful exponent of modernization as an instrument of achieving national cohesion. He believed that economic development was a prerequisite for national integration, social transformation of the largely feudal society, and more importantly, political order and stability.[40] His view of Islam as a progressive, dynamic, and creative force in society clashed with the dogmatic and conservative interpretation of the ulema.[41] But like many other mainstream, moderate leaders, he also constantly referred to Islam as the basis of Pakistani nationalism.

Ayub was not a democratic leader, nor did he believe in democracy for realizing the national objectives of the nascent state. He thought that the military, by dominating other institutions of the state, had to assume the role of the modernizing agent in the society, as, in his view, the democratic politics was a wastage of time and resources. He thought that building a strong and prosperous Pakistan was a task that was beyond the skills and capacity of the political forces of his time. The military bureaucratic hierarchy had a very low opinion of politicians, who they dismissed as too traditional, parochial, and particularistic to initiate or manage economic and social change. The Pakistani establishment's views on nation-building were close to that of Western policy circles that attached greater value to armed forces than traditional institutions or even democratic politics. The modernization theory in the 1960s also reinforced the notion that the military elites in the new nations possessed distinctive skills and beliefs that were essential for nation-building. As a modern institution, the military was thought to transform traditional political order, function as a stabilizing force, accommodate aspirations of the new middle class, and manage an orderly change.[42] The critique of this paradigm does not belong here, but it would be enough to say that it stands largely discredited; Pakistan had four of them and all have left a long blazing trail of trouble, discontent, and violence. The set of solutions offered by the military regimes postponed the political crisis without resolving the central dilemma of evolving political consensus or creating acceptable institutions. Some of the early expounders of the modernization theory have changed their minds about the role of the militaries in modernization and state-building, and accepted democratic development as the true route to political institutionalization.[43]

Let us turn to the nation-building program or modernization ideology of the state elites in Pakistan. By disaggregating it, one would find that the program had three main components: centralization, authoritarian power structure, and economic development. The state elites devoted their attention and resources to building the infrastructure of a centralized state, while leaving the political aspects of nation formation to the dynamics of economic and social change. Even the state-building efforts centred on increasing the functional capacities of the state machinery more than its political institutionalization. The underlying premise of strengthening the coercive institutions of the state and expanding its administrative networks was perhaps on the grounds that the challenges to the territorial integrity required a 'strong state'. But this might be interpreted more in the sense of a powerful state than a 'strong state', because the latter would imply political legitimacy and popular support.[44]

The Pakistani state elites were not alone in creating a highly centralized state structure. This has been a dominant paradigm in state formation in the West. Ortega Y. Gasset argues quite convincingly that state came before the nation. And it was through the medium of the state that different linguistic, cultural, or ethnic groups were recast into a nation.[45] But this was the initial phase of state formation in Europe in the seventeenth and eighteenth centuries when the assimilative policies and use of force against recalcitrant groups invoked little external response or organized political resistance. The developing states are operating in a different global environment in which multiplicity of political, security, and informational factors impinge on national policies and political choices.[46] In the vastly changed circumstances of the postcolonial world, centralization or the use of coercive means to subdue diverse national groups has quite often internationalized domestic contestations. My view is that the Western ideal of an ethnically homogenous nation-state is not achievable in our times and circumstances, and it must be either given up, or left to the modernization process—both economic and political. Presently, a viable alternative lies in political unity based on power sharing and cultural autonomy of the constituent units of the Pakistani federation.

In the case of Pakistan, the centralization of state powers did not take into consideration the ethnic and regional realities. The bureaucratic-military elites that dominated the state formation

process in the formative phase of Pakistan conveniently ignored
the fact that the ethnic groups that came into the fold of Pakistan
had strong regional interests, which required a greater degree of
autonomy and political participation. From the start, they regarded
even the voicing of very legitimate regional interests as anti-state—
particularly from East Pakistan and smaller provinces in the Western
part of the country. They suppressed demands for regional autonomy,
and even an expression of regional cultures, instead of encouraging
inclusive and participatory state-society relations. It was quite
legitimate for the provincial elites to demand recognition of their
cultures, a share in political power, and appropriate constitutional
safeguards to protect their political interests. The identity and security
narratives and policy frameworks of the new state ran counter to
some essential historical facts: that provinces existed before any
institutional or physical infrastructure of the new state of Pakistan
was even established. Although Pakistani leaders, both military and
civilian, accepted federalism, they frequently worked against its
spirit and basic principles. In practice, they turned Pakistan into
a quasi-unitary, authoritarian state that was in conflict with the
democratic, parliamentary, and federal vision of the founders. This
is evident from the frequent dissolution of the provincial assemblies
and the enforcement of the governor's rule, from the first decade of
independence to the end of the fourth military regime in 2008.

Intervention of the central government in provincial affairs had
been more of a norm than an exception. The One Unit scheme
even merged all the existing provinces of then West Pakistan in
1955.[47] The 1956 and 1962 constitutions further reinforced the
submerging of separate provincial entities, denying them a separate
identity, power, and representation. They were restored in 1970,
but considerable damage to the principle of federalism and to
national security and integration had already been done. It was one
of the troublesome consequences of the bureaucratic-military-led

state formation process that East Pakistan seceded and became an independent state of Bangladesh.

The truncated Pakistan, now under the leadership of the charismatic Zulfikar Ali Bhutto, began to reshape and restructure itself with the first democratic transition in December 1971. One of the major challenges that failed in Pakistan was the writing of a constitution based on national consensus. This consensus occurred for the first time in 1973. The quantum of provincial autonomy allowed in the constitution was acceptable to the provincial elites, but the central government retained the power to dismiss the provincial governments. Zulfikar Ali Bhutto used this power arbitrarily and removed the Balochistan government lead by the National Awami Party (NAP) in February 1973.[48] The practice of removing opposition governments in the provinces, or preventing opposition parties from forming governments, did not end there. Some of the past central governments have created artificial majorities in the provincial assemblies through the allocation of ministerial positions and outright bribes to win over independents and dissidents from other parties. Almost all civilian and military governments have used interventionary politics in various forms to put in place pliant governments at the provincial level. This has begun to change with the fourth democratic transition since 2008, and with the passage of the 18th Amendment, which has granted greater autonomy to the provinces—something that was unprecedented.[49]

Another aspect of the centralization process relates to the dominance of the executive in the political system of Pakistan; all other institutions in power and influence pale in relation to it. The parliamentary system of government that invariably, all the civilian governments in Pakistan have supported, has reduced the importance of the legislature. The place and power of the prime minister, political patronage, and wide-spread corrupt practices tied most of the legislators to the executive. Since the restoration of parliamentary democracy in 1985 to its subsequent dissolution in October 1999, all the successive elected parliaments failed to play any independent role in keeping the executive in check or even in performing a proper legislative role. They rubber-stamped all the ordinances and passed bills presented by the executive without much debate or scrutiny. The issue of accountability of actions of the prime minister and his cabinet members never gained any importance on the floor of the assemblies except a few solitary voices from the opposition questioning legislative bills, policies, and conduct of the government.

The second element in the state and nation forming strategy of the centralist ruling groups was political stability or order by imposing an authoritarian system of governance. The authoritarian rule in Pakistan was both a cause and an effect of the expansion of the state, particularly the modernization of the armed forces.[50] This resulted in an institutional imbalance between the bureaucratic-military establishment and the elected civilian governments. Judging from the shadow of the military over civilian rule since 1985, and the imposition of military rule on 12 October 1999, the development of the state, particularly the political economy of defence, had a lot to do with Pakistan's crises of democracy.[51] Also, the fragmentation and weakened legitimacy of the political forces offered opportunities to the ambitious military leaders to take over.[52] But it would be wrong to assume that the state elites had no hand in destabilizing the elected governments and weakening the political process.[53] In fomenting the political crisis in the 1950s, the civil bureaucrats, and the military generals pulling strings from behind the scenes, had created difficulties for the normal functioning of the Constituent Assembly and the elected prime ministers. They used their institutional power to topple the governments, and raise new political groups, playing one against the other.[54] Learning no lessons from the troubled history of the country, the security establishment of the country, from 1977 to 1999, removed elected governments, and suspended and amended the constitution to suit individual interests of the coup-makers. In establishing their autocratic rule, they parroted the familiar list of allegations against the elected governments—inefficiency, nepotism, corruption, and the deterioration of economic conditions. We discuss the guardian and patronizing role of the military and its place in the political order of the country in another chapter. The primary objective of military intervention has been to maintain dominance over the political system and supervise its functioning and development. When the military was not in power, it used its proxy presidents, or these proxies wrested political power on their own.[55]

The power structure in Pakistan has been oligarchical in composition, though state elites have played a central role in its operation. Land-owning aristocracy, new industrial and commercial elites, and certain sections of the Islamist constituency during the rule of Zia ul-Haq, have formed an informal power alliance with the establishment. However, not all elements of the political spectrum were thought fit for partnership; co-option was selective and limited to those who shared the military rulers' view of political structuring. This was also true of General Pervez Musharraf, who cultivated a liberal image of himself, and selected individuals for important governmental assignments who, disregarding the question of his legitimacy, would support his agenda of reforms in the economic, political, and administrative spheres.

Inter-elite networks under the military have always been incomplete, transitory, and insufficient to consolidate the nation-making process. Conversely, the dominance of the military has caused deeper polarization among the elites and alienated the new middle classes. By usurping power, the generals took away whatever autonomy the provincial elites had acquired. With the advent of any military regime, the political influence and power that the provincial elites exercised in the provinces as elected representatives and the clout they had with the elected governments at the centre was replaced with non-representative civilians, bureaucrats, and the military officers behind the scenes as 'monitors'. The military's style of governance, political ideology, and rule through the highly centralized civil and military organizations has historically worked against provincial interests. Small provinces are not as well represented in the civil service or the military as the Urdu speaking migrants or the Punjabis. It was natural for the East Pakistanis, or in the post-1971 period, for the educated youth in Balochistan and Sindh to be attracted by the counter-elite politics of the regionalist elements. Consequently, the long periods of authoritarian rule that Pakistan has endured strengthened ethnic identities more than building the intended unified nation.[56]

The third, and most important element in state-building, was economic development. Ayub Khan was the chief architect of Pakistan's industrial base. The military's economic policies favoured free enterprise, and the expansion of domestic markets with wide ranging networks of financial and industrial institutions. Private investment and privatization of state-built industrial units, often ending up in the hands of family and friends, constituted the core value of development planning in the 1960s. There is no disagreement as to the rate of economic growth that Pakistan achieved under the military rule, but creating and strengthening private business enterprises was not divorced from political objectives. Pakistan's fledging bourgeoisie class emerged as the staunchest supporter of a petty bourgeoisie state dominated by the bureaucratic-military elite. Also, the expansion and modernization of the industrial sector fitted well into the imperatives of the political economy of defence, for it made more resources available to the state to pay for the modernization of the armed forces and sustain a certain level of defence preparedness.

There is no doubt that economic development is an important ingredient of both nation as well as state-building. However, Pakistan's economic growth strategies were guided more by the interplay of powerful interests than pure economic considerations. Monopoly, import substitution, and protectionism served the interests of the big businesses more than the objectives of a balanced development of all important sectors and regions. Stress on 'trickle down' effects of the private economy produced a concentration of wealth within limited number of industrial houses, while a focus on West Pakistan, and within it around Karachi, led to serious regional disparities. Likewise, preferences for certain sectors introduced economic distortions.[57] The economic development model that Pakistan pursued under the military rested on the assumptions of what is known as 'the social utility of greed'. Whatever surplus was accumulated was either pocketed by the industrialists or consumed by the state for its own expansion. Social development received very little attention. In theory, the highest rate of economic development in the Ayub decade (1958–69) should have laid the foundations for political stability. But the storm of agitations that erupted with the celebration of the 'developmental decade' in 1968 was a manifestation of the inequitable distribution of rewards of economic development and was reflective of political frustration. It would not be an exaggeration to say that it was Ayub's political and economic structuring of the Pakistani state that strengthened separatism in East Pakistan. Likewise, economic growth under the Zia period was impressive, but his dictatorship resulted in the politicization of ethnic groups, particularly in Sindh.

Today, Pakistan faces deep structural problems that continue to impede its economic recovery. These are: a massive debt burden, high cost of over-extended state apparatus, non-performing loans, economic recession, closure of industry, and, the holy cow, the defence burden. The capacity of the state to collect revenues has declined and a parallel informal economy has grown on a vast scale. Some, concerned with the larger question of political stability of the state, extend support to the military government under the assumption that only dictatorial rule would help stem the rot and put Pakistan back on the rails of good governance and economic development. This optimism about the capacity of the armed forces has waned in a vastly changed national and international environment. The military itself perhaps realizes the problem of its limited capacity that is already stretched to the limits fighting insurgencies and the war on terror.

Ethnic Elites, Nationalities, and Nation Formation

The provincial elites prefer to define and structure the Pakistani nation in terms of a composite political entity.[58] This implies roughly three things. First, the constituent units have inviolable rights, and these rights must form the basis of a relationship with the central authority. Second, the cultural and political hegemony of the state is impermissible as it violates the basic tenet of being of the units. Third, the distribution of political power in the system must be rearranged or work in such a fashion that it satisfies fundamental concerns of the various groups. The political language of this prescription is autonomy, decentralization, participation, and democracy.[59]

In as diverse a political community as Pakistan, nation formation must be regarded, first and foremost, as a political process based on a 'social contract' among the member groups to share political power and the material rewards of living together. This is precisely what the ethnic elites or provincial leaders have demanded of the Pakistani state. Most of the provincial parties and ethnic groups have consistently struggled for the preservation of cultural and political rights. Their demands have ranged from greater political autonomy to the recognition of nationalities and national rights but within the framework of a unified Pakistan. The issue of four nationalities—Punjabi, Baloch, Pashtun, and Sindhi—has been misrepresented by the state-controlled media, the Islamists, and some mainstream national political parties. A recognition of four or more nationalities, such as those demanded by the Mohajirs (Urdu speaking migrants) or Seraiki (southern Punjab), would in no way undermine national solidarity. Rather, inclusionary politics would integrate ethnic interests with the notion of Pakistani nationhood.

Understanding the ethnic mix in Pakistan would be necessary to understand the question of identity. The existing provincial boundaries of Pakistan, as inherited from British India, are not ethnic boundaries. Although main ethnic entities form the major clusters in the provinces, most of the ethnic and linguistic groups are interspersed and widely distributed across provincial boundaries. Large concentrations of Pashtuns in Balochistan, the Baloch in Sindh and Punjab, Punjabis in Khyber Pakhtunkhwa, and Mohajirs in urban areas of Sindh blur the ethnic boundaries. Such a mosaic and inter-mixing carries the potential for both conflict as well as integration. Excluding the Mohajir social group, all other ethnic transmigrations have occurred over the centuries and have established defined territorial domains. Therefore, the ethnic issue does not lend itself to a clear definition along provincial lines. It is a three-in-one problem: provincial autonomy, preservation of group cultures, and distributive justice.

However, provincial identities are tagged with the identities of the majority ethnic groups. This is the way they have evolved, and are recognized by others. A sense of separate identity of each group is deeply rooted in history, the interplay of which cultural forms even a common religion can't dissolve. And there is hardly any need for taking away or giving up the historic identity of any ethnic or social groups regardless of their weakness or strength. We need to recognize that the politics and ideology of identity are primarily about self-preservation as a cultural entity, and a basis of claiming political rights.

The diversity of the units and their internal compositions do not pose any threat to the state in and of themselves. As Anwar Syed has noted, it is the repression of the state and its authoritarianism that poses a threat to its territorial integrity.[60] Under an authoritarian system, the provincial elites in particular felt deprived of their due share in power; they looked upon the state elites as masters, not friends. Their concerns for autonomy, citizenship rights, and participation in the economic and political process of the state are as justified as the demand for Pakistan itself. It was the absence of democracy and inadequate power sharing arrangements that produced frustration with the state, strengthened group feelings, and even led to armed struggle for the restoration of rights in certain cases, especially in Balochistan. Had these issues been remedied, the grievances could have been ameliorated. The case of the National Awami Party, frequently labelled by its detractors as secessionist, illustrates this point. Allowing the party to form governments in Balochistan and North-West Frontier Province (now Khyber Pakhtunkhwa), in 1972 vastly changed its perspective on the national question. The party was the first to adopt Urdu as the provincial language and confined its demand for Pashtunistan to renaming the Frontier province. But when its Balochistan government was dismissed in February of 1973, the Baloch wing took up arms and launched an insurgency that lasted four years.[61] We need to rethink the nation formation strategy in terms of regional identities, an official recognition of ethnic groups, and acceptance of their political participation. The policy of a strong central government combined with authoritarian rule has resulted in a weak Pakistani state—weak in terms of the political capacity to integrate ethnic groups or cultivate a sense of strong Pakistani nationalism among them.

Multiculturalism and New Federalism

The end of the fourth military regime, and the inauguration of the third democratic transition in Pakistan in 2008, has begun a new process of accommodation between the centre and the provinces. Two remarkable developments are noticeable. First is the emancipation and proliferation of electronic media, which is quite a vibrant sector of cultural and political communication. Actually, the media began to free itself using the technology of satellite television and the globalization of information during the Musharraf regime. It didn't come as a gift from the military but as a recognition of a ground reality, as the foreign and the first Pakistani private television channel, Geo, began to reach out to Pakistani viewers in distant lands. The true cultural and linguistic diversity of Pakistan is nowhere more visible than in the electronic media. The media entrepreneurs have approached all segments of Pakistani society and have launched 24-hour news and entertainment channels in national and regional languages. The FM radio revolution is yet another phenomenon in Pakistan with more than one station in almost every district of the country. The presentation of news and entertainment material in local languages has given people a choice and an opportunity to celebrate and enjoy their own culture.

The historical diversity of Pakistani culture today is neither constrained nor subverted by the state. Rather, its expression is open, free, and competitive with each language channel having created a niche among the population. The electronic media also offers an opportunity for regional, ethnic activists, writers, and literary figures concerned with conservation of their cultural heritage and traditions to preserve, create, and celebrate. In this respect, Pakistan has come a long way from only Urdu and state-controlled television and radio, to all languages and private media broadcasts of nearly a hundred channels. Regional languages and cultures have found entry in the homes of local populations as well as those of communities that speak other languages or belong to other cultural groups.

However, the national language, Urdu, and Islamic programmes continue to dominate viewership, but in the market of many cultures—national, regional, and global—at least the old sense of deprivation and denial is gone. Equality of cultures is, and will be, to the extent of equal opportunity and not of the outcome in terms of numbers proportionate to the ethnic populations staying focused on regional cultures. Cultural change, learning new languages, and social and physical mobility associated with urbanization will be some of the factors that will influence the choosing of an identity. This, at best, will have to be layered and multiple, and each expressed according to the occasion and situation one is in.

The second momentous change that will reshape the identity politics of Pakistan is the restructuring of federalism in the country through the passage of the 18th Amendment into the constitution. It has already set into motion a remarkable, though slow, political revolution in restructuring Pakistan's polity. This has greater historic value than restoring the parliamentary character of the constitution, or even granting provincial autonomy. The word autonomy cannot capture the true letter and spirit of the new federalism that has started unfolding in the country. Rather, it is about remodelling Pakistan's political system according to a new principle of distribution of power, with the provinces as new centres of authority, power, and resources.[62]

Thinking of the provinces as new centres of power and laying something down into the constitution to make them powerful, runs counter to both the colonial tradition of supervising political evolution, and the centralized state and nation-building strategy followed for the past six decades. It goes to the credit of political parties and their leadership that they have realized that the old ways of governing Pakistan have failed and that they need to give up a greater part of the power and resources of the centre, which had grown arrogant, paternalistic, and insensitive to the provinces.

This structural change in the political order has created new conditions in which some groups and sections are bound to lose, while others will make gains. Who loses and who gains is an issue that will greatly impact the ongoing process of shifting power to the provinces, as the old, deeply entrenched political and bureaucratic groups fight to the last to save their little turfs and fiefdoms. In Pakistan's case, the federal bureaucracy is the loser, as it cannot hope to rule the provinces under the guise of national integration, solidarity, and security anymore. It will take a great deal of internal reflection on the part of the federal bureaucracy, as well as time, to adjust to the power shift.

Since personal and group loss of this kind is not that easy to adjust to, the traditional ruling groups, as it appears at the moment, will pull all strings from wherever they can to slow down the transfer of power and create difficulties. We have heard too often, for most of our history, two self-serving arguments in support of centralizing power in Islamabad. First, the elite at the centre—political, bureaucratic, and military—are the only patriotic lot and know what the people and provinces need. Second, that the provinces cannot be trusted with power and that they do not have the capacity to wield it—as if those at the centre are angels who have descended from some other planet with all the human virtues and the noblest of intentions. The new structure is meant to defeat these arguments that have shaped power and identity discourse in Pakistan.

The inner spirit of the new federalism is to let the provinces take responsibility for doing good for the people, as those who are close to the people understand what they want and how public interest can best be served. This spirit is behind the implementation of the devolution of power to the provinces. However, in some cases where the big monies and real powers are involved, the political class at the centre has not been willing to allow authority to the provinces. This, we believe, is a teething issue, and that the new federalism will take its natural course when governments formed by different parties set different standards and political traditions.

National identity formation is a common enterprise, and at the end, identity is shared and pluralistic, and is not exclusive to any group. It is shared in the sense that all ethnic groups own it, recognize it, and participate in its development.[63] Pakistan, like other countries in the region, appears to be overly possessed by the idea of a common national identity, which in our view may not be desirable, as it would amount to the subjugation or elimination of regional and ethnic identities and cultures. It is better to maintain a pluralistic order of identities, cultures, and values, which fits the cultural and ethnic needs of the diverse communities of Pakistan.

Notes

1. Farhan Hanif Siddiqi, *The Politics of Ethnicity in Pakistan* (London & New York: Routledge, 2012), 95–112.

2. Moonis Ahmar, 'Ethnicity and State Power in Pakistan: The Karachi Crisis,' *Asian Survey* 36/10 (October 1996), 136–40.

3. These finding are based on the author's personal observation over the past few decades during repeated travel in Sindh, Punjab, Balochistan, and Khyber Pakhtunkhwa.

4. Paul R. Brass, *Language, Religion and Politics in North India* (Lincoln, N.E: Backinprint, 2005), 182–234.

5. 'In 2015, Karachi The Most Violent Region of Pakistan,' *The News International,* January 2, 2016, accessed: December 8, 2016. *See* year wise entries at the Global Security Website, <http://www.globalsecurity.org/military/world/war/karachi.htm>.

6. Razeshta Sethna and Zia Ur Rehman, 'Karachi's Sectarian Backyard,' *Dawn*, November 7, 2016 accessed: December 8, 2016. <https://www.dawn.com/news/1080324>.

7. Richard Sisson and Leo Rose, *War and Secession: Pakistan, India and the Creation of Bangladesh* (Berkeley: University of California Press, 1990).

8. Jonathan Spencer, 'Postcolonialism and the Political Imagination,' *The Journal of the Royal Anthropological Institute* 3/1 (March, 1997), 1–19. It is not only about choosing a path, but postcolonial identity construction goes into the issue of 'representation' and 'being represented'.

9. Bob Lingard, and Sajid Ali, 'Contextualising Education in Pakistan, a White Paper: Global/National Articulations in Education Policy,' *Globalisation,*

Societies and Education 7/3 (2009), 237–56. Within educational policy, there has always been the need to integrate 'Islamic-ness' in order to form a national identity. This paper also discusses how education has been affected by the political events after partition.

10. One view quite often expressed by Indian historians is that Nationalism in Pakistan could possibly be defined only in reference to a Hindu India. See: Sanjay Chaturvedi, 'Process of Othering in the Case of India and Pakistan' *Centre of The Study of Geopolitics, Department of Political Science, Punjab University*, (October 2001), 149–59.

11. Nasir Islam, 'Islam and National Identity: The Case of Pakistan and Bangladesh,' *International Journal of Middle East Studies* 13/1, (February, 1981), 55–72

12. Hamza Alavi, 'Nationhood and Nationalities in Pakistan,' *Economic and Political Weekly* 24/27 (July 1989), 1527–134. In the eyes of the articulate leadership of sub-national groups, the Pakistan 'nation' has been appropriated by Punjabis who dominate the ruling bureaucracy and the military that has effectively been in power in Pakistan since its inception.

13. Alan Marriott, 'Nationalism and Nationality in India and Pakistan,' *Geography* 85/2 (April 2000), 173–8. This article identifies three sub-groups within Pakistan: Sindhi, Baloch, and Gilgit and Baltistan (Northern Areas) and highlights their respective demands for autonomy and independence.

14. Thorstein Veblen, 'The Predatory State,' ed.Waldo R. Browne, *Leviathan in Crisis* (New York: The Viking Press, 1946), 25.

15. Charles Tilly, 'Reflection on the History of European State-Making,' ed. Tilly, *The Formation of National States in Western Europe* (Princeton: Princeton University Press, 1975), 15.

16. The concept 'civil society' might be defined as a set of private and autonomous associations of the individuals that exist out of the state. While promoting citizenship rights and interests in wide and varied areas, such as economy, culture, and politics, they act as a restraint against the arbitrariness of the state. See: John Keane, 'Despotism and Democracy: The Origin and Development of the Distinction between Civil Society and the State, 1750–8150' Keane, ed. *Civil Society and the State: New European Perspectives* (London: Verso, 1988), 43–8.

17. John H. Kautsky, 'Nationalism', Harvey G. Kebschull, ed. *Politics in Transitional Societies* (New York: Appleton-Century-Crofts, 1968), 107–20; Michael F. Lofchie, ed., *State of the Nations* (Berkeley: University of California Press, 1971); S.N. Eisenstadt and Stein Rokkan, eds., *Building States and Nations* (Beverly Hills: Sage Publications, 1973); Karl Deutsch and William Foltz, eds., *Nation-Building* (New York: Atherton Press, 1963); Clifford Greetz, ed., *Old Societies*

and New States (New York: Free Press, 1963); Rupert Emerson, *From Empire to Nations: The Rise to Self-Assertion of Asian and African Peoples* (Cambridge: Harvard University Press, 1960).

18. Such an accumulation is primitive in a sense that it is not premeditated by the constituent groups. In many developing countries, it reflects the same trend as witnessed by the European state formation in its early phase. See, Youssef Cohen, Brian R. Brown, and A.F. K. Organski, 'The Paradoxical Nature of State Making: The Violent Creation of Order,' *American Political Science Review* 75/4 (1981), 901–10.

19. David B. Knight, 'Identity and Territory: Geographical Perspectives on Nationalism and Regionalism,' *Annals of the Association of American Geographers* 72/4 (December, 1982), 514–31.

20. Mohammed Ayoob, 'The Security Problematic of the Third World,' *World Politics* 43 (January 1991), 265–2 .Contrary to Ayoob's view, Caroline Thomas contends that the contemporary international system is benign for state formation as it recognizes the sovereign legitimacy of the new states. But this sovereignty has not immunized the post-colonial states from adverse external influences like intrusion or intervention. See: Caroline, Thomas 'New Directions in Thinking about Security in the Third World,' ed. Ken Booth, *New Thinking about Strategy and International Security* (London: Harper Collins Academic, 1991), 270.

21. Hamza Alavi, 'Misreading Partition Road Signs' *Economic and Political Weekly*, (November 2002) 2–9.

22. Jamil-ud-Din Ahmad, *Speeches and Writings of Mr. Jinnah*, Vol. 1 (Lahore: Sh. Mohammad Ashraf & Sons, 1960), 160.

23. For a detailed account of the controversies, views, and development of Muslim nationalism, see, K.K. Aziz, *A History of the Idea of Pakistan* (Lahore: Vanguard, 1987), 4 volumes.

24. S. A. Vahid, *Thoughts and Reflections of Iqbal* (Lahore: Sh. Ashraf & Sons, 1964), 396.

25. See for instance, Stanley Wolpert, *Jinnah of Pakistan* (New York: Oxford University Press, 1984).

26. See Abul A'la Maududi, *Islami Riyasat [Islamic State]* (Lahore: Islamic Publications Ltd., 1969).

27. Abul A'la Maududi, *Nationalism and India*, (Pathankot: Maktaba-e-Jammat-e-Islami, 1967).

28. Pervez Amirali Hoodbhoy and Abdul Hameed Nayyar, 'Rewriting the History of Pakistan.' Asghar Khan, ed. *The Pakistan Experience: State & Religion* (Lahore: Vanguard, 1985), 164–77.

29. Afzal Iqbal, *Select Writings and Speeches of Maulana Mohammed Ali* (Lahore, 1944), 452.

30. Hafeez Malik, *Moslem Nationalism in India and Pakistan*, (Washington, DC: Public Affairs Press, 1963), 240.

31. Freeland Abbott, 'The Jam'at-i-Islami of Pakistan' *The Middle East Journal*, 11 (Winter, 1957), 40.

32. For details see: Abul A'la Maududi, *Musalman aur Maujuda Siyasi Kashmakash* [Muslims and the Present Political Struggle], Vol. II (Pathankot: Maktaba-e-Jamaat-e-Islami, 1938); Maududi, *Tehrik-e-Azadi-e-Hind aur Musalman* [The Indian Independence Movement and Muslims) in Urdu (Lahore: Islamic Publications, 1974).

33. Abul A'la Maududi, *Islamic Law and Constitution*, trans. and ed. Khurshid Ahmad (Lahore: Islamic Publications, 1960), 5–6.

34. Saeeduddin Ahmad Dar, *Ideology of Pakistan* (Islamabad: National Institute of Historical and Cultural Research, 1998).

35. Charles H. Kennedy, *Islamization of Laws and Economy: Case Studies on Pakistan* (Islamabad: Institute of Policy Studies, 1996).

36. Justice (rtd.) Dr Javid Iqbal, *Islam and Pakistan's Identity* (Lahore: Iqbal Academy Pakistan and Vanguard Books, 2003), 355.

37. Sharif al Mujahid, *Quaid-i-Azam Jinnah: Studies in Interpretation* (Karachi: Quaid-i-Azam Academy, 1981).

38. *Quaid-i-Azam Mahomed Ali Jinnah: Speeches as Governor-General of Pakistan 1947–1948* (Karachi: Pakistan Publications, n.d.), 65.

39. Ibn-e-Khaldun, *The Muqaddima*, trans. Franz Rosenthal, (New York: Pantheon Books, 1958), Vol. 1, 393.

40. For Ayub's views, see Mohammad Ayub Khan, *Friends Not Masters* (London: Oxford University Press, 1967).

41. Mohammad Ayub Khan, *Speeches and Statements*, Vol. 1 (Karachi: n.d.), 57.

42. Hans Speier, 'Preface' *The Role of the Military in Underdeveloped Countries*, ed. John J. Johnson (Princeton: Princeton University Press, 1962), v. There is a plethora of literature on this subject. See: S. E. Finer, *The Man on Horseback: The Role of the Military in Politics* (New York: Praeger, 1962); William F. Gutteridge, *Military Institutions and Power in the New States* (New York: Praeger, 1965); Morris Janowitz, *The Military in the Political Development of New Nations* (Chicago: University of Chicago Press, 1964); Samuel Huntington, *Political Order in Changing Societies* (New Haven: Yale University Press, 1968).

43. Samuel P. Huntington, *The Third Wave: Democratization in the Late Twentieth Century* (Norman and London: University of Oklahoma Press, 1991).

44. Caroline Thomas explains state strength and weakness in terms of institutional

capacities which she differentiates as despotic—arbitrary, and infrastructural—effectively exercised through the institutions. Caroline Thomas, 'Southern Instability, Security and Western Concepts: On an Unhappy Marriage and the Need for a Divorce' in Caroline Thomas and Paikiasothy Saravanamuttu eds. *The State and Instability in the South*, (New York: St. Martin's Press, 1989), 182–8.

45. Quoted by Anwar Hussain Syed, *Pakistan: Islam, Politics, and National Solidarity* (New York: Praeger, 1982), 4

46. Mohammed Ayoob, 'The Security Problematic of the Third World' *World Politics* 43/2 (1991), 265–6.

47. In order to create an artificial parity with the numerically larger East Pakistan, the four provinces of West Pakistan, the present-day Pakistan, were merged together into a single unit. See: Anas Malik, 'Pakistan' in Neil DeVotta, ed. *An Introduction to South Asian Politics* (New York: Routledge, 2016), 44.

48. Gulshan Majeed and Rehana Saeed Hashmi, 'Baloch Resistance during Zulfiqar Ali Bhutto Era: Causes and Consequences' *South Asian Studies* 29/1 (January–July, 2014), 321–31.

49. Mian Raza Rabbani, *A Biography of Pakistani Federalism: Unity in Diversity* (Islamabad: Leo Books 2014), 137–276.

50. There is no single explanation of praetorianism in Pakistan. Hamza Alavi argues that the institutions of the colonial state as transferred to the new state of Pakistan were vastly 'overdeveloped'. A counterpoint is developed by a prominent Pakistani historian, Ayesha Jalal, who contends that the notion of 'overdeveloped' state is 'ahistorical'. See: Hamza Alavi, 'The State in Postcolonial Societies: Pakistan and Bangladesh' *New Left Review*, (July–August 1974); Ayesha Jalal, 'Pakistan's Predicament' *Third World Quarterly*, 3 (July 1989): 234.

51. On this argument see: Ayesha Jalal, *The State of Martial Rule: The Origins of Pakistan's Political Economy of Defence* (Cambridge: Cambridge University Press, 1990), 93–135.

52. For this perspective, see: Hasan Askari Rizvi, *The Military & Politics in Pakistan 1947–86* (Lahore: Progressive Publishers, 1986).

53. On their manipulations and palace intrigues see: Syed Nur Ahmad, *From Martial Law to Martial Law: Politics in the Punjab, 1919–1958*. trans. Craig Baxter (Boulder: Westview Press, 1985).

54. M. Rafique Afzal, *Pakistan: History and Politics, 1947–1971* (Karachi: Oxford University Press, 2001), 95–116.

55. Interventions took place in 1977, 1988, 1990, 1993, 1996, and 1999.

56. Tahir Amin, op. cit., 77.

57. For a critique see: Shahid Kardar, *The Political Economy of Pakistan* (Lahore: Progressive Publishers, 1987).

58. Anwar H. Syed, 'Political Parties and the Nationality Question in Pakistan' *Journal of South Asian and Middle Eastern Studies* 12/1 (Fall 1988): 42–75.

59. For this perspective, I have benefitted from Anwar H. Syed, *Pakistan: Islam, Politics, and Nationalism*, 157–97.

60. Ibid.

61. For details see: Selig S. Harrison, *In Afghanistan's Shadow: Baluch Nationalism and Soviet Temptations* (New York: Carnegie Endowment of International Peace, 1981).

62. Raza Ahmad, 'The Endemic Crisis of Federalism in Pakistan' *The Lahore Journal of Economics*, Vol. 15, (September 2010): 25–9.

63. David Rousseau and A. Maurits van der Veen, 'The Emergence of a Shared Identity: An Agent-based Computer Simulation of Idea Diffusion' *The Journal of Conflict Resolution* 49/5, (October 2005): 686–712.

Chapter II

Security Structure and Identity

Selecting or adopting a particular national identity from a wide range of competing categories—ethnic, territorial, religious, and secular—or even inventing a new one to suit national needs is primarily a political act. Behind such endeavours, one can find a will, an idea, and a scheme of thought, or even some calculation that can be supported by social reference, history, and ideology. No nationalism or identity associated with it has ever been left to the forces of nature. These are human constructs and have some political purpose to serve. In this sense, identity construction may be termed an instrument of branding and marketing nationalism. The two become mutually interdependent, supporting and reinforcing each other in a dynamic social and political process. Once we assume human agency in the construction of identity, then we must identify the actors, their political purpose, and the resources they use. In Pakistan, as in other societies, the resources, capacity, and power to influence identity formation are distributed disproportionately among ethnic groups, state institutions, and political parties. Generally, the politicians and intellectuals take 'a site that is privileged in formatting and transmitting discourses'[1] on national identity. What the relative power and strength of the politician and intellectual in any society is will depend on social and political structures that produce them and sustain them. Pakistan has not been very conducive to the growth and influence of either of the two; they have existed and played some role, but only a marginal one. Their role in articulating national identity depends on freedom and democracy; as they grow, so might their role. For the most part, they have been overshadowed by a military-dominant political order for more than three decades.

As we have argued in the introductory chapter, the actors, and structures of power and influence they create, are 'mutually constituted'.[2] Therefore, a pertinent question in the context of Pakistan's political history is to ask what role the security structure and the military has played, as an 'autonomous' actor, in creating and sustaining that structure in the narrative of national identity.[3] Our answer to this question rests on two propositions that can be supported by a plethora of literature that has been produced to explain the role of the army in politics and the civil-military relations in Pakistan.[4] The first proposition is that the military has played a disproportionately bigger role in articulating the identity of Pakistan, far greater than any other constituent group—ethnic, religious, political, or intellectual. Many of these groups have functioned as auxiliaries, proxies, and at best, subordinate allies. Our second proposition is that Pakistan's security structure—military, as an institution, as well as security and foreign policies, and nuclear strategy—have sustained a specific narrative about the meanings of Pakistan, its foundational idea and vision. Before we go any further, it is necessary to preface this discussion by raising the issue of the unfixed role of the competing actors and the question of changing the balance of influence among them. There is always a possibility of realigning and reorienting the discourses on national identity, whether it is done by the military or the politicians and intellectuals. However, structures of power and influence associated with the security establishment of Pakistan have reflected both a quality of flexibility and of stubbornness, and the change is never without continuity in certain elements. For instance, in the war against terrorist groups, the military appears to have now distanced itself from the jihadist elements that it previously nurtured in support of the Afghan Mujahedeen and militants in the

Indian-occupied Jammu and Kashmir region. So there is a change in the meanings of Pakistan and what kind of state and society Pakistan should be.

We have explained, and somewhat exhausted debate and discussion on, competing social forces attempting to shape and construct national identity in their own ways. In this chapter, we focus on the security structure in broader terms, and not just on the military or what is popularly referred to as the 'security establishment'. This includes other elements of the security structure—threat perceptions, the enemy debate, security and foreign policy, and the role of the nuclear weapons and strategic culture.[5] The military, as a political actor, as has been evident by four takeovers; the mainstream political parties and the intellectuals disagree over the meanings of Pakistan. The latter has attempted to root the meanings of Pakistan on the vision of its founders. The political parties and the intelligentsia, in general, have interpreted the founding vision as aiming to create a secular, moderate, and democratic Pakistan, with the exception of right-wing academics, journalists, and intellectuals who are aligned with the right-wing parties. The mainstream intelligentsia believes that secularism—the neutrality of the state in religious matters and constitutional democracy—must define the national identity of Pakistan. Only this paradigm can ensure political stability, progress, internal cohesion, and security of the country. On the other hand, the four military regimes have subverted the constitution, which is the foundation of a democratic order, and have attempted to fashion a political system that placed the military in a preeminent position, controlling, directing, and supervising political facades, parading themselves as 'representative' of the people. In doing so, the regimes delegitimized constitutional politics, political parties, and the democracy. In a political culture shaped by opportunism and considerations of being around the corridors of power—a feudal trait—the military found support and allies more than it could accommodate in its wide ship of power.

The security structure of Pakistan and its role in identity formation has rested on the assumptions about threats, enemies, and in its judgment of what could be the appropriate strategies to counter them. In this regard, four postulates seem to have embedded the ideas about the identity of Pakistan articulated by the security structure. First and foremost, is the ideology of Pakistan.[6] What the ideology of Pakistan is, is a question that has begged many more questions. For the military, religious parties, and the right-of-the-centre political parties, it is the two-nation theory and Islam that is the basis of Pakistani nationalism and its identity.[7] Second, India is the main adversary and a challenge for a sovereign, equal, stable, and prosperous Pakistan. With a new 'existential' threat posed by radical Islam and militancy, there is a shift in focus, but not a change in perceptions of India as the enemy. Rather, the military sees a connection between some factions of the Tehrik-i-Taliban Pakistan and the Baloch militant groups, and the Indian intelligence assisting them in their acts of terrorism.[8] Others have argued that radical Islam is the consequence of wars in Afghanistan, Pakistan's policy of assisting the Afghan Mujahedeen and armed struggle of the Kashmiris and its alliance with the United States in its war on terrorism in Afghanistan.[9] The regional climate of sectarianism, rivalry among the Middle Eastern powers, namely Iran and Saudi Arabia and their sponsorship of militancy in Pakistan, have also contributed to the rise of radical Islam, as well as the Islamic revolution of Iran and the Islamization policies of the country. Third is the idea of Muslim nationhood of Pakistan which goes beyond the political debates of the two-nation theory and encompasses a wide range of characteristics from Muslim history, its heroes and pan-Islamism—a deep feeling of being a part of the universal Muslim community and spirit to stand by the causes of oppressed Muslims anywhere in the world. Fourth is an expansive idea of Pakistan as a pivotal Muslim state, a power with vital interests in Afghanistan and Kashmir but aspiring to play a greater role in the proximate Muslim regions. In consequence, these assumptions, which are often taken as 'facts', have greatly influenced the security structure of Pakistan. In the following sections, we turn to some of the elements of this structure and how they determine the narratives of identity.

Threat Perceptions and Enemy Debate

Historically, India has remained the centre of Pakistan's security discourse for reasons relating to the circumstances of partition, Muslim nationalism, the two-nation theory, and territorial disputes. These are some of the factors that have nurtured and sustained the India-centric view of national security, foreign policy choices, and geopolitical conceptions. However, there is no single, unified, or consensual position about what kind of threat India poses to Pakistan. Popular perceptions of the Indian threat widely range from her desire to undo Pakistan to establishing a hegemonic security regime in the region and destabilizing the country through proxies.[10]

The historical roots of antagonism between the two states are well known, but what has added to mutual bitterness is the inability of the post-independence leaders on both sides of the borders to normalize relations by healing the wounds of partition or creating a climate of trust and empathy. Rather, bilateral engagement has been hostile, adversarial, and driven by distrust and rivalry. Three and half wars, which resulted from the unresolved territorial question of Kashmir, have greatly contributed to confrontational attitudes. Besides this issue, the dominant view within the security community of Pakistan that India seeks dominance, encirclement, and isolation of Pakistan has influenced its perceptions of the threat environment and has determined her strategic responses for many of the past decades.[11] In our view, while it is necessary to respond to external threat conditions appropriately, as all states do, an exclusive focus on the territorial dimension of security obscures more complex threats emanating from internal contestations of power, identity, and legitimacy.[12] Ethnic militancy in Balochistan, political violence in Karachi, the rise of religious extremism, and the emergence of radical Islamic groups engaged in terrorism are some of the dimensions of national security that Pakistan was not able to foresee in its long-term strategic calculations, if they were ever the subject of security planning. The point is that in societies that are politically less integrated like Pakistan, national security as a concept and policy evokes different images and reactions from different sections (ethnic groups, political institutions, security establishment, and civil society) within the state. In the dynamic conditions of post-9/11 global security and insecurity challenges, when the notions of security are undergoing radical redefinition, these variations can no longer be ignored in understanding the security predicament of Pakistan. What is necessary is to bring all different conceptualizations of security, threats, challenges and what would be appropriate responses together and create a national framework of security. The creation of a national consensus would require national dialogue by widening the scope of institutions and groups participating in the narratives of national security. This has yet to take place in Pakistan. The formulation of security doctrines, policies, and strategies continues to remain the preserve of the security institutions of the country; the civilian institutions, including the Parliament and its committees, exercise little or no influence because of capacity and leadership issues. The imbalance in civil-military relations also discourages the political leadership and representative institutions from questioning the military-dominant view of national security.

Every postcolonial state has a different institutional heritage and political history but what we generally find common among them is an uncritical acceptance of the view that foreign state or states, often neighbours, present challenges to national security. And the response to them is through the conventional means of the balance of power, alliances, and adding to the national power. This is what constitutes a neo-realist understanding of the security dilemma that fails to address the internal security complexities and peculiarities of countries like Pakistan. While we cannot discount the authenticity of external threats to national security, we need to broaden the agenda of national security threats that must include the actors, forces, and movements that endanger national and societal security—like radicalism, terrorism, and sub-national militancy. The ideas of democracy and human rights, stability and order, and equality and justice cannot be peripheral ideas but must be central to a broader understanding of national security. It is their absence that creates a social and political climate conducive to the germination and growth of extremism and radicalism.[13]

There is a fundamental difference in the state and identity formation process of the industrial societies and the developing world. The historical circumstances of state formation, autonomy of political institutions, and the essential relationship between the state and society happens to be very different. The Western democratic states have achieved a satisfactory level of political integration in developing a strong sense of nationalism, national identity, and social cohesion. This has enabled them to resolve or significantly reduce the potential of internal threats to the state and its institutions. But even they are no longer immune from the new internal threat from radical elements that the globalized network of terrorism has spanned during the past two decades. It is the marginalized, the religious or ethnic other, less integrated or alienated young elements of the immigrant populations with allegiances to radical Islam that has turned guns on the host communities.[14] It is more imperative in the context of Pakistan and other developing states that the internal aspects of security shouldn't be excluded from any meaningful analysis of national security. In their case, the vision of state-building through a hegemonic view of nationalism and national identity has quite often come in conflict with the popular aspirations for political representation and participation in the discourse on nationalism and national identity of diverse ethnic groups. Their agenda for autonomy and extensive rights often clashes with the centralization of state powers.[15]

Democracy as Identity and Security

One of the ways contemporary states and societies are classified is by deciding whether they are democratic, feudal-tribal, authoritarian, or non-democratic. With the 'triumph' of Western liberalism, democratic identity has acquired powerful meanings and likeable characteristics.[16] There is an abundance of academic literature and an accumulation of historical experience, which suggests that state institutions based on consensus, political participation, citizenship rights, and consent of the governed determine the degree to which a state can be 'weak' or 'strong'.[17] On the contrary, the coercive means through which the authoritarian states exercise power, generate a sense of national solidarity, or produce narratives of national identity, have failed to produce desired results. All such states, from Afghanistan to the larger Middle East, have either collapsed or have been confronting internal turmoil and deadly civil wars.[18] The hegemonic, single party and ideological states espousing Arab nationalism, revivalism, and socialism have failed in the Arab world both for reasons of internal contradiction and external interventions, including drawing of the state boundaries by European powers.[19] Therefore, in our opinion, the holistic perspective of national security must involve both the territorial defence as well as the larger issues of societal security. Similarly, the issue of democratic development in its broadest meanings can't be divorced from it. However, military dimension remains crucial because failure to defend the physical base of the state would wipe out the political and societal elements of security. But raising and sustaining a territorial security apparatus, even in its conventional sense, must be based on consent, and not on coercion, because such an enterprise requires valuable economic resources that other sections of the society must sacrifice for. The issue is that heavy investment in the military might run the risk of tilting the institutional balance against the political forces when the supremacy of civilian institutions has yet to be established.[20]

The contemporary states, whatever their form or bases of authority, including Pakistan, have been successful in mobilizing resources towards implementing their defence strategies in realizing their vision of national security. That leaves, however, a big impact on the conflictive demands of development and national security. The experience of many states indicates that the degree of political legitimacy—level of popular support—that a regime enjoys, and the democratic or non-democratic character of the state makes a qualitative difference in balancing the opposing demands of defence and development. At least theoretically, democratic governments cannot spend public funds without debate and scrutiny because they are held accountable for what they do, or fail to do, regarding popular demands for distributive justice and addressing issues of social and economic progress. A wide array of autonomous institutions, public vigilance and values of dissent and discussion restrain the arbitrariness of those responsible for national security from ignoring development in the name of primacy of national security. There are other reasons for the democrats to be restrained in defining the threats, boundaries, and means of national security; they have to work through the intricate system of institutional checks and balances. By its operational requirements, democracy brings flexibility into government in setting priorities and implementing programmatic changes in allocation of resources for defence and development. The conditions of economic underdevelopment, social instability, threats of civil conflict, and surging demands of a needy population, create enormous pressures for a government waiting for the next round of elections to be responsive.[21] While the authoritarian regimes can get away with unsuitable priorities, the elected governments have to pay a heavy political price for neglecting the constituents that bring them into power. In the context of some of these theoretical strands of democracy, a legitimate question to be raised here is: does Pakistan represent a democracy that has these characteristics with control over all institutions, including the military and narratives of national security and national identity construction? A categorical answer is no. The security structures of Pakistan have remained too powerful for the successive civilian governments to challenge its perceptions of threats, foreign policy choices, and its strategic culture. Since previous attempts to challenge the security and foreign policy narratives as well as the power of the security establishment in their 'reserved' powers of foreign and security policies have resulted in military intervention or destabilization, they have treaded on a cautious path of passive submission.[22]

Pakistan has a mixed experience of democracy and military regimes. The real progress in the case of Pakistan is that a broader consensus on democracy has emerged among the political parties. It has witnessed democratic continuity for about a decade and the first peaceful transition of power from one party to another in 2013. The media has proliferated, and its power to influence national debate and discussion has greatly increased. However, progress on developing a stable democracy has been frequently stalled by the military's intervention in politics in the past. When in power, the military has attempted to create a 'garrison state' as the military appeared to permeate every walk of life—business, industry, services, bureaucracy, and massive housing development throughout the country.[23] It took upon itself the sole responsibility of creating new political institutions, establishing ethical norms, and even venturing into the difficult terrain of religion and society, culture, and identity formation.[24] They have left a heavy imprint on the civil-military relations and the identity of Pakistan. Every democratic government, after a transition, has faced difficult legacy issues.

In Pakistan, like elsewhere, the military regimes have ruled through outright repression or by forming narrow-based oligarchies of powerful elites in the society under their domination. Strong, centralized, or hegemonic state apparatus under the military regimes offered no viable option for welding together the ethnically diverse regional communities into Pakistani nationhood in the name of the 'development first, democracy later' model, a common security threat, or Islam. Here, while foregrounding the issue of identity and democracy, it is important to note that the military's repeated takeovers and restructuring of the political order to suit the institutional and personal political interests of the top generals in power perpetuated societal fragmentation which exposed the state to a variety of ethnic, communal, and religious conflicts. The successor democratic governments have found it hard to end them. These conflicts have been as much about power and access to resources as they have been driven by a particular quest for communal identity issues that raised their head in the vacuum of democratic politics. Compared to the troubled legacies of the military rule, we find that the democratic regimes in Pakistan have a significantly enhanced capacity to mediate internal conflicts, share power, build political coalitions, and work together to resolve thorny issues like provincial autonomy and the allocation of national resources among the provinces through the National Financial Commission Award.[25] In our view, a national security analysis of Pakistan or any other developing country must bring to light the issues of democratic development, nation-building, and internal threat conditions that emanate from the flawed model of state formation, elite corruption, bad governance, and criminalization of politics.

Insecurity Predicament and Praetorian Rule

In this section, we will attempt to explore the relationship between the security problem of Pakistan and the political ascendancy of the bureaucratic military elites, along with the power and influence they have exercised in developing national identity and security narratives. Our findings, and based on them, our argument, is that four spells of military rule have worsened the 'insecurity dilemma'[26] of the country by destabilizing democratic evolution, subverting a natural balance in politics and sponsoring social, religious, and political forces that worked counter to the vision of a democratic, moderate, and secular Pakistan. The rise of the military on the grounds of national security also explains how Pakistan lost track of its constitutional development and people-centred ideas of national integration.

We can contrast Pakistan's losing democratic track with India that has been steadily trekking on it despite bigger challenges of diversity. The fact is that Pakistan inherited more or less similar levels of institutional development as did India, and its founding fathers were no less committed to a constitutional notion of democracy and rule of law than India's.[27] Pakistan and India shared historical, civilizational, and cultural similarities with the only difference of an emergence of Muslim nationalism and separatism in the last decade of the British rule. Partly, the political trends and the legacy of the decade leading to the creation of Pakistan became the major handicap of the new state. It failed to convert and integrate the idea of Muslim nationalism with the territories that constituted it. Its leaders were unwilling to leave the comfortable ideological ground of Muslim nationalism to tread on the difficult terrain of territorial Pakistani nationalism, which would have required them to come to terms with ethnicity, pluralism, and political accommodation of regionalism in Pakistan. Such a transition would have also required answering some uncomfortable questions about the histories of the people that constituted Pakistan, about their individual identities, and how they could be used as integral strands of a new identity narrative for the country.[28] Such narratives required a pluralistic, democratic, and constitutional framework to allow all ethnic groups to participate, making the system inclusive to defining what the nation was and how it could move together to achieve its common objectives—the objectives that were at the heart of the struggle for winning a separate homeland for the Muslim majority areas.

Reconciling regional particularism, demographic and economic imbalances, divergent interests, and the dream of a cohesive, effective nation and statehood emerged as the biggest challenge of Pakistan. However, it was not a challenge unique to Pakistan, as all other states inheriting ethnic diversity from the colonial powers had to face it as well. The issue all of them, including Pakistan, faced was how to build a nation within the new state. Assuming that a common thread of Islam would subsume ethnic interests and identities proved false, and worked counter to the basic assumptions about the political world being driven by concrete interests in power. Only federalism and democracy could provide the institutional template to accommodate regional aspirations with the idea of Pakistani nationalism. Pakistan lost that framework in the early years of independence, and its drift towards the bureaucratic-military authoritarianism was precipitous. Fears, insecurity, rising demands of ethnic groups, and institutional weaknesses, along with a shift of power from the parties and politicians to the bureaucracy, are some of the factors that contributed to the loss of vision and direction in the formative first decade.[29]

There is no single explanation for how or why the bureaucracy, and then the military, emerged as dominant players in the political process.[30] For some clarity, if not a definite answer, one must look at the complex linkages between state formation in the postcolonial setting, the regional threat environment, and the trends in global security relations—the beginnings of the Cold War, for example.

It is necessary to underline the point that state formation and its institutional infrastructure or development has never been immune to the influence of factors of international systems. Pakistan's vulnerability to external influences at the formative stages was far greater than other developing countries, as it wanted to balance a much larger India with very little power endowment available to it. Also, the new state had to grapple with the issues of institutional and political consolidation in the face of transmigration of millions of people, a crippled economy, and the hostility of a more powerful India that was manifested in its annexation of the larger parts of the Jammu and Kashmir region.[31]

While we should keep the regional and international environment in the background, the failure to institutionalize a democratic political process was more a result of the interplay of internal forces than the malignant regional security environment. Operating a parliamentary system—that Pakistan accomplished in the first decade—required, at the minimum, disciplined political parties, a federal constitution and some measure of political consensus on the tricky questions of representation and provincial autonomy. Unfortunately, the Muslim League, the party that led the struggle for the creation of Pakistan, disintegrated into rival factions led by self-centred, ambitious figures. A framing of the constitution was pitifully delayed over the issue of the distribution of power between the federal government and the provinces. A host of other factors, such as the dominance of the executive and increasing imbalance between the bureaucratic-military establishment and the autonomous political institutions further deepened the democratic crisis of Pakistan. In consequence, political power began to shift in favour of the state elites who had succeeded in manoeuvring their way in to the highest political offices in the country.[32] A group of elites played a central role in redefining Pakistan's internal politics and its relations with key players in the post-Cold War international system.[33] Therefore, it is very important to understand what constituted the elites and how their interests created an authoritarian political framework of the politics of the country. Evaluating Pakistan's history, Professor LaPorte argues that Pakistan's politics have evolved around an elite group that is composed of top-level military officers, central administrative officers, and members of large landowning families from every province of the country. They share a common 'social base…traditional wealth and power in land in the Punjab and Sind and tribal leadership [and land] in Balochistan and Northwest Frontier.'[34] He thinks the complexity of such a diverse elite formation which has been 'underestimated, cohesiveness overestimated, and whose composition is undergoing significant change' as it is evident in the rise of economic and business elites.[35] In the first decade, they exploited every political situation to weaken the democratic political forces and strengthen their own personal and institutional power base. More dangerously, the state elites had a narrow vision of a secure and stable Pakistan that was rooted in their ideology of 'controlled democracy', a strong central government, and a preeminent position of the executive. Trained and socialized in the colonial bureaucracy, they tended to see the clamorous political process through the colonial lenses of law and order. They were quick to accumulate power of the central state apparatus mainly by expanding the infrastructural capacity of the coercive institutions, while wilfully stultifying the growth of a representative political system. The civilian bureaucracy assumed a central position in determining the direction Pakistan would take in shaping its internal institutions, and foreign and security policy choices. It nurtured the military and sought its support in turning the politicians into subordinate positions. The alignment between the military and bureaucracy subverted the development of political institutions[36].

The most critical element in tilting the balance in favour of the bureaucratic-military elites was the allocation of relatively larger resources towards raising the defence forces of Pakistan than other sectors. The assumption then, and even now, is that no cost is big enough when it comes to national security, as perceived by the elite and powerful security structures. From day one, the military establishment had received disproportionate political attention and entitlement to funds. Strengthening of the armed forces was considered central to the strategy of survival through a strong state that could effectively counter hostile India. Although internal divisions and the potential of secessionist movements required a strong army, much of the rationale came from the assessment of the regional security environment in which an Indian threat loomed large in the Pakistani perception of security. Pakistani leaders thought that India was not reconciled to its independence and wanted to undo the partition.[37] Enemy images that were born in the communal frenzy of the pre-independence era were somewhat transferred to the independent states of India and Pakistan. By the force of latent emotions of Muslim nationalism and confrontation with India, the two-nation theory became embedded in the identity and security narrative of Pakistan as a nation and state. This implicitly linked the Pakistan identity to India. The latter contested the idea of two nations, which construed a large Muslim community as a nation within India, conflicting with the idea of the Indian nation being secular and territorial.[38] Some have argued that this ideological divide has determined the hostile relations between the two states that emerged out of the British Raj.[39] The migrant middle class from India and the same class from the Punjab that dominated the military and the bureaucracy supported the idea of two nations, the one threatened by the other for its non-reconciliation with the other nation. The weak and threatened nation of Pakistan has to be defended at all cost against the more populous and more powerful India. This narrative of identity paved the way for the military to assume a central role in defining and defending the nation and the state—a role of the guardian of the state that continues to overshadow the role of other institutions within the state. Going to war over Kashmir (1948), as well as ideological, political, and territorial contestation over the region cast the die of hostility between the two states; they have yet to chart any new course in their relations.

Having been born in communal hatred, bloodshed, hostility and war, the narrative that India was not reconciled to an independent Muslim state of Pakistan got some credence and popular support. Factors like an imbalance of power also began to trouble the Pakistani security managers. India's size, its real and potential military power, and an implicit desire for a restructuring of the security relations in her image of regional dominance pushed Pakistan further towards building a stronger defence. This was a typical realist solution to the complex problem of national security that had serious internal dimensions. The issue is not that the defence forces were irrelevant to the threats that Pakistan confronted, but that such endeavours resulted in distortions of the balance of power between the state and civil society—the civilian and the military sectors. The impact of early decisions, security orientation, narratives of nationalism, and alliances with the United States to offset the Indian threat have left a lasting influence on everything that defines Pakistan today—security, politics, and foreign relations.

In the realist-dominant view of security, Pakistan's own resources were severely limited for building credible military capacities to counterbalance the perceived Indian threat.[40] Taking a leaf from the history of weaker states attempting to balance more powerful neighbours, Pakistan's top military leaders and their allies in the civil bureaucracy looked for external factors to compensate for the weak resource base, a usual practice in the balancing game. Having failed to solicit support in the first few years, they found the international constellations of Cold War power relations propitious for their search for external military assistance.[41] Located in the strategic triangle of Central, South, and West Asia, Pakistan had enough relevance for the Western idea of a wider security zone in the Middle East. The

US policy of containing communism in the 'northern tier' brought her squarely into its strategic plans for the region. Although a strong propensity towards building an optimal defence capability already existed, the alliance with the US provided the essential and most critical means to Pakistan, for the first time, for expanding and modernizing the armed forces. The decisions to place Pakistan in the US camp were not taken by the political elites; they were essentially shaped by the bureaucratic-military elites.[42] That led not only to the expansion of the military capabilities but also to the power and influence of the military in Pakistani politics, and in determining its identity. Pakistan's history since that time provides enough evidence about the linkages between the growth of the armed forces, external alliance, and the political role of the military. In a normal evolution of the state, when larger issues of political power have been settled and constitutional norms run supreme, one would find no causal link between the expansion of the defence capability of a country and the military's intervention in domestic politics. In Pakistan's case, it happened when the state was stabilizing itself, the ideas of nationhood were contested, and the political framework was weak and in the making.

The emergence of the military as a dominant player occurred in Pakistan at a time when the country was going through severe crises of state formation, national identity, and search for political order. The political forces in the country had been weakened by the manipulations of the state elites. Living in the colonial mode of thought and mindset, the military-bureaucratic elites were loath to accept the supremacy of the representative institutions. They worked hard at conspiring to rob the political institutions of their natural growth and power. They succeeded in aggrandizing the real political power and in playing a puppet show of political factions that allowed the politicians to exercise nominal authority. The major reason for their rise was their position within the state power structure, but what added to their capacity to manoeuvre themselves to the centre of power was the weakness of the social structures that had produced leadership in West Pakistan. Changing of political loyalties, making and breaking of political alliances, and the politics of intrigue had badly stained the character of the feudal politicians in the opinions of the populace. However, they were not alone in producing political instability and chaotic conditions; the bureaucratic-military leaders played their part in raising and pitting one group against the other.[43] It was all justified in the name of security and stabilising the new state, for which task the political class was seen lacking in competence, skills, and education. This negative view of politicians and political parties among the military leaders has persisted over the decades.

It is evident from the military's dominance in politics that the generals who took over power by force—from Ayub Khan to Pervez Musharraf—read a similar riot act in rationalizing intervention. It accused the politicians of failing to deliver to the country a workable political structure. They were neither capable nor could they be trusted to run the affairs of the state; they were corrupt, irresponsible, power hungry, and lacked the essential vision of constructing the Pakistani state in the true spirit of the independence movement.[44] More deeply, it reflects how the state elites viewed the political process, the concept of public representation, and their own role as the guardians of the state of Pakistan. In the pursuit of personal power, ambitions, and dominance over other state institutions, international alignment was also a factor in the calculations of the military in capturing the state apparatus. In its containment strategy, the United States of America had considered the military officer corps of Pakistan and other allies in the region as a major source of defence against communist expansion and penetration.[45] The military might have been encouraged by this assessment, as is evident from the wide-ranging support Ayub Khan received from the United States and the West. Pakistan went under martial law thrice more, in March 1969, July 1977, and October 1999, spanning thirty of its existence. Judging from the timespan, developmental strategies, and political institutionalization undertaken by the generals, they did not intervene simply to restore political order, build a 'genuine' democracy, and restore the economic health of the country, as they had promised. They had a larger mission: structuring the Pakistani state according to their image of national security, stability, and development. Everything they did in this regard, or failed to do, had serious implications for the balance of power between the society and the state, the centre and the provinces, and the nation and nationalities. At the end, they left the country in more chaotic, unstable, and polarized conditions than when they took over. Their ideas and policies of security produced more insecurity—ethnic nationalism, religious extremism, sectarianism, and terrorism. This brings us to the geopolitically centered idea of security and what consequences it has produced over time for the state and society.

National Security and State Formation

While the personal power ambitions of the military rulers cannot be ruled out as a motivating factor, their assessment of the security situation within and around the country played an equally significant role in their decision to topple the civilian regimes. India, as indicated earlier, has remained central to Pakistani threat perceptions. The main concern of the military establishment in the domestic environment was to suppress ethno-national movements, prevent the country from slipping into social chaos, and ensure political stability. The political ideology of the military leaders had two components: stability and economic modernization. The ultimate national security of the country hinged on these twin pillars. The free play of democratic forces was considered counterproductive to the objectives of a stable, and in economic terms, a modern, secure, and strong

Pakistan. In their simplistic reading of the history of Pakistan and other countries, neither the 'illiterate' masses nor their mostly feudal politicians constituted the right stuff for democratic development. Provincial rights, often articulated through the idea of autonomy and ethnic identities, have been regarded by the military as threats to the territorial integrity and the ideology of Pakistan. The military, the right-wing intelligentsia, and the religious parties have all based their conception of the ideology of Pakistan on Islam and on Muslim nationalism, with ethnicity being seen against the spirit of unity and Pakistani nationalism.

The articulation of Pakistani nationalism as Muslim nationalism is flawed in the sense that it fails to recognize, let alone positively consider, ethnic identities, and local cultures and languages as composite colours of a larger Pakistani nationalism, which has to be territorial, sensitive to, and celebrative of, the histories and unique strands of cultures of the region. What it intends to be is territorial and composite Pakistani nationalism, which the acronym of Pakistan signifies. This looks a bit complex. Political narratives about identity and nationalism have to grow out of the real world more than the constructs articulated in different time contexts. The idea of territorial nationalism with a focus on the constituent regions, the people, and their histories has not won wider support, as most of the critical actors have failed to appreciate the organic value and strength of this idea.

One of the most critical actors in the political drama of Pakistan and in the development of security and identity narratives is the security structure. Quite opposite to the secular ideology of the Turkish military, which for decades has been held as a model in Pakistan (more for its role in politics than for its ideology though), the Pakistani military has embraced the idea of Muslim nationalism and the ideology of Pakistan in its expansive interpretation. The ideology remains the most important source of inspiration. However, the military's solution to the complex problems of nation-building and political integration was derived from its own organizational experience, which provided a considerable mass of social learning. The political reality of larger national communities that are divided along narrow caste, ethnic, religious, and tribal affiliations is, however, different from the homogeneity of military organizations. Looking at that reality through the lens of a disciplined and centrally commanded organization would never present a picture of chaos and disorder; therefore, there is an urgent need to grasp the complex social realities in their own specific contexts, and then devise solutions that balance individuality with collective national needs. Never have the military rulers of Pakistan, their ideologues and cultural strategists, shown any sensitivity to the complex ethnic order of Pakistani society. The reasons for this neglect are simply their organizational culture and the uncritical acceptance of the ideology of Pakistan as fixed and unilaterally defined.

The military, while in power or when in a position to exercise influence out of the shadows, has extended support to a security-driven narrative of nation and state-building. The military's role in such a foundational sphere, which must have been the mandate of the democratic governments, has created a different identity of the Pakistani state, which some of the scholars have described as the 'garrison state'.[46] Harold D. Lasswell employed the phrase 'garrison state', defining it as a political entity where 'the dominant group is constituted by the specialists on violence, since force is the distinctive skill of soldiers and police. The specialist on violence rises in power as other skill groups subside, such as the specialists on civil administration, party and pressure-group administration, and specialists on propaganda or persuasion.'[47] The formation of the 'garrison state' started with the first martial law (1958–69) with the objective of building a strong and effective state structure to ensure stability, order, and national unity.

The military has adopted three strategies to build the Pakistani state that would achieve the above objectives: de-politicization, centralization, and modernization of the economy. They mutually reinforce and work towards the realization of the military's vision of a strong and unified state. De-politicization, thus, was aimed at clearing the way for the military to monopolise the political arena by banning political parties, fragmenting them, and writing new rules for the political game. To further this project, the military suspended the constitution, wrote a new constitution, or amended it to place the military rulers in an unassailable position of power. In this regard, the military regimes have produced a politics of their own brand with the character of patronage, cultivation of groups that would serve as its 'democratic' or political façade, and restructuring of political and state institutions to ensure its domination of the state.[48] In every aspect, military rule has been different from a constitutional government, including its management of, and control over, the state and the narratives of national security and identity. Domination might be a weaker expression; in fact, it has exercised a form of internal hegemony by creating allies in every sphere of national influence including media, culture, and textbooks to circumscribe what is a 'good', 'patriotic' Pakistan.

The military regimes believed in and acted according to an exclusionary political framework by keeping every party and group out of the power structure that they thought might threaten their authority. By offering incentives, they created a big room and space only for the individuals, groups, and fragments of political parties that would serve as their political proxies: the Conventional Muslim League of Ayub Khan, Zia ul-Haq's propping up of religious parties and later the cultivation of Islamic Jamhuri Itehad (IJI) by his successors, and the Muslim League, Quaid-i-Azam, under Pervez Musharraf. The basic instruments of de-politicization were: a ban on political activities, suppression of civil rights and control over the media through censorship, and severe punishments for those who challenge their power. Every time a martial law was enforced, prominent politicians and loyal political activists were arrested and dragged before the military courts for 'accountability'. Since military regimes had no popular legitimacy, they had to remove, and if possible, eradicate, all sources of opposition to their rule by using every coercive means. However, the severity of these means has varied, on the level of opposition, depending on who the real target of each of the military regime was and what the objective conditions of the country were.

The de-politicized model of governance rested on building a coalition of interests around the military leader—the general in power. Using the instrument of state patronage, none of the military rulers had any difficulty in shaping a broad coalition consisting of big businesses, feudal and tribal politicians, and bureaucratic elites as their subordinate partners. The generals selected their partnership because they shared the military rulers' vision of political structuring, and saw their interests promoted, and protected, by the regime they created. In every case of political co-optation, the majority of the political families joined the military regime, which is a sad reflection on the weak commitment of the Pakistani politicians to democratic principles. The question arises, why does a large majority of the politicians prefer joining hands with the military regimes, and not defend democracy and our constitution? The answer might be found in the social basis of leadership and the weak political party system in Pakistan. The feudal politician has an independent power base in his constituency against which no political party has ever been able to compete effectively. The political parties had no control over the feudal politicians who were quick to join military-dominated coalitions. They owed nothing, or very little, to the political parties for their electoral victories, their own rise, and political identity at a local level which has depended on kinship, patronage, and personal connections. This is because no matter which party they belonged to, or even when running independently, many of them have generally won by mobilizing caste, tribe, and other relevant social and kinship networks. There is also a deep history of the emergence of this class of political players as intermediaries between the colonial government under Britain and the local populations. That has set an enduring tradition of being in power without principles through a tertiary clientelism flowing from top to bottom—the feudal client of the military acted as a patron at the level of electoral constituency. Understanding the stronghold of the culture of power and privilege, the military rulers have effectively used the state patronage to wean away the feudal politicians from the political parties.[49]

After neutralizing the political forces, and selectively co-opting those who would serve as their political front in the country, the military rulers reorganized the political structure of the state. Ayub Khan introduced 'basic democracy', while Zia ul-Haq subverted the 1973 constitution by drastically amending it, practically changing it from parliamentary to presidential. Pervez Musharraf did the same and reverted the Constitution to semi-presidential by restoring the power of the President to dissolve elected assemblies and the governments.[50] By rigging the constitution, they pursued certain common objectives, and controlled or limited participation, keeping the political parties out of the electoral process by fashioning supportive political alliances, and strengthening the centralization of political authority. The differences among the three military regimes were more in terms of justification for coming into power and a selection of allies than central issues over the character of the state. Ayub rationalized his rule by focusing on economic development and modernization, while Zia attempted to seek support by using Islamic symbols with a smattering of Islamic laws in order to keep the Islamic constituency in the fold. Pervez Musharraf presented himself as a 'liberal' and drew closer to the vision of Ayub Khan by choosing a strategy of selective suppression, fragmentation of political parties, and co-optation to legitimize and prolong his rule.

Every military regime has worked against the spirit of federalism, which ethnic diversity and regional characteristics of Pakistan's provinces require. Military rule by its intent, policy, and character, has been centralizing, as they brought all governmental and political institutions from top to bottom under the control of one organization—the military establishment. The institutional arrangements that they thought were close to the 'aspirations' or 'genius' of the people, or were replacing 'sham democracy' with 'genuine democracy', were aimed at enforcing the trend towards centralisation of the federal government. In every case, such a strategy, being unnatural to the social conditions of Pakistan, has proven to be counterproductive. Over-centralization and subversion of national political parties gave rise to tribal, ethnic, linguistic, and sectarian affiliations, undermining the very objective of national unity.[51]

A third element in the military's state-building enterprise was centrality of economic development that would lend its leaders credibility, performance legitimacy, and social stability. Ayub Khan was the first to recognize the link between the economy and a strong and effective state. He may even be considered the chief architect of planning and of executing plans to lay down a firm industrial base of the country. The military has tightly embraced the basic ideas of neoliberalism by favouring free enterprise, and expanding domestic markets with wide-ranging networks of financial and industrial institutions. But in Ayub Khan's plans, the state and the public sector played a leading role and created conditions to build up a capacity for the private sector, which was quite weak. It often built up industrial units and then gave them into private hands. That gave rise to a crony capitalism—a part of coalition building under the military regimes. Driven by this motive, the privatization of state-built industrial units (often ending up in the hands of family and friends), constituted the core value of development planning. Pakistan's fledgling bourgeoisie class emerged as the staunchest supporter of a petty bourgeoisie state dominated by the bureaucratic-military elite. Also, the expansion and modernization of the industrial sector fit well into the imperatives of the political economy of defence, for it made more resources available to the state in its effort to counterbalance the Indian threat.

There is no doubt that economic development is an important ingredient for both nation as well as state-building. However, Pakistan's economic growth strategies were guided more by the interplay of powerful political interests than pure economic considerations. A permissive environment for monopolies, import substitution, and protectionism served the interests of big businesses more than the interests of consumers. Neither of the development priorities was geared towards balancing various sectors, nor was it aimed at giving equal opportunity for development to all regions that each had a unique, natural, and human development.

Democracy and Security

The separation of East Pakistan amply demonstrates the failure of the centralist authority structure to promote national integration. Ethnic movements in Sindh and KP, and two major Baloch insurgencies (1974–77, 2006–16), have largely been a reaction to the economic policies promoting inequality and political manipulations by the centre. This also illustrates that the national security policy of the state, made up of ethnically diverse regions, cannot, and must not, ignore the issue of democratic rights, adequate representation in political power structures and provincial autonomy. In the contemporary world system, the political conflicts within the state quite often spill over to the adjacent states, pulling in external factors. The South Asian region represents perhaps the worst examples of internationalization of internal conflicts (Afghanistan, Sri Lanka,

Kashmir and Punjab, and Balochistan). Even if internal political contestation is forcefully contained or muted, it would enhance vulnerabilities of the state to external influences, and at worst, intervention.[52] Although the military's role as the most developed institution, and its state-building policies under Ayub Khan, have often been widely praised, paradoxically, the military was the catalyst for the country's dismemberment.[53] A deep understanding of the issue would show that the strangulation of democratic forces, repression by the authoritarian state and the resultant sense of political deprivation fomented the Bangla nationalism.[54] The Pakistani praetorian state, though highly developed in terms of structural capacity, was politically weak and its organic links with the mass society were shallow. The military then failed to connect itself with the vital institutions of the civil society. Rather by suppressing them, it became isolated. In former East Pakistan, for example, it was at war with the civil institutions and finally with the citizens, and thus isolated and vulnerable to Indian military intervention and defeat.[55]

The other two military regimes (Zia ul-Haq, 1977–88; Pervez Musharraf, 1999–2008) have produced equally dangerous consequences for national security given the choices in the wars in Afghanistan they made, alliances with the militants and foreign powers they struck, and the erroneous national security policies they introduced. The Zia ul-Haq regime supported the Afghan Mujahedeen by arming, training, and patronizing several of the factions, along with millions of Afghan refugees, to defeat the Soviet Union. It took great risks in sustaining the Afghan insurgency for about a decade, which also allowed tens of thousands of foreign militants to train in Pakistan and trek through the western borderlands into Afghanistan. The Arab and other fighters came with jihadist ideology, ideologues, and developed transnational Islamist connections to wage jihad against every 'unjust' government, national or foreign. The idea was to raise the cost of the Soviet occupation that it believed would force it to withdraw.[56]

Besides the Afghan Mujahedeen, it cultivated the religious parties that were willing to raise funds, mobilize young Pakistani fighters, and host the Arab Jihadists. The United States, under the Republican administration of Ronald Reagan, saw the Soviet move in Afghanistan as an imminent threat to its security arrangements in the Gulf region. Its credibility as a 'guarantor' of security in the regions had suffered a grave blow with the fall of the Shah of Iran and takeover by the success of the Islamic revolution. It interpreted the Afghan-Soviet war in terms of the Cold War ideological conflict, and offered itself to lend support to the Mujahedeen as well as Pakistan so that, in its strategy of countering the Soviet Union, it would serve as a 'frontline' state.[57] After about four decades, the country remains on the 'frontline', as the wars in Afghanistan, which are being fought by new actors under a very different regional and international environment, have not ended. When it comes to the security consequences of the Afghan and Kashmir policy—the privatization of a national security policy with the role of militant groups—one may find a troubling connection of the present conflicts and dangers with the beginning of the war in Afghanistan. Due to limitations of space and the subject under discussion, we can only identify three major, long-term consequences for national security. First, it is the emergence of the jihadist culture with deep roots in Islamic radicalism, that has a transnational character, and thus that has created a security impact beyond the battlegrounds of Afghanistan and Pakistan. Second, the radical Islamic groups have emerged as relatively autonomous and anti-state, and have created their own narrative of national security—with imagined and real enemies, a clear policy, and organizations to carry out their agenda. Third, the radical thought propaganda and militancy have strained pluralism in Pakistan by giving rise to intolerance, extremism, and sectarian identities. The eleven years of Zia ul-Haq's state-driven Islamization and orientation of Islamist-security policy—the employment of Islamic radicals in support of the state objectives—have left a deep, negative, impact on society and national security.

The fourth military regime (1999–2008) continued with the same polices but under the thin veneer of 'liberalism'. An unconstitutional military regime and political liberalism were contradictions in principles and philosophies. What about the civilian governments (1988–1999) and their policy choices when they succeeded the third military regime? They had hardly any power or influence over the national security policy and critical elements of foreign policy. They had to survive politically, and that depended on accepting the drastic power-shift toward the military that had taken place during the Zia ul-Haq years. That legacy has remained in place in the fourth democratic transition (2008–present). It was that heritage of accumulation of power by the military, and its domination of the state that prompted General Pervez Musharraf to avenge his dismissal in October 1999 by taking over the country. The state and institutional affairs became reduced to a tribal warfare between an elected prime minister with two–third majority and a single general infuriated by his removal just a year before his retirement. It also reveals a lot about the weakness of the political parties, the democratic culture, and the institutional power of the military.

Musharraf's pursuit of power at the national scene, including the branded security policy, was no different than what other military dictators had done. He targeted a popular political leader, destroyed the party he led, and used state resources to create supportive political factions, much in the footsteps of Zia ul-Haq. However, there was a change in the tactical part of the strategy towards Afghanistan, even if not in the objectives. Having supported the Taliban regime in Afghanistan, he reversed the course under American pressure, as the regional and international environment changed with the terrorist attacks in New York and Washington, DC on 11 September 2001.[58] He quickly changed allies from the Taliban to the Americans by creating virtue out of necessity. It earned him much needed international support and recognition as a valuable ally who would provide every bit of assistance in support of American efforts to dislodge the Taliban and help create a stable and peaceful Afghanistan.[59] One can debate whether or not Musharraf had more choices other than aligning Pakistan with the American 'war on terror', but no matter what he did, it was considered 'inadequate' and 'lacking' by the United States with its mantra of 'do more'. A transactional relationship, formed under compelling security circumstances, has tended to expose inherently conflicting interests over Afghanistan. As the war dragged on with similar effects on the staying power of another great power, the lessons of history (that Afghanistan is a 'graveyard' of empires—memorialized for a long time) introduced ambiguities, doubts, and conflicting urges in Pakistan's policy. Such a policy had its own effects, not just on bilateral relations with the United States, but it also allowed Afghanistan to move in the direction of India, which in its view uses the war as a front to wage war in Balochistan.[60] The terrorist outfits proliferated under Musharraf's rule as a reaction to his policies, as well as to the weakening of the state. The Tehrik-e-Taliban factions ousted the state from Swat, and tribal regions by destroying both the traditional social order and the administrative and security institutions. By aiding the US 'war on terrorism', Pakistan became a victim of terrorism, costing the lives of around 12,977 citizens according to the statistics of the National Counter-Terrorism Authority.[61] The economic cost of the war is estimated to be around U.S. \$218 billion.[62] Insurgency in Balochistan resurfaced after the ouster of the civilian government, gaining strength by attracting the support of traditional and new rivals feeling insecure by the development of the Gwadar port. The insurgencies, terrorism, and political crises are some of the consequences of the fourth military regime. The legacies of the military continue to cast a heavy shadow on every aspect of national security, which the civilian leaders find troubling, and have been unable to deal with on their own because of the domination of the military over the security policy.

There is an enduring lesson from the troubled history of Pakistan: the praetorian state and democratic society cannot exist together; one must weaken the other in order to expand and develop itself. The consequences of this contradiction influence all elements of the state and society, and redefine the essential relationship with the political authority in contemporary Pakistan, as it did in the previous decades. Constitutionalism, democratic values, and political institutions have been the first casualty of military regimes. Repeated deviations from the constitutional path, though validated by the courts under the 'law of necessity', have undermined its juridical and institutional supremacy. Two further consequences are subtler, but equally detrimental to the development of democracy, peace, and stability in Pakistan. First is the decline of the moral authority of the state, which has produced serious implications for national security and identity. Arbitrary applications of coercive means to seek allegiances of the citizens has not only weakened the bond between the state and individual, but has also pushed the targeted sections of society towards equally violent responses. The spiral of state oppression and insurgency in Balochistan (1973–7) was a grave manifestation of the weakened moral authority of the state when it dismissed an elected government of the province.[63] In the same way, the dismissal of elected governments by Musharraf contributed significantly to political disaffection that has fuelled ethnic, sectarian, and religious conflicts. The end result is that the security-state has created more insecurity for itself and for the society.

An accommodation of economic or cultural interests of ethnic groups through an undemocratic order has failed to integrate them into the national mainstream. Even though military rulers co-opted some of the ethnic elites to share power, the popular appeal of ethnic nationalism at the grassroots level did not diminish.[64] Rather, the absence of democracy provided a fertile ground for the growth of ethnic sentiments, particularly in Sindh and Balochistan provinces. The blocking of political and constitutional solutions made the ethno-national movements unmanageable and potentially dangerous for the territorial integrity of the country.

Second, Pakistan has suffered considerable institutional decay under the military dictatorships. The development of political parties has been stunted. Woefully, most of the parties represent loose factions and their leadership is personalized and confined to the landed aristocracy. Had Pakistan's political system evolved along the lines of representative legitimacy, a new generation of politicians from business and professional classes might have emerged. While the size of the Pakistani middle class has vastly expanded over the decades, it remains unrepresented in political power. The reason is that the main political parties have favoured members of landed elite when awarding party tickets, as they are considered electable. Nothing can symbolize political and social stagnation more than the monopoly of the feudal class over political power. It is a free political process that stimulates the growth of autonomous institutions within society that expresses its dreams and ideals. By denying such freedoms, the military rule in Pakistan prevented the evolution of independent intellectual, social, and political networks that could challenge the dominance of traditional power elites. As Western experience shows, the growth of civil society and democratic development go together, one strengthening the other.[65] The weakening of the civil society in Pakistan has weakened the very institutional basis of democratic politics. However, this has begun to change with the democratic transition, and the trend may grow if the process is not disrupted again.

One of the central facts of Pakistani politics is that the power of the military with its latent capacity and deep legacy to intervene in politics looms very large. It has carved out a constituency of political support, which is often clamorous in demanding the overthrow of elected governments. It has captured powers that constitutionally belong to elected governments. In certain areas of national policy, such as defence spending and national security, the military has decisive influence. Although, since 2008, the military has supported the transition to democracy, its apolitical character as an institution has yet to grow and the democracy has to be consolidated enough to be irreversible.

Pakistan's national security is more complex than can be explained solely in terms of external military threats or conventional defence strategies. We need a holistic perspective of security in order to comprehend the whole range of domestic issues that enhance vulnerability of the state and its institutions. I have argued that national security analysis cannot be divorced from the internal process of state formation. The military rule that was aimed at developing a powerful state proved counterproductive to the requirements of an ethnically diverse and divided society. Democracy, not dictatorship, could mould the regional identities into a Pakistani nationhood. The functioning of democratic institutions since 2008 has begun to demand greater accountability and subordination of the military to the parliament.[66] There is persistent and wider criticism of the role of the intelligence agencies in politics and for their inability to provide security against terrorism.[67] With further progress in democratization, the influence of the military may hopefully decline and its political culture change. Success in achieving national integration through a mix of institutional arrangements that promote representative legitimacy and political consensus would increase the political capacity of the state to deal with the turbulence of nation-building, insurgencies, and many other complex legacies handed down from the military regimes. An effective security policy would rest on these measures.

Notes

1. David Rousseau and A. Maurits van der Veen, 'The Emergence of a Shared Identity: An Agent-based Computer Simulation of Idea Diffusion,' *The Journal of Conflict Resolution* 49/5 (October 2005): 689.

2. Ibid.

3. Aqil Shah, *The Army and Democracy: Military Politics in Pakistan* (Cambridge: Harvard University Press, 2014).

4. Hasan Askari Rizvi, *The Military and Politics in Pakistan* (Lahore: Progressive Publishers, 1974); Ayesha Siddiqa, *Military Inc.: Inside Pakistan's Military Economy* (London: Pluto Press, 2007); Hussain Ḥaqqānī, *Pakistan: Between Mosque and Military* (Washington: Carnegie Endowment for International Peace, 2005); Hasan Askari Rizvi, *Military, State, and Society in Pakistan* (New York: St. Martin's Press, 2000); Shuja Nawaz, *Crossed Swords: Pakistan, Its Army, and the Wars Within* (Oxford: Oxford University Press, 2009).

5. Rasul Bakhsh Rais, 'Pakistan's Strategic Culture and Deterrence Stability on the Subcontinent,' in eds. Michael Krepon, et. al. *Deterrence Instability and Nuclear Weapons in South Asia,* (Washington: Stimson, 2015), 95–118; Feroz Hassan Khan, 'Rough Neighbours: Afghanistan and Pakistan' *Strategic Insights* 2/1 (January 2003); Hasan-Askari Rizvi, 'Pakistan's Strategic Culture' in ed. Michael R. Chalmers, *South Asia in 2020: Future Strategic Balances and Alliances* (Carlisle: Strategic Studies Institute, 2002), 305–28; Ijaz Khan, *Pakistan's Strategic Culture and Foreign Policy Making: A Study of Pakistan's Post 9/11 Afghan Policy Change* (New York: Nova Science Publishers, 2007); Peter R. Lavoy, 'Pakistan's Strategic Culture: A Theoretical Excursion' *Strategic Insights,* 4/10 (October 2005); Lisa Curtis 'The Reorientation of Pakistan's Foreign Policy Toward its Region' *Contemporary South Asia* 20/2 (2012): 255–69.

6. C. Christine Fair, *Fighting to the End: The Pakistan Army's Way of War* (New York: Oxford University Press, 2014); Shuja Nawaz, *Crossed Swords: Pakistan, Its Army, and the Wars Within* (Oxford: Oxford University Press, 2009); H. Rizvi, *Military, State and Society in Pakistan* (London: Palgrave Macmillan, 2014); Husain Haqqani, 'The Role of Islam in Pakistan's future' *Washington Quarterly* 28/1 (2004), 83–96; Vali Nasr, 'Military Rule, Islamism and Democracy in Pakistan' *The Middle East Journal* 58/2 (2004),195–209.

7. Javid Iqbal, *Islam and Pakistan's Identity* (Iqbal Academy: Vanguard, 2003.); Stephen P. Cohen, *The Idea of Pakistan* (Washington: Brookings Institution Press, 2004); Akbar S. Ahmed, *Jinnah, Pakistan and Islamic Identity: The Search for Saladin* (London: Routledge, 1997); Farzana Shaikh, *Making Sense of Pakistan* (New York: Columbia University Press, 2009); Nasir Islam, 'Islam

and National Identity: The Case of Pakistan and Bangladesh' *International Journal of Middle East Studies* 13/1 (1981), 55–72; Ayesha Jalal, *The Struggle for Pakistan: A Muslim Homeland and Global Politics* (Cambridge: Belknap Press of Harvard University Press, 2014); Ziad Haider, *The Ideological Struggle for Pakistan* (Stanford: Hoover Institution Press/Stanford University, 2010); Farhan Mujahid Chak, *Islam and Pakistan's Political Culture* (New York: Routledge, 2015)

8. 'TTP Fighting against Pakistan as India's Proxy: Defence Minister' *The News* (Islamabad), May 2015, <https://www.thenews.com.pk/article-186067-TTP-fighting-against-Pakistan-as-Indias-proxy:-Khawaja-Asif>. Accessed 3 November 2016.

9. Stephen P. Cohen, *The Future of Pakistan* (Washington: Brookings Institution, 2011).

10. For instance, see Agha Shahi, *Pakistan's Security and Foreign Policy* (Lahore: Progressive Publishers, 1988); Noor A. Hussain, 'India's Regional Policy: Strategic and Security Dimensions,' in *The Security of South Asia*, Stephen Philip Cohen, ed. (Urbana and Chicago: University of Illinois Press, 1987), 24–49; Hasan-Askari Rizvi, *Pakistan and the Geostrategic Environment* (New York: St. Martin's Press, 1993); S.M. Burke and Lawrence Ziring, *Pakistan's Foreign Policy: A Historical Analysis* (Karachi: Oxford University Press, 1990); G.W. Choudhury, *Pakistan's Relations with India, 1947–66* (London: Pall Mall Press, 1968).

11. Aslam Siddiqi, *Pakistan Seeks Security* (Lahore: Longmans, Green, Pakistan Branch, 1960); Pervaiz Iqbal Cheema, *Pakistan's Defence Policy, 1954–8* (Basinstoke: Macmillan, 1990); Rais Ahmad Khan, Rasul B. Rais and Khalid Waheed, eds., *South Asia: Military Power and Regional Politics* (Islamabad: Islamabad Council of World Affairs, 1989); K. Subrahmanyam, *Indian Security Perspectives* (New Delhi: ABC Pub. House, 1982); K. Subrahmanyam, 'India's Security Challenges and Responses: Evolving a Security Doctrine' *Strategic Analysis* 11/1 (April 1987), 6–15; Mohammed Ayoob, 'India in South Asia: The Quest for Regional Predominance' *World Policy Journal* 7/1 (Winter 1989–90),107–33; Mohammed Ayoob, 'India as Regional Hegemon: External Opportunities and Internal Constraints' *International Journal* 66 (Summer 1991), 420–48; Bharat K. Wariavwalla, 'Security with Status: What Motivates India's Security Policy' in W. Thomas Wander & Eric H. Arnett. eds. *The Proliferation of Advanced Weaponry: Technology, Motivations, and Responses,* (Washington, DC: AAAS, 1992); Douglas C. Makeig, 'War, No-war and the Indo-Pakistan Negotiating Process' *Pacific Affairs* 60/2 (Summer 1987), 271–94.

12. On this issue, a plethora of literature has emerged during the past decade. For

instance, see: Brian L. Job ed., *The Insecurity Dilemma: National Security of Third World States* (Boulder & London: Lynne Rienner Publisher, 1992); Ken Booth ed. *New Thinking About Strategy and International Security* (London: Harper Collins Academic, 1991); Edward E. Azar and Chung-in Moon, eds. *National Security in the Third World: The Management of Internal and External Threat* (College Park: Center for International Development and Conflict Management, University of Maryland, 1988); Nicole Ball, *Security and Economy in the Third World* (Princeton: Princeton University Press, 1988); Caroline Thomas, *In Search of Security: The Third World in International Relations* (Boulder: Lynne Rienner, 1987); Barry Buzan, *People, States and Fear: The National Security Problem in International Relations* (Brighton: Wheatsheaf, 1983).

13. Keith Krause and Michael C. Williams, 'Broadening the Agenda of Security Studies: Politics and Methods' *Mershon Review of International Studies* 40/2 (1996), 229–54; Barry Buzan, Ole Wæver, and Jaap de Wilde, 'Introduction' in *Security: A New Framework for Analysis*, (Boulder, Lynne Rienner: 1998), 1–20.

14. Magnus Ranstorp, *Understanding Violent Radicalisation: Terrorist and Jihadist Movements in Europe* (London: Routledge, 2010.); Frank Peter and Rafael Ortega. *Islamic Movements of Europe: Public Religion and Islamophobia in the Modern World* (London: I. B. Tauris, 2014); Nathal M. Dessing et al., *Everyday Lived Islam in Europe* (Burlington, VT: Ashgate, 2013); R. Coolsaet, *Jihadi Terrorism and the Radicalisation Challenge: European and American Experiences* (Farnham, Surrey: Ashgate, 2011); Angel Rabasa and Cheryl Benard, *Eurojihad: Patterns of Islamist Radicalization and Terrorism in Europe* (New York: Cambridge University Press, 2015); Daniela Pisoiu, *Islamist Radicalisation in Europe: An Occupational Change Process* (Abingdon, Oxon: Routledge, 2012); R. Coolsaet, *Jihadi Terrorism and the Radicalisation Challenge in Europe* (Aldershot: Ashgate, 2008); E. G. H. Joffé, *Islamist Radicalisation in Europe and the Middle East: Reassessing the Causes of Terrorism* (London: I.B. Tauris, 2013); Ed Husain, *The Islamist: Why I Joined Radical Islam in Britain, What I Saw inside and Why I Left* (London: Penguin, 2007).

15. See Mohammed Ayoob, 'The Security Problematic of the Third World' *World Politics*, 43 (January 1991), 265–73.

16. Francis Fukuyama, *The End of History?* (Washington: National Affairs, 1989).

17. Caroline Thomas explains state strength and weakness in terms of institutional capacities which she differentiates as despotic—arbitrary, and infrastructural— effectively exercised through the institutions. See: Caroline Thomas, 'Southern Instability, Security and Western Concepts: On an Unhappy Marriage and the Need for a Divorce' in Caroline Thomas and Paikiasothy Saravanamuttu,

eds. *The State and Instability in the South* (New York: St. Martin's Press, 1989), 182–88. Michael Mann identifies infrastructural power with the ability of the state to implement its decisions and 'penetrate civil society'. See: Michael Mann, 'The Autonomous Power of the State: Its Origins, Mechanisms and Result' in Job A. Hall, ed. *States in History* (Oxford: Basil Blackwell, 1986), 113.

18. On the collapse of the Middle East states, see Michael C. Hudson, *Crisis of the Arab State: Study Report.* August 2015. <http://belfercenter.ksg.harvard.edu/files/CrisisArabState.pdf>. Accessed on December 24, 2016; Ariel I. Ahran, and Ellen Lust, 'The Decline and Fall of the Arab State', *Survival: Global Politics and Strategy* 58/2 (2016), 7–34.

19. See for instance, David Fromkin, *A Peace to End All Peace* (New York: Henry Holt and Company, 1989), 351–455.

20. Ayesha Jalal, *The State of Martial Rule: The Origins of Pakistan's Political Economy of Defence.* (Cambridge: Cambridge University Press, 1990).

21. Parvez Hasan, *Pakistan's Economy at the Crossroads: Past Policies and Present* (Karachi: Oxford University Press, 1998), 84, 269, 318; James H. Lebovic, 'Spending Priorities and Democratic Rule in Latin America' *The Journal of Conflict Resolution* 45/4 (August, 2001), 427–52.

22. Nawaz Sharif had two–third majority in the 1997 general elections, unprecedented in the history of Pakistan. He started a back channel with the then Indian Prime Minister Atal Bihari Vajpayee to resolve the Kashmir issue, hosting him in Lahore on a historic visit. This was all indicative of assuming real powers under the constitution. The Chief of Army Staff, General Pervez Musharraf and a coterie of generals started the Kargil conflict without informing the Prime Minister, and later took over power when Nawaz Sharif fired Musharraf. Learning from the past, in his third tenure (2013–17), Nawaz Sharif was very sensitive to what the military said about security and foreign policy choices.

23. On garrison state, see: Ishtiaq Ahmed, *Pakistan the Garrison State: Origins, Evolution, Consequences, 1947–2011* (Karachi: Oxford University Press, 2013); Harold D Lasswell, 'The Garrison State' *The American Journal of Sociology* 46/4 (January 1941); Robert LaPorte, 'Succession in Pakistan: Continuity and change in a Garrison State' *Asian Survey* 9/11 (Nov 1969), 842–61; K.L. Kamal, *Pakistan: The Garrison State* (New Delhi: Intellectual Publishing House, 1982); Tan Tai Yong, *The Garrison State: Military, Government and Society in Colonial Punjab, 1849–1947* (SAGE Series in Modern History, 8; New Delhi: Sage Publications India, 2005).

24. All the military rulers formulated two inter-related policies on education and culture. The cultural orientation of Ayub Khan and Pervez Musharraf was

modernist-liberal but authoritarian. Zia ul-Haq's policies aimed at transforming Pakistan into an Islamic state.

25. There is considerable evidence of this in political consensus on the 18th Amendment and the NFC Award in 2013–14.

26. Job defines 'insecurity dilemma' as internal predicament; lack of social cohesion, obscurity of political legitimacy, lack of effective institutions to provide peace, threats to and from regimes in power. These conditions might increase external threats: Brian L. Job, 'The Insecurity Dilemma: National, Regime, and State Securities in the Third World' in *The Insecurity Dilemma*, op. cit., 17–19.

27. Stanley Wolpert, *Jinnah of Pakistan* (New York: Oxford University Press, 1984); Mujahid, Sharif et. al. *Quaid-i-Azam Jinnah: Studies in Interpretation* (Karachi: Quaid-i-Azam Academy, 1981).

28. Balraj Puri, 'From Ideology-to Territory-Based Nation: Pakistan's Transition and Lessons for India,' *Economic and Political Weekly* 37/9 (March, 2002): 834–5.

29. M. Rafique Afzal, *Pakistan, History & Politics, 1947–1971* (Karachi: Oxford University Press, 2001).

30. See Hasan-Askari Rizvi, *The Military and Politics in Pakistan, 1947–86* (Lahore: Progressive Publishers, 1986); Stephen P. Cohen, *The Pakistan Army* (Berkeley: University of California Press, 1984); Bilal Hashmi, 'Dragon See: Military in the State' in *Pakistan: The Roots of Dictatorship,* Hassan Gardezi and Jamil Rashid eds. (London: Zed Press, 1983), 148–72.

31. On the origins of the Kashmir conflict, see: Alastair Lamb, *Kashmir: A Disputed Legacy, 1846–1990* (Hertinfordbury: Roxford Books, 1991).

32. Syed Nur Ahmad, *From Martial Law to Martial Law: Politics in the Punjab, 1919–1958.* trans. Craig Baxter (Boulder: Westview Press, 1985).

33. Syed Fida Hasan, *Pakistan the Promise of the Early Years: A Memoir* (Lahore: Zeenat Publishers, 2016).

34. Robert LaPorte, 'Power and Privilege: Influence and Decision-Making in Pakistan,' *Pacific Affairs* 50/4 (1977–1978), 673–9.

35. Ibid.

36. Sumit Ganguly, 'Pakistan's Never-Ending Story: Why the October Coup Was No Surprise' *Foreign Affairs* 79/2 (March/April, 2000), 3.

37. For the earlier view of Pakistani elite that India wanted to undo Partition, see: G.W Choudhury, 'Pakistan-India Relations' *Pakistan Horizon* 11/2 (1958), 57–64; Yasmin Khan, *The Great Partition: The Making of India and Pakistan* (New Haven: Yale University Press, 2007); Tai Yong Tan and Gyanesh Kudaisya, *The Aftermath of Partition in South Asia* (London: Routledge, 2000).

38. See S. K. Ghosh, and Shri K. F. Rustamji. *Secularism in India: The Concept and Practice* (New Delhi: A.P.H. Publications, 2001); Christian W. Troll, *Islam in*

the Indian Subcontinent: Muslims in Secular India (Tokyo: Sophia University, 1986); M.M. Sankhdher, *Secularism in India, Dilemmas and Challenges* (New Delhi: Deep & Deep Publications, 1992); Ragini Sen, Wolfgang Wagner, and Caroline Howarth, *Secularism and Religion in Multi-faith Societies: The Case of India* (Cham: Springer, 2014); Taylor C. Sherman, *Muslim Belonging in Secular India* (Cambridge: Cambridge University Press, 2015); Donald Eugene Smith, *India as a Secular State* (Princeton: Princeton University Press, 1963); C.S. Adcock, *The Limits of Tolerance: Indian Secularism and the Politics of Religious Freedom* (New York: Oxford University Press, 2014).

39. Klaus Schlichte, *The Dynamics of States: The Formation and Crises of State Domination*, (England: Ashgate, 2005), 183–210.

40. E.H. Carr, 'The Nature of Politics' in E.H. Carr, ed. *The Twenty Years' Crisis, 1919–1939: An Introduction to the Study of International Relations.* (London: Macmillan, 1946), 533–7; Stefano Guzzini, *Realism in International Relations and International Political Economy: The Continuing Story of a Death Foretold* (London: Routledge, 1998); Kenneth Waltz, 'The Anarchic Structure of World Politics' *Theory of International Politics* (Reading: Addison-Wesley Pub., 1979), 49–69; Robert Gilpin, 'War and Change in World Politics' in Paul R. Viotti and Mark V. Kauppi eds. *International Relations Theory* (New York: Macmillan, 1987),115–124.

41. Robert J. McMahon, 'United States Cold War Strategy in South Asia: Making a Military Commitment to Pakistan, 1947–1954' *The Journal of American History* 75/3 (1988), 812–40; Dennis Kux, *The United States and Pakistan, 1947–2000: Disenchanted Allies* (Washington: Woodrow Wilson Center Press, 2001); E.I. Brodkin, 'United States and India and Pakistan: The Attitudes of the Fifties' *International Affairs (Royal Institute of International Affairs 1944)* 43/4 (1967), 664–77; Henry W. Brands, 'India and Pakistan in American Strategic Planning, 1947–54: The Commonwealth as Collaborator' *The Journal of Imperial and Commonwealth History* 15/1 (1986), 41–54; David Shavit, *The United States in Asia: A Historical Dictionary* (New York: Greenwood Press, 1990); M. S. Venkataramani, *The American Role in Pakistan, 1947–1958* (New Delhi: Radiant, 1982)

42. It was Ayub Khan as Defence Minister and Foreign Office and civil bureaucracy that had a very strong pro-West orientation that began seeking American economic and military assistance. Liaquat Ali Khan's visit to the US, earlier, had adequately conveyed to the Americans that they could count on Pakistan in the emerging Cold War international climate. See: Karamatullah K. Ghori, 'Sixty Years of Pakistan's Foreign Policy' *Pakistan Horizon* 60/2 (April, 2007),

9–12; Rais Ahmad Khan, 'Pakistan-United States Relations' in *Proceedings of the National Symposium*, Islamabad (1982).

43. Syed Nur Ahmad, *From Martial Law to Martial Law: Politics in the Punjab, 1919–1958*, trans. Craig Baxter. (Boulder: Westview Press, 1985).

44. Mohammad Ayub Khan, *Friends Not Masters: A Political Autobiography* (New York: Oxford University Press, 1967). Zia ul-Haq, Yahya Khan, and Pervez Musharraf repeated the same lines.

45. *Supplement to the Composite Report of the President's Committee to Study the United States Military Assistance Program* 11 (Washington, DC: US Government Printing Office, 1959), 79.

46. Robert LaPorte, 'Succession in Pakistan: Continuity and Change in a Garrison State' *Asian Survey* 9/11 (1969), 842–61.

47. Harold D. Lasswell, 'The Garrison State,' *The American Journal of Sociology* 46/4 (January, 1941), 455–468.

48. Aqil Shah, 'Pakistan's "Armored" Democracy' *Contemporary South Asia*, 4/3 (1995), 26–40.

49. Every political family embraced Ayub Khan as the leader and accepted his 1962 Presidential Constitution. They considered joining the Conventional Muslim League then as a privilege. It is estimated that about 70 per cent of the members of Zia ul-Haq's Majlis-i-Shoora (a consultative assembly) belonged to the Pakistan Peoples Party at one time or another. Almost 90% of the Muslim League-N, defected to Pervez Musharraf and established the PML-Q.

50. The 8th amendment was adopted as a condition set by Zia for the lifting of Martial Law in 1985. For the text, see *The Constitution of the Islamic Republic of Pakistan,* (Islamabad: Government of Pakistan, Federal Judicial Academy, 1989), 27–30, 174.

51. Aqil Shah, 'Pakistan's "Armored" Democracy' *Contemporary South Asia* 4/3 (1995), 26–40.

52. On externalization of internal conflicts see De Silva Kingsley, *Internationalization of Ethnic Conflict in South Asia* (Kandy: International Centre for Ethnic Studies, 1991).

53. Altaf Gauhar, *Ayub Khan, Pakistan's First Military Ruler* (Karachi: Oxford UP, 1996); Lawrence Ziring, *The Ayub Khan Era: Politics in Pakistan, 1958–1969* (New York: Syracuse University Press, 1971); S.A. Saeed, A *President without Precedent: a Brilliant Account of Ayub and His Regime* (Lahore: Lahore Book Depot, 1960); Wayne Wilcox, 'Pakistan: A Decade of Ayub' *Asian Survey* 9/2 (1969), 87–93; Khalid B. Sayeed, 'Development Strategy Under Ayub Khan' *Journal of Developing Societies* 14/2 (1979), 76–84; W. M. Dobell, 'Ayub Khan as President of Pakistan,' *Pacific Affairs* 42/3 (1969), 294–310.

54. Rounaq Jahan, *Pakistan: Failure in National Integration* (New York: Columbia University Press, 1972).

55. Gary Jonathan Bass, *The Blood Telegram: Nixon, Kissinger, and a Forgotten Genocide.* (New York: Knopf, 2013)

56. Muhammad Yousaf and Mark Adkin, *Afghanistan-the Bear Trap: The Defeat of a Superpower,* (Havertown: Casemate, 2001).

57. Arvind Goswami, *3D: Deceit, Duplicity, Dissimulation of US Foreign Policy towards India, Pakistan & Afghanistan* (Bloomington: Author House, 2012); Khalid Mahmud Arif, *Working with Zia: Pakistan's Power Politics, 1977–1988* (Karachi: Oxford University Press, 1995); Thomas P. Thornton, 'The New Phase in US–Pakistani Relations' *Foreign Affairs* 68/3 (1989), 142–59; Leo E. Rose and Kamal Matinuddin, *Beyond Afghanistan: The Emerging US–Pakistan Relations* (Berkeley: Institute of East Asian Studies, University of California, 1989).

58. Naseem Ahmed 'General Musharaf's Taliban Policy, 1999–2008' *The Dialogue* 5/2. (June 2010); 96–124; Daniel Seth Markey, *No Exit from Pakistan: America's Tortured Relationship with Islamabad* (New York: Cambridge University Press, 2013); K. Alan. Kronstadt, *Pakistan–US Relations* (Washington, DC: Congressional Research Service Library of Congress, 2009); C. Christine Fair, 'Time for Sober Realism: Renegotiating US Relations with Pakistan' *The Washington Quarterly* 32/2 (2009), 149–72.

59. K. Alan. Kronstadt, *Pakistan–US Relations* (Washington, DC: Congressional Research Service, Library of Congress, 2009); C. Christine Fair, 'Time for Sober Realism: Renegotiating US Relations with Pakistan' *The Washington Quarterly* 32/2 (2009), 149–72.

60. Baqir Sajjad Syed, 'Threat emanates from India-managed Afghan Soil, Generals Told' *Dawn*, August 10, 2016; 'India Finances Trouble in Pakistan: Hagel', *Dawn*, 27 February 2013.

61. 'Significant Incidents' NACTA, accessed 21 November 2016, <http://www.nacta.gov.pk/>.

62. *Pakistan Economic Survey* (Islamabad: Govt. of Pakistan, Finance Division, Economic Adviser's Wing, 1978).

63. For details see: Selig Harrison, *In Afghanistan's Shadow: Baluch Nationalism and Soviet Temptations* (New York: Carnegie Endowment of International Peace, 1981).

64. See: Tahir Amin, *Ethno-National Movements of Pakistan: Domestic and International Factors* (Islamabad: Institute of Policy Studies, 1988), 223.

65. Adnan Rafiq, 'New Politics of the Middle Class' in Ishtiaq Ahmad and Adnan

Rafiq eds. *Pakistan's Democratic Transition: Change and persistence.* (London and New York: Routledge, 2017), 72–94.

66. Raza Khan, 'Khursheed Shah Asks Government to Summon Military Leadership Before the Parliament', *Dawn*, August 10, 2016.

67. 'PM Should Sack Officers of Intelligence Agencies if they Fail to Trace Quetta Attack Perpetrators: Achakzai", *Dawn*, 9 August 2016.

Chapter III

State, Nation-Building, and Identity

Today, the nation-state is a universal political construct, embraced by all political communities for establishing order, forging social cohesion by integrating diverse ethnic groups into a nation. Its origin, history, and institutional development are spread over centuries of political and social transformations, empire building, long wars, and political settlements like the Peace of Westphalia in 1648.[1] In its present form, the nation-state has its roots in Western political experience. It has resulted from a 'competitive enterprise of war and politics';[2] thousands of rival authorities were eliminated or subordinated before the emerging state succeeded in expanding the boundaries of its centralization.[3] Beginning with its basic, rudimentary character, the evolution of the Western state went much further than establishing control, order and conditions of internal peace. In an interactive process with society, over time, it developed a host of autonomous and differentiated institutions that set it apart from all traditional forms of authority structures. Although the dynamics of its own institutional needs propelled its growth, it promoted and sustained the growth of civil society as an essential political requirement, transforming it into a core social value.[4] In essence, it was the creation and strengthening of the civil society that redefined the bond between individual and the state in terms of rights, contract, and corresponding obligations, giving rise to the idea of a constitutive and legitimate political authority. As the twin processes of state and nation-building coincided, a sense of national identity evolved that further reinforced the social and cultural process of integration of diverse social and cultural groups into a nation. However, with so many states in Europe, neither the approaches, nor the processes of building a national state have been uniform. Each state and nation has learnt something from others but has essentially evolved within its historical and cultural, and in relation to its approximate, geopolitical order.[5] There has not been, nor can there be, a single, universal template of nationalism because of the diversity of the socio-political forces that have influenced and shaped various nationalisms.[6]

The states, if not nations, have acquired some definite characteristics that make them structurally similar though vastly differentiated along ideological lines, and economic models as well as in adopting forms of state-society interactions. Chief among them are fixed territorial boundaries, sovereignty, norms of non-intervention, mutual acknowledgement and conduct of relations by diplomatic means. The evolution of international order, global institutions, hegemony of great powers, and evolution of international regimes are some of the factors that have generated common norms and values among the nation-states. These have further contributed to the internal restructuring of the states and their connectivity with others. Even with similar structural elements, as referred above, states vary greatly in their capacity to govern, produce, and distribute economic goods, establish writ of law, deliver justice, and contribute to human development. On account of the progress or failure of these functions, states have been classified according to ideological or economic performance criteria—liberal, democratic, authoritarian, developed, or developing.[7] The ideal and objectives of the states and the question of power, its centrality and organizing principles have been used to identify the kind of state or government that has come to rule. The principle of organization of political power and its legitimacy—the right to rule—may also help classify the states as republican or monarchical.[8] Similarly, the issue of the distribution of power horizontally among the state institutions, or vertically between the centre and the units will determine whether they have a system of separated powers or a federal form.[9] The type of state system, its efficacy, policies, and outcome, matter for nation-building.

There has been a close and dependent relationship between the state and nation-building processes; one reinforces the other. Historically, they have evolved together, more in the European context, when a community considered itself as a nation and established self-rule within the territorial limits it claimed as its historic homeland.[10] Asserting a claim over the 'homeland' was never a neat and clean process, because too many contests staked a claim over the 'homeland' and each of them wanted to establish 'self-rule'. It was through war, bloodshed, victory or defeat on the battleground that the questions of boundaries and the ruler were settled.[11] But these struggles within, and in relation to, other quasi-states or states had a major bearing on the relationship between the civil society and the national state—sentimentality, ownership, and stakes. As John Hall argues, 'states certainly mattered for nationalism'[12] Their need for self-development and self-preservation in wars with neighbours required economic, social, and political assistance of the society, which in return, generated the two-way-demands process of allegiance and rights of representation. This produced national cohesion, a spirit of nationalism, and an active civil society engaged with the national state.[13]

State as it operates in the contemporary world has gone through many transformations with modernity, trade, commerce, hegemony, wars within the states and among the states and changes in the world order.[14] The breakup of empires that contained nations within themselves and the emergence of new nation-states in the twentieth century, from Latin America to Asia and Africa, have resulted in a great variety of states, nationalisms and approaches to nation- and state-building.

The emergence of nationalism and nationalist movements in European colonies, the two great wars, and the weakening of British and other European empires, produced one of the greatest waves of decolonization. The empires became exhausted by the wars, and the colonies became a burden, as they were no longer as profitable as they had been in the nineteenth century. The cost of maintaining order, and ruling over mobilized communities demanding statehood was too high to prolong colonialism. At the heart of such demands was the Western idea of nationalism, but without the Western prerequisites of being a nation in a homogenous ethnic or cultural sense.[15] The nationalist myths and narratives and popular mobilization contributed to the sentiment for independence and self-rule. However, there is a big debate about whether it were the forces of nationalism in India or the colonial fatigue that gave birth to India and Pakistan in 1947. Regardless, it was a matter of time before British rule would have come to an end; the war had changed the fundamental structure of world power and power relations, including the relationship of the colonies with the imperial powers. What changed this relationship more was the strength of the Indian nationalist movement, which had struck deep and broad roots within the subcontinent.[16] The new nations of India and Pakistan, like many other postcolonial nations, emerged as a direct consequence of the Great War as well as from the decades-long struggle and sacrifices for independence. In their case, conflictive nationalisms, unresolved issues of minority rights, communalism, and violence played a major role in the circumstances of their birth. It was a sorrowful endgame of the British rule.[17]

India and Pakistan were not nations in the Western sense of the word. Neither of the two was culturally homogeneous or ethnically defined. They were then, and they are even now, nations in the political sense. They have contained, in their partitioned territories, communities with different cultures, ethnicities, histories, languages, and social identities, which in the European sense, would entitle them to be 'nations' in their own rights. India inherited a much larger and more complex diversity, which produces one of the greatest experiences of nation- and state-building, perhaps unique in terms of the size and the variety of social groups, cultures, and ethnicities living within its borders.[18] Pakistan's diversity resembles that of India but at a much smaller scale. Pakistan's distinctiveness as having two parts, East Pakistan and West Pakistan, separated by one thousand miles of Indian territory, was an exceptional case of being a state. What brought culturally, ethnically, and linguistically very distinct people together into the fold of Pakistan was the common spirit of Muslim nationalism.[19] That imposed a big challenge to state- and nation-building in addition to ethnic diversity and the fragmented character of social groups.

State- and nation-building has not been an easy process in the postcolonial states, including Pakistan, for three reasons:[20] First, the society is divided along many social groups with different sizes, multiple layers of identities and existing at different levels of social and economic development. Colonialism with selective modernity produced uneven effects of disparity and inequality among ethnic groups and regions. In the context of nationalist mobilization, the inheritance of inequality raised very high expectations of equality at the time of independence, which the nascent, struggling, weak state of Pakistan couldn't meet. One failure after another removed every uniting bond of Muslim nationalism replacing it with ethnicity and feelings of discrimination. Second, in West Pakistan, tribalism and feudalism, which remain constant social barriers in the path of state- and nation-building in Pakistan, created two distinctive streams of politics, political demands and composition of elites in respective wings of the country. In my view, the elites from West Pakistan, their social characteristics being tribal and feudal, sought dominance, and clashed with the middle and lower middle class social base of Bengali ethnic nationalism who were demanding equality, fairness, and representation. The early seizure of state apparatus by the migrants from India and a section of the Punjabi bureaucrats, as well as the rise of the military, turned West Pakistan into a formidable centre of power. It exasperated regional equality further, promoting a sense of marginalization among the Bengalis.

Finally, once the emotions of Muslim nationalism died down, the pragmatic interests of the ethnic communities began to assert themselves. In only a few years' time, the unifying spirit of the Pakistan movement and its inspiring leaders was gone. A natural landscape of major ethnic divisions, subdivisions, religious forces with sectarian tendencies, and clash of ideas and ideologies, all claiming some voice and space in shaping the new state of Pakistan emerged. These conflict-generating forces overloaded the state with too much burden in its initial stage of institutional development. Pakistan resembled 'quasi-societies' of developing countries.[21] Societies divided horizontally, along ethnic lines, with disparate social groups and deeper regional, ethnic, and religious identities than the national identity, have different ideas for, and interests in, shaping a nation. Creating a nation out of social and ethnic fragments of varying sizes requires appropriate approaches toward state- and nation-building. Generally, postcolonial states have adopted mixed clusters of approaches—ideology, centralization, modernization, representation, and repression of separatist movements. Flexibility is the key in making policy adjustments, adapting to the domestic and international environments, and responding to the changing demands of society and ethnic groups. National identity narratives, political participation, and economic and social development serve as some of the most effective tools of national integration and solidarity.

Our argument is that creating a nation out of diverse ethnic groups is a historical process that may take a long time to complete and may face turbulences and troubles on this journey. There are no set rules, policies or principles to pursue nation- and state-building. Every state has to learn its own lessons, change direction when needed, and apply all resources towards the objectives of national cohesion and state effectiveness. The problem is that what European nations achieved through internal wars, repression, and dominance of the core group over a long period to build a culturally homogenous nation, cannot be emulated in the contemporary world. Not that those nations, like Pakistan, have not gone to war with other states or have not fought internal wars against secessionist elements to 'rationalize their societies'; they 'have not had enough war, or, perhaps enough war of the right type.[22] While national unity, solidarity, and integration are important goals towards nation-building, achieving national character or characteristics of the European states or following their routes in today's world is neither necessary nor desirable. Unfortunately, academic and political discourses on state-building in the postcolonial world have taken an essentialist approach to develop characteristics of the Western nations.[23] Pakistan or other developing countries cannot pass through the same sequences of state-making as the Europeans did. The issues that Pakistan faces are complex and the constraints, domestic as well as regional, are too many. While the internal obstacles to national integration are well-known, as summarized above, one must also consider the geopolitical pressures that emanate from the regional and international environments.[24] I believe developing nationhood, state-making, and acquiring a national identity are evolutionary processes that cannot be engineered or artificially imposed, but only aided by policies that are sensitive to the needs of the constituent groups and open for participation by these groups. What are the policies that various Pakistani regimes have attempted to strengthen the idea of Pakistani nationhood? What are the cultural, historical, and religious referents of these policies? How have various ethnic, linguistic, and religious groups responded? Which elements of the state and society influence the politics of national identity? In answering these questions, we will focus on the following two propositions:

a) Ethnic diversity does not melt away with the accommodation of economic or cultural interests of ethnic groups alone or in a few generations; nor can such a melting away to make a nation in the European sense be considered as a desirable goal. What is appropriate and necessary is the integration of genuine interests in a wholesome way that must allow social groups to participate in the political process, share power, and develop stakes in the national state.

b) Regional autonomy, devolution of powers and a recognition of multiple linguistic and cultural identities within a pluralistic, democratic framework would contribute to national solidarity and lay the foundations for the development of a nation-state. Pakistan's state- and nation-building projects are a work in progress and may remain so for some time. It has faced severe setbacks, failures, and some success toward this long-distant goal. Let us critically evaluate the approaches and policies of state- and nation-building during the past seventy years, what the progress is so far, and which policies have worked and which haven't.

Centralization

The dominant elites in Pakistan, and elsewhere in developing countries, have uncritically accepted the Western notions of nation-state and tools of centralization in structuring the state and promoting national integration. This idealization rests on two interrelated assumptions: first, it is through centralization of power that a state can be strengthened enough to establish order in the society, ensuring conditions of peace and stability. Second, centralization can be the means for using institutional capacities of the state for economic and social development, security, and modernization. These assumptions rest on the reading of history, the experience of state-building in the

Western world, and education and socialization of the nationalist elites. In internalizing state-building ideas, they looked more at the finished product of the West than at the rough material of nations they inherited from the colonial powers. My contention is that a uniform model of nation-building for all developing countries cannot be fashioned. Such an enterprise would be dangerous, and might result in adverse consequences, even self-destruction. There are many reasons for this cautionary note, but one will suffice to explain the pitfalls of pursuing the policies of nation-building through a strong central government. It is a historical accident that most of the postcolonial states like Pakistan have inherited a mosaic of ethnic, religious, and linguistic groups that have a proud past, a strong sense of ethnic or communal identity and rich cultural traditions. Needless to say, these groups had a semi-autonomous existence, territorial boundaries, if not a self-rule, for centuries before Western colonization. The construction of a cohesive national identity by the central state, primarily through 'primitive accumulation of power',[25] and without political legitimacy would instead provoke resistance, alienate important sectors of the society, and might even undermine the legitimacy of the state itself.

This is exactly what happened in Pakistan's first twenty-five years. Centralization primarily meant concentration of power in the central government in Pakistan. Within the centre, the balance of power slipped away from the political elites to the bureaucracy, trained and socialized in colonial service. It did not change its outlook towards the society, people, and general public. The bureaucrats who assumed top positions in the central government had shallow roots, if any, in the society, were arrogant and exhibited patronizing attitudes towards the people, very much like their British bosses.[26] They had very pessimistic views of the political classes, and took upon themselves the responsibility of building the new state of Pakistan. They sincerely believed that a feudal social background, poor education, and issues of integrity regarding the politicians made them poor material for leading Pakistan. They thought the political leaders could not measure up to the challenges of order, development, stability, and security of the country.[27] Political confrontations, lack of unifying leadership, and a weak party system coupled with a delay in framing the constitution and the holding of elections had delegitimized the political elites. The bureaucrats took full advantage of the difficulties and problems of the political elites and began to assert themselves, eventually taking over the state. By displacing politicians, a few of them took over positions of heads of the state and heads of the government in the formative phase of the country.[28] This left a deep impact on the political direction the country took and shaped the foreign and security policies of the country. The bureaucrats factionalized the politicians and used them as pawns in making and breaking cabinets.[29]

Owing to the foreign policy choices that the bureaucracy made on account of their Western orientation, the military began to gain influence. With the beginning of the Cold War between two great powers—Soviet Union and the United States—Pakistan found an opportunity for an alliance with the United States. The US wanted Iran, Pakistan, and Turkey to form a 'northern tier' in its containment policy towards communism.[30] More than the distant, and somewhat unreal, threat of communism, Pakistan was more concerned about the immediate and near threat, which it perceived from India. This was the prime motivation of Pakistan in joining the Western security pacts, Central Treaty Organization (CENTO) and South East Asia Treaty Organization (SEATO).[31] The flow of economic aid, military assistance, training programs for the military officers and their connectivity, particularly with the United States, added a new dimension to the centralization process in the Pakistani polity. The military began to emerge as a powerful national player. The civilian bureaucrats lacking political legitimacy wanted to have the military on their side to manipulate the political process in their favour. They co-opted General Ayub Khan, Chief of the Armed Forces as a member of the cabinet with the portfolio of Defence Minister. But the General had his own designs, vision, idea, and concept for building Pakistan. He thought the parliamentary democracy was not workable in a country like Pakistan. The political class with its origins in the feudal, tribal social system had neither the vision nor the capacity to develop the country. He found the chaos of democratic politics too disorderly, political instability as a weakening of the country, the politicians as self-centred, devoid of patriotism, and the people as illiterate, poor, and manipulated by the political leaders. He thought the country, even after adopting the 1956 Constitution with remarkable consensus, and preparing for the first general elections, was in turmoil. He became 'concerned' with the troubles of the country and began to think 'hard' about how a chaotic Pakistan ruled by unruly politicians could be transformed into a 'strong', modern, and prosperous country.[32] He argued that order, stability, economic development, and a controlled-basic democracy would suit the social and economic conditions of Pakistan.[33] He wanted the military to be the centre of power, with himself at the top, the co-opted members of the political class to work with him to modernize Pakistan on which, in his view, would rest stability, security, and prosperity of the country.[34] He ventured into new, innovative ideas of political development, state- and nation-building and a state-society relationship.[35]

With reformist thoughts in mind, the General took over power in October 1958 by imposing Martial law, which he termed as a 'revolution'.[36] The 'revolution' kept him in absolute power for the next eleven years. Never in the short history of Pakistan, then, has any single leader exercised so much power without any constraints as Ayub Khan did. He wrote a new constitution in 1962 that introduced a presidential form of government, organized a new political party—Conventional Muslim League—and restructured every political and bureaucratic institution to implement his vision of a modern Pakistan. The political template that Ayub Khan followed was not entirely new but reflected ideas of development economists in Western academia about state and nation-building in postcolonial states. They had argued for order and stability as the basic function of new states because of the low development of political culture, poverty, and ethnic fragmentation.[37] Such a pessimistic social and political analysis had a context in the rise of communism and the emerging popularity of socialist thought and likelihood of revolutionary movements in postcolonial states. The first military takeover in Pakistan was very much connected to the Cold War, tilted towards the United States, military pacts, and the view that militaries could be agents of modernization, stability, and development.[38]

The new regime perfected a dangerous triangle of centralization—concentration of power in the central government, in the military, and within West Pakistan, practically in the Punjab—the largest constituent. The military-centred centralization produced three adverse consequences for state- and nation-building. First, the constituent ethnic groups felt they had become a colony more than equal partners with equal stakes in the state of Pakistan. They saw the centralized state- and nation-building process as going against the spirit of ethnic pluralism and working against their interests. In the new centre of power, all other ethnic groups except the Mohajir and the Punjabi elites, found themselves on the margins. They became bitter, frustrated, and disillusioned about the direction that the country had taken. Marginalization of the ethnic groups had started earlier with the formation of One-Unit—consolidation of four existing provinces into West Pakistan to 'solve' the problem of representational parity between East and West Pakistan. In order to reach a constitutional consensus, the East Pakistanis, numerically stronger, had gingerly conceded to this scheme of equal numbers in the National Assembly.[39] The one-unit scheme disappointed every province of the country, except the Punjab. East Pakistanis thought that they had the right to representation on the basis of 'one-man-one-vote', which was denied to them. The rest of the provinces lost their identity, power, and representation. When the second military ruler, Yahya Khan, restored the provinces in 1969, too much damage had been done to nation-building. Ethnic nationalism emerged as the strongest political force in reaction to the politics and policies of the military regime (1958–69), leading to greater demands for autonomy, and the Awami League's six points that bordered on creating a quasi-independent state of East Pakistan, which became Bangladesh after the civil conflict, military action, and Indian intervention in 1971.

The second negative effect of the one-unit policy was on centre-province relations. Excessive centralization created a flawed federal structure, which was federal only in name. The power to extract and distribute resources, planning for development, and vital decisions to shape the structure of the state, and the ideas of nations became located at the centre. This stream of thought, policies, and political economy ran contrary to the very idea of Pakistan, which was rooted in the struggle for the minority (Muslim) rights, autonomy for the Muslim majority regions, and adequate representation for the rest in the Indian centres of power. Construction of a nominal federal state during the Ayub era worked counter to the expectations of the General to build a 'strong' Pakistan. From the outset, East Pakistan and smaller provinces forcibly clubbed together into West Pakistan had demanded adequate autonomy, and the issues of representation and autonomy had been settled with consensus on the 1956 Constitution.[40] The military regime and its 1962 Constitution reordered the federation, leaving only a narrow space for provincial autonomy. The country weakened in terms of a common spirit of nationhood, because the constituent ethnic groups viewed the federation as a usurper, and exploiter, dominant, and autocratic. The allegiance, loyalty, and emotional commitment of the ethnic nationalists that was already weak, shifted further away from the idea of a Pakistani nation towards that of sub-nationalism.

Third, the rise of the military created an imbalance in the power between the civilian and the military sectors of the political system. The legacy of this imbalance has lived on with three more martial laws and the development of the security establishment as an autonomous centre of power within the state. Four military rules, equalling the tenure of civilian governments in the first sixty-years of the country, have caused great damage to the natural evolution of political institutions, the development of a political party system, and the constitutional tradition.[41] Every military ruler disrupted democratic development by subverting the political process and fragmenting political parties. Above all, its effects have been greater on the ethnic groups and smaller provinces, as they view military rule as 'Punjabi' rule. The reason is that for decades, the military had been dominated by Punjabi military officers and soldiers. The composition of the Pakistan military over the past quarter of a century has slowly changed with greater Pashtun representation and increasing induction from Balochistan and Sindh.[42] The feeling that Punjab dominates Pakistan has lingered because of its demographic dominance and higher representation in all centres of power.

Lastly, uneven regional development during Ayub Khan's rule, economic disparity, and social inequality gave rise to sub-national forces. This reflected in the absolute victory of the Awami League in East Pakistan and a stronger showing of the Baloch-Pashtun National Awami Party in Balochistan and the North-West Frontier Province (NWFP)—now KPK—in the 1970 elections.[43] As a reaction to the 'decade of development' which Ayub celebrated in 1968, two major ideological streams of socialism and ethnic nationalism came to dominate those crucial elections: the first ever national parliamentary elections. The economic and political conditions under Ayub Khan produced ethnic nationalism, and separatism, questioning Pakistani nationalism.

The 'development decade' cost Pakistan the separation of East Pakistan when the military and political leaders failed to honour the result of the 1970 elections, as it would have given the Awami League of East Pakistan mandate rule on the basis of majority. The party rode to popularity on the slogan of provincial autonomy, rights, discrimination, and inequality. The military rule also alienated other ethnic groups. However, Ayub Khan's basic premise of modernity, essentially a political project aiming to transform ethnic groups with multiple identities into a single nation, was not off-the-mark. The European modernist, the state builders, had applied social and political engineering from above to this same effect. One of the modernists' beliefs is that they, by inaugurating industrial society, can 'break down the segments of traditional order to create a common culture capable of integrating all citizens'.[44] The epoch, the national and regional environment, the regional identities, geopolitical order, and flawed security and foreign policy all worked against the objectives the military regime had set for state- and nation-building.

Islam and Nation

Although the formation of Muslim nationalism in British India was influenced by a variety of cultural and political factors, Islam gave it coherence, direction, and meanings. The Muslims, the largest minority in a vastly Hindu majority country, imagined themselves as a nation, but within an Indian fold. There has been a long history of self-imagining as a Muslim nation that began to take shape hundreds of years before modern-day nationalism. They regarded themselves as a Muslim *qaum* (nation).[45] It was this history of self-imagining that became the foundation of Muslim nationalism in the waning decades of the British imperial rule in India.[46] However, the role of

Islam in promoting a sense of Muslim political community in the pre-independence era, and its mobilizing appeal during the Pakistan movement, has produced conflicting interpretations of its relevance to the construction of a Pakistani nation. The question that Pakistan confronted then, and does even now, is whether Islam alone can be the basis of nationhood in Pakistan. As the case of the separation of East Pakistan suggests, a common religion provides some sociological basis for collective nationalism, but that alone cannot be a sufficient factor to hold ethnically-diverse people, with territorial concentration, together into a single nation-state.

The reason why the Pakistani leaders have generally held the view that Islam is a binding force among people belonging to different ethnicities is the deep impact of the 'two-nation theory'. In contrast to the 'Hindu' nation—actually the Indian—the theory defined the 'other' nation as Muslim, disregarding the fact there were Buddhists, Christians, and Sikhs as well. The leaders of the Pakistan movement, including Quaid-i-Azam Mohammed Ali Jinnah, had centred the demand for Pakistan on the idea of a 'Muslim nation'. Jinnah argued that Islam was not just a religion, but represented a separate social order, culture, and a civilization that gave the Muslims a distinctive character as a political community.[47] Various sections of the Muslim communities spread out in the subcontinent supported the concept of Muslim nationalism, although for different reasons, with different motivations.[48] The religious, conservative layers of the society, and even the mainstream, modern supporters of the Pakistan movement, rejected the notion of territorialized ethnic nationalism on the grounds that Islam transcended narrow ethnic and lingual differences. Allama Muhammad Iqbal, the poet philosopher who proposed the idea of Pakistan in the 1930s, held the view that 'it is not the unity of language or country or the identity of economic interests that constitutes the basic principle of our nationality…we are members of the society founded by the Prophet.'[49] It is generally the conception of the *Ummah* or the universal Islamic community bonded together by faith, and not by territorial demarcations. Such views have generated strong feelings of pan-Islamism among the Muslims of the subcontinent, feelings that are stronger than in any other parts of the world.[50] However, Jinnah did not conceive Pakistan in purely pan-Islamic terms. His conceptualization of Muslim nationalism was in the context of Indian politics under imperial rule. It was based on the protection of minority rights, and is defined essentially in relation to the Hindu majority.[51]

The idea of Muslim nationalism and the two-nation theory served its purpose by playing a historic role in mobilizing the Muslim population behind the demand for a separate state of Pakistan in the Muslim majority areas. The question is, what was its relevance after the Muslim-dominated regions constituted an independent Pakistan? A simple answer is that, in the chaos of politics and struggle for survival, the leaders of the new country were not prepared to have more controversies on their table. Any transition from Muslim nation to a secular Pakistani nation, redefined in terms of histories, cultures, identities, and the respective heritage of the constituent regions of the country, would have required rethinking of the entire project of Pakistan. Even today, neither the leaders nor the intellectuals of the country are willing to rebrand nationalism in Pakistan. That would require a composite territorial conception, which actually Pakistan is. The name it has taken has nothing to do with Islam or its civilization; it is the literal representation of the territories and provinces that constitute Pakistan today.[52] What is generally ignored is the role that territorial concentration of the Muslim populations in Bengal and other regions that became Pakistan played in realizing the dream of Pakistan. Muslim self-imagining as a nation would have been farcical without this geopolitical fact. Without this territorial anchor, in fact, the Muslims would have been a huge minority, as they are today in India. The issue is whether, once the demand for Pakistan was accepted, Islam as a common faith of the new majority could serve as an effective unifying force the same way it did during the struggle for the creation of Pakistan. My answer is no, as is evident from the separation of East Pakistan. Beyond faith, there are other affiliations, commonalities, interests, and dependencies that the leaders of Pakistan can, and should have, explored to construct Pakistan's identity. A simple historical fact, often forgotten, is that the people of the regions constituting present-day Pakistan had lived together for centuries under states, empires, and kingdoms with open borders from Central Asia to the vast India. Indus and its tributaries, and the fertile lands around them as well as towns built on the banks—historic and rich in commerce, arts and culture—served as a magnet for invaders, migrants, and traders. What brings diverse people in every situation of nation and state together, is converging interests and shared ideas, common fears and insecurities, and the confidence that they are a nation in their own right. Pakistan had both the subjective content—self-imagining as a nation—and objective articulation that required referencing in the territorialities of the units. That would have required nation-building from below, and an account of the aggregate identities of the units, as well as a promotion of their common stakes in the Pakistani state. This is a route Pakistan has taken very late, and has often travelled at slower speeds than it should have. There have been other factors at play in bringing communities, peoples, regions, and ethnicities together— like the national economic market, industrialization, migration and urbanization, and development—to compensate for the well-thought out policy of state- and nation-building.

Pakistan's state- and nation-building has been from above rather than from the centre. Islam and Muslim nationalism have constituted the core ideas of being a state and nation among the centralist elites and centralizing institutions—the military and bureaucracy. How much Islam can be a binding force is a question that never got a unanimous answer among the non-elite sections of the society or even among the ethnic, nationalist elites and intelligentsia of the country. Since the question of Islam's relationship with the state and nationalism is tied with the more complex question of identity, answers take ideological lines. There are, roughly, three different sets of ideas that contend for shaping the identity of the state and nationhood. Let us characterize these perspectives approximately as Islamist, modernist, and sub-nationalist. The Islamist position on the idea of 'nation' needs a little explanation. The Islamists believe that Islam is a complete code of life, has answers to all modern problems, and must be considered a source of personal conduct and guide for public affairs. They define Islam essentially as a political ideology, and set the mission of the faithful, at least in areas where they have formed an independent state, to create an Islamic state, establishing supremacy of the sharia (Islamic law or way of life).[53] The Islamists doctrinally refuse to consider a territorial definition of nation as relevant to Muslims. Their conception of an Islamic *millat* (nation) would embrace all believers irrespective of their race, language, or domicile. Faith in Allah, Qur'an, and the Prophet gives them a far greater sense of togetherness than any other factor, like territory, common history, culture, and language.[54] Using this phraseology, or, if you wish, symbolism, the Islamists stress the role of religion in achieving national unity.

Second, the Islamists extend the role of religion from personal to public life by endeavouring to create an Islamic state. By deconstructing the history of the Pakistan movement, they claim that the country's independence was won in the name of Islam, and that the driving force behind the idea of Pakistan was the creation of an Islamic state.[55] This seems to be a total reversal of the position that they took during the political struggle for Pakistan. The ulema (Islamic scholars) from Ahrar, Jamiat-i-Ulema-i-Hind, and even Jamaat-i-Islami had refused to support the creation of Pakistan because they believed that a future territorial state would not be an Islamic state. Some of them had other reasons to oppose the idea of Pakistan; it would fragment the Muslim populations in India, and staying within the Indian fold together would give greater power and influence to the Muslims.[56] Nor did they trust the leadership of Westernized Muslims like Jinnah.[57] The Jamiat-i-Ulema-i-Hind and the famous Deoband Islamic seminary, in fact, associated themselves with Indian nationalism.[58] The position of Maulana Abul A'la Maududi, the most articulate and celebrated exponent of an Islamic state, was not different from the orthodox ulema on the creation of Pakistan.[59] The only difference is that he was equally opposed to Indian nationalism.[60] However, their opposition to Pakistan, in no way, could exclude them from participating in the political process, or prevent them from migrating to the new country, as many of them did. After the creation of Pakistan, the Islamists have contended that Pakistan is an ideological state, meaning that the sole purpose of making Pakistan was to create ideal conditions for Islamic values and way of life. Maulana Maududi goes one step further in characterizing any failure to implement Islam in state affairs as 'a form of national apostasy'.[61]

Ideology of Pakistan

The twentieth century was also an age of ideologies, among other great ideas and innovations, progress, and wars. Ideologies are systems of thought, set of ideas and political beliefs to understand and explain the world and to change the world according to their principles and philosophies.[62] The idea of ideology is much broader than it is generally understood; it ranges from less formal attitudes, culture, popular beliefs, and personal orientations to more formal, abstract, and logically coherent philosophies to motivate human actions for reordering or defending an existing system. The debate about the ideology of Pakistan, from the early decades to the present time, has been as much about the identity of the country as it is about restructuring the state and society. The ideology of Pakistan has been conceptualized essentially as an Islamic ideology. Even the modernist nation-builders, like Ayub Khan, established the Advisory Council on Islamic Ideology—renamed as the Council of Islamic Ideology in the 1973 Constitution—that guides state institutions to change laws and policies according to Islam.[63] Its role has always been advisory, and more recently controversial, because of its conservative position on women's rights.[64]

The debate on the ideology of Pakistan was dormant and confined to the discourse writings of the Islamist intellectuals and parties. The ideology of Pakistan was thrown into public debate for the first time, and got official support during the dictatorship of Zia ul-Haq (1977–88). None of its advocates has yet clearly defined what it means exactly beyond saying that Islam is the ideology of Pakistan, but by implication, the 'ideology of Pakistan' refers to two things: Islam is the basis of nationhood in Pakistan, and that Islam must be accepted as the supreme guiding principle of the state.[65] Even the most professed secular leaders have frequently brought the 'ideology of Pakistan' into political debate, not realizing that it would strengthen the politics of Islamization. It is partly this ambivalence and political use of Islam by the secular elites that has allowed the Islamists to set the agenda of Islamic politics.[66] In practice, neither the mainstream's political parties, nor the modernist sections of the society, accept claims of the Islamists about the ideology of Pakistan. Political ideologies are reflected by the constitution of a country, and the Pakistani constitution, as discussed earlier, has accepted the principle of repugnancy, meaning that no law will be made against the Islamic principles. Beyond this, the constitution embodies principles and institutions of parliamentary democracy.

The Islamist position on nation-building suffers from serious contradiction, and is often misleading. First, it is historically incorrect to state that the demand for Pakistan rested on the promise of creating an Islamic state in the vision of the Islamic fundamentalists. There is a vast difference between claiming a state for Muslims, which was the case, and Islamizing a state. It was consistent failure to reach an acceptable agreement on the constitutional guarantees for the rights of the Muslims in British India that strengthened the demand for the creation of a separate state of Pakistan in the Muslim majority areas. Islam itself, in India, was never in danger, and will never be in danger, as long as India remains a secular country. The objective was preserving a cultural identity and the protection of economic and political interests of Muslims by having a state of their own. As indicated earlier, Islamic symbolism was considered necessary for the political mobilization of the Muslim masses, and it served that purpose very well. Second, the founders of Pakistan, particularly Iqbal and Jinnah, have been grossly misinterpreted by the Islamists in support of their views on the relation between Islam and the state. None of them was even remotely associated with the idea of an authoritarian, hegemonic, or theocratic state, which the Islamists pursue with so much dedication. There is no doubt that, on occasion, Jinnah made brief references to Islam in seeking support for Pakistan, but dragging him closer to the Islamist position is a very recent phenomenon. An objective reading of history would reveal that the creator of Pakistan was a constitutionalist, democrat to the core, and a secular Muslim.[67] His presidential address to the Constituent Assembly of Pakistan, on 11 August 1947 stands testimony to this: 'You are free, you are free to go to your temples, you are free to go to your mosques, or to any other places of worship in this state of Pakistan. You may belong to any religion or caste or creed—that has nothing to do with the business of the state'.[68] Unfortunately, Jinnah's real personality and ideological outlook fell victim to the political exigencies of the authoritarian state and obscurantist ulema. This continues to be the case.

As it is evident from the tragedy of East Pakistan, once Pakistan was achieved, Islam by itself couldn't be the basis of national solidarity. When the environment of pre-Partition, communalized politics changed, the central dynamics of politics also changed, requiring a utilitarian approach to strengthen the bonds of unity among diverse political communities within the fold of Pakistan. After separation from the Hindu majority, new polarization along centre-province lines emerged, which generated new demands, and raised new expectations. At the heart of the new politics of the new country were issues of provincial rights and fair share of power in the structure of the state. In this struggle for rights, Islamic sloganeering was no substitute for participatory politics, representation, and equality. Ibn-e-Khaldun (1332–1406), a North African Muslim scholar, recognized this dilemma long ago by asserting that religion was a weak force compared to *asabiya* (ethnic solidarity) in promoting a common identity or preserving a state.[69] The separation of East Pakistan, now Bangladesh, amply demonstrated the fact that faith and political interests are two different matters. A politics of accommodation and integration of interests is required to keep communities that may have a single faith but different ethnicities, together. This episode must have put an end to the wishful thinking that the material interests of diverse regional groups are insignificant, or can be superseded by the holy politics of Islam.

The lessons that Pakistan can and must learn from its failure to integrate East Pakistan are these: economic disparity, denial of political power, and the superimposition of new forms of cultural or ideological identity foment ethnic nationalism. This should have ended the reliance on Islam as the sole basis of nation formation. The Islamists have continued their rhetoric, however, paying little or no attention to pragmatic issues that might involve the genuine and concrete interests of the people of different regions. What I am suggesting is that basing national solidarity on religion obscures real issues pertaining to the distribution of political power and participation, eroding trust and confidence in the political union. And, thus, it is a poor but dangerous political tool to cause fragmentation more than achieving the intended national cohesion.

Modernization and Nation-Building

The Pakistan Army and the civil bureaucracy that formed the core of the country's ruling establishment for well over thirty years, have approached the issue of nation-building from the angle of modernization. Ayub Khan, who imposed the first Martial law in 1958, was the most forceful exponent of modernization as an instrument of achieving national cohesion. He believed that economic development was a prerequisite to national integration, social transformation of the largely feudal society, and more importantly, to political order and stability.[70] His view of Islam as a progressive, dynamic, and creative force in society clashed with the dogmatic and conservative interpretation by the ulema.[71] But like many other leaders, he also constantly referred to Islam as the basis of Pakistani nationalism.

Ayub thought that the military, by dominating other institutions of the state, had to assume the role of a modernizing agent in the society. In his judgment, such a task was beyond the skills and capacity of the political forces that were too traditional, parochial, and particularistic to plan or manage economic and social change. The Pakistani establishment's views on nation-building were close to that of Western policy circles that attached greater value to armed forces than traditional institutions. The modernization theory in the 1960s also reinforced the notion that the military elites in the new nations possessed distinctive skills and beliefs that were essential for nation-building. As a modern institution, the military was thought to transform traditional political order, function as a stabilizing force, accommodate aspirations of the new middle class, and manage an orderly change.[72] A critique of this paradigm does not belong here, but suffice to say that it stands largely discredited, given the Pakistan experience. The set of solutions offered by the military regimes postponed the political crisis without resolving the central dilemma of evolving consensus on acceptable political norms and institutions. Some of the early expounders of the theory have accepted democratic development as the true route to political institutionalization.[73]

Let us turn to the nation-building program through the modernization ideology of the state elites in Pakistan. By disaggregating it, one finds that the program had three main components: centralization, authoritarian power structure, and economic development. The state elites devoted their attention and resources to building the infrastructure of a centralized state, while leaving the political aspects of nation formation to the dynamics of economic and social change. Even the state-building efforts centred on increasing the functional capacities of the state machinery, more than its political institutionalization. The underlying premise of strengthening the coercive institutions of the state and expanding its administrative networks was that the challenges to the territorial integrity required a 'strong state'. But this might be interpreted more in the sense of a powerful state than a 'strong state', because the latter would imply political legitimacy and popular support.[74]

The Pakistani state elites were not alone in creating a highly centralized state structure; this was also happening in India, next door. This has been a dominant paradigm in state-formation in the West. Ortega Y Gasset suggests that state came before the nation. And it was through the medium of the state that different linguistic, cultural, or ethnic groups were recast into a nation.[75] But this was the initial phase of state formation in Europe when the policies for amalgamation and use of force against recalcitrant groups invoked little external response or organized political resistance. Most developing states are operating in a different global environment, in which multiplicity of political, security, and information factors impinge on national policies and political choices.[76] In the vastly changed circumstances, centralization and the use of coercive means to subdue diverse national groups might internationalize domestic contestations, as it did in the case of East Pakistan. It would be prudent to give up the Western ideal of an ethnically homogenous nation-state. A viable alternative lies in political unity based on power sharing and the cultural autonomy of the constituent units.

In the case of Pakistan, centralization of state powers did not take into consideration ethnic and regional realities, particularly under the military regimes. I have no hesitation in saying they sowed the seeds of ethnicization of regional communities. They acted like outsiders when ignoring the fact that the ethnic groups that came into the fold of Pakistan had strong regional identities, which required a greater degree of autonomy, representation, and political participation. From the start, the state elites regarded even the voicing of regional interests as anti-state; they suppressed demands for regional autonomy instead of accommodating them. It was quite legitimate on the part of the provincial elites to demand recognition of the cultures of their respective groups, share in political power, and appropriate constitutional safeguards to protect their interests. By doing so, they ignored the most important historical fact: the provinces existed before any institutional or physical infrastructure of the new state of Pakistan was established. Although the Pakistani leaders, both military and civilian, accepted federalism, they frequently worked against its spirit. In practice, they turned Pakistan into a quasi-unitary, authoritarian state. This is evident from the frequent dissolution of the provincial assemblies and the enforcement of governor's rule. Intervention of the central government in provincial affairs has been more of a norm than exception. The One Unit scheme even merged all the existing provinces of then West Pakistan in 1955. The 1956 and 1962 constitutions further reinforced the submerging of separate provincial entities. They were restored in 1970, but considerable damage to the principle of federalism had already been done. The quantum of provincial autonomy allowed in the 1973 constitution was (although acceptable to the provincial elites) that the central government retained the power to dismiss the provincial governments. Zulfikar Ali Bhutto used this power arbitrarily and removed the Balochistan government of the National Awami Party (NAP) in February 1973. The practice of removing unwanted governments in the provinces did not end there. It continued under various regimes. More recently, the Nawaz Sharif government in the centre suspended the Sindh Assembly in August 1999 and appointed Ghous Ali Shah, a federal minister and member of the National Assembly, as advisor to the Prime Minister on Sindh. In practice, Mr Shah exercised all the executive powers of a chief minister. The Assembly was suspended because the Pakistan Muslim League government in Sindh could not sustain a majority in the House after its alliance with the MQM fell apart. The PPP-led coalition government suspended the provincial assembly of the Punjab in 2009 and imposed the governor rule, later restored after political bargaining. Some of the central governments have created artificial majorities in the provincial assemblies through allocation of ministerial positions and outright bribes to win over independents and dissidents from other parties. Political intervention from the centre during the entire history of Pakistan has been more a norm than an exception, and one that all civilian and military governments have used to put in place pliant governments. With the restoration of democracy, for the fourth time in our history since 2008, there appears to be a better climate of inter-party relations with a sentiment of reconciliation. But at the same time, we have seen conflictive and confrontational attitudes as well, which symbolize a country going through a democratic transition.

Another aspect of the centralization process relates to the dominance of the executive in the political system of Pakistan, which diminishes all other institutions in power and influence. The parliamentary system of government that invariably all the civilian governments in Pakistan adopted, reduced the importance of the legislature. The place and power of the prime minister, political patronage, and wide-spread corrupt practices tied most of the legislators to the executive. All the successive elected parliaments have been unable to play any independent role in keeping the executive in check or even performing a proper legislative role. The reason is that its members function under the influence of dynastic party leaders. They rubber-stamp all the ordinances and pass bills presented by the executive without much debate or scrutiny. The issue of accountability of actions of the prime minister and his cabinet members has never gained any importance at the floor of the assemblies except a few solitary voices from the opposition. The political executive uses the federal bureaucracy in the provinces more for political control and helps the local politicians form the ruling party to exercise greater influence than support normal governance. The autonomy of all the departments of the government and civilian administrators in the districts has eroded considerably with persistent interference from the elected representatives in their postings and transfers. Competition among the bureaucrats for better administrative positions has also been a factor in the politicization of the bureaucracy. This has promoted a culture of corruption and graft in the country that has caused the collapse of many of the civilian institutions. Politicians in the central government have often used unscrupulous and dishonest bureaucrats to advance their political interests in the provinces.[77]

The second element in the state and nation forming strategy was political stability or order through imposing an authoritarian system of governance. The authoritarian rule in Pakistan was both a cause and an effect of the expansion of the state, particularly the modernization of the armed forces.[78] This resulted in institutional imbalance between the bureaucratic-military establishment and the representative political process. Judging from the shadow of the military over civilian rule since 1985, and the re-imposition of military rule during 1999–2008 suggests that the development of the state, particularly the political economy of defence has a lot to do with Pakistan's crises of democracy.[79] Also, the fragmentation and weakened legitimacy of the political forces offered opportunities to the ambitious military leaders to take over.[80] But it would be wrong to assume that the state elites had no hand in destabilizing the elected governments and weakening the political process.[81] In fomenting the political crisis in the 1950s, the civil bureaucrats, and the military generals pulling strings from behind the scenes, had created difficulties for the normal functioning of the Constituent Assembly and the elected prime ministers. They used their institutional power to topple the governments, and raise new political groups, playing one against the other. The allegations of inefficiency, nepotism, and corruption against the politicians were used primarily to wrest political power. General Zia ul-Haq and presidents Ghulam Ishaq Khan and Farooq Ahmad Khan Leghari exercised institutional power to dissolve the elected governments four times (1988, 1990, 1993, 1996). Although the Supreme Court declared the removal of Prime Minister Nawaz Sharif in March 1993 to be unconstitutional, the President succeeded in crippling his government, forcing him to resign from office and call for new elections.[82] The President did this with clear support from then Chief of Army Staff, General Abdul Waheed Kakar. The Chief of Army Staff, General Pervez Musharraf, in a dramatic move, dismissed the elected Prime Minister Nawaz Sharif, and the federal and provincial governments, and suspended the national assembly, senate, and the provincial assemblies, declaring that the Constitution will stay in abeyance on the evening of 12 October 1999.[83] It is ironic that Mr Nawaz Sharif had dismissed the Chief of Army Staff a few hours before the military action when the General was still in the air on his way back to Pakistan from Sri Lanka.[84] The army took over power for the fourth time. It amended the Constitution to restructure the political system to suit its political interests, which it touted as building a 'true democracy'.[85]

The fourth military coup demonstrates once again that the state elites consider the free play of political forces to be a 'threat' to national security. Whatever the declaratory objectives, the generals had personal ambitions woven into their perspectives on state- and nation-building. The military regimes had a consistent policy to control the political process, restrict participation and guide the political process from the top. In their elitist view of politics, the popular will of the poor and illiterate masses can't be trusted; they are vulnerable to the manipulations of the socially influential landed aristocracy. This has been an old theme that the regimes have continuously brought into the political discourse of Pakistan.

The military, when taking over political power, acquired vast powers to remove, and if necessary, eradicate, all sources of societal opposition. Political parties that have been dominated by the dynastic political class, the media, judiciary, and institutions of the civil society have proved too weak to offer any resistance to unconstitutional rule. Because of a long history of political opportunism and confrontation among the political parties, unlike solidarity between the ruling party and the opposition in the failed coup in Turkey on 17 July 2016, those in the opposition in Pakistan have not only hailed removal of elected governments but have also demanded such an unconstitutional act on the ground that the government was not functioning according to the Constitution.[86] There cannot be greater political absurdity than such demands and celebrations over the unconstitutional removal of elected governments. Even today, some of the opposition parties demand that the military take over power and present it as a popular demand.[87] This shows low levels of commitment to democratic norms, political opportunism, and a lack of character among the political class of Pakistan. In this respect, one finds a strong imprint of feudal political culture on the political process of the country. Also, the prolonged military rule and its alliances with a section of the political elites has strengthened the view that democracy should not be the most preferred way of political and economic development of Pakistan; that democracy has only legitimized the power of the most influential classes. These are debatable points. In my view, deviation from democratic, constitutional norms has only deepened the political crises and delayed further development of institutions, like political party system, parliament, judiciary that are considered so vital for the development and consolidation of democracy.

The power structure in Pakistan has been oligarchical in composition, within which the military and bureaucracy have played a central role in its operation. Land-owing aristocracy, new industrial and commercial elites, and during the rule of Zia ul-Haq, certain sections of the Islamist constituency have formed an informal power alliance with the security establishment. However, not all elements of the political spectrum were thought fit for partnership; co-option was selective and limited to those who shared the military rulers' view of political structuring. This was also true of General Pervez Musharraf, who cultivated a liberal self-image. He carefully selected individuals for important governmental assignments who, disregarding the question of his legitimacy, supported his agenda of reforms in the economic, political, and administrative spheres.

On the whole, inter-elite networks under the military have always been incomplete, transitory, and insufficient to consolidate the nation-making process. Conversely, dominance of the military has caused deeper polarization among the elites and alienated the larger sections of the ethnic groups and parties, as they saw domination of the Punjab under the military rule. Besides this, military rule has damaged the federal structure of the country. By usurping power, the generals took away whatever autonomy the provincial elites had acquired through their democratic struggle. The political influence and power that they exercised in the provinces as elected representatives, and the clout they had with the elected governments at the centre, has been replaced with non-representative civilians, bureaucrats, and the military officers behind the back as 'monitors'. The style of governance of the ethnic coalitions, cultivated to support the military governments, has also worked against provincial interests. Lacking genuine local support, they depended on the highly centralized civil and military organizations. Never have the smaller provinces, like Balochistan, been as well represented in the civil service or the military as the Urdu speaking migrants or the Punjabis. It was natural for the East Pakistanis, or in the post-1971 period, for the educated youth in Balochistan and Sindh to be attracted by the counter-elite politics of the regionalist elements. Consequently, the military regimes have strengthened ethnic identities more than achieving the declared objective of achieving national solidarity.[88]

Third, and most important element in state-building, was economic development. Ayub Khan was the chief architect of Pakistan's industrial base.[89] The military's economic policies favoured free enterprise, and the expansion of domestic markets with wide ranging networks of financial and industrial institutions. Private investment and privatization of state-built industrial units, often ending up in the hands of family and friends, constituted the core value of development planning in the 1960s. There is no disagreement as to the rate of economic growth that Pakistan achieved under military rule, but creating and strengthening private business enterprises was not divorced from political objectives. Pakistan's fledging bourgeoisie class emerged as the staunchest supporter of a petty bourgeoisie state dominated by the bureaucratic-military elite. Also, the expansion and modernization of the industrial sector fit well into the imperatives of the political economy of defence, for it made more resources available to the state to pay for the modernization of the armed forces and sustain a certain level of defence preparedness. In the fourth military takeover, apart from other factors, economic decline and inability of the elected governments to pull the country out of the economic crisis played an important role in the military's decision to wind up democracy.

There is no doubt that economic development is an important ingredient of both nation- as well as state-building. However, Pakistan's economic growth strategies were guided more by the interplay of powerful interests than pure economic considerations. Monopoly, import substitution, and protectionism served the interests of big businesses more than the objectives of a balanced development of all other important sectors and regions. Stress on 'trickle down' effects of the private economy produced a concentration of wealth within a limited number of industrial houses, while focus on West Pakistan, and within it, around Karachi, led to serious regional disparities.[90] Likewise, preferences for certain sectors of the economy introduced economic distortions.[91] The economic development model that Pakistan pursued under the military rested on the assumptions of what is known as 'the social utility of greed'. Whatever surplus was accumulated was either pocketed by the industrialists or consumed by the state for its own expansion. Social development received very little attention. In theory, the highest rate of economic development in the Ayub decade (1958–69) must have laid the foundations for political stability. The storm of agitations that erupted with the celebration of the 'developmental decade' in 1968, was a manifestation of the inequitable distribution of the rewards of economic development, and reflective of political frustration. It would not be an exaggeration to say that it was Ayub's political and economic structuring of the Pakistani state that strengthened separatism in East Pakistan. Likewise, economic growth under the Zia and Musharraf dictatorships, cumulatively for two decades, was impressive, but military dictatorship resulted in the politicization of ethnic groups, and the rise of religious extremism and militancy. Largely because of military interventions, Pakistan faces deep structural problems that continue to impede its institutional recovery. The capacity of the state to govern, establish the rule of law, even collect revenues, has declined. Some concerned with the larger questions of economic downturn, political instability and social disorder wish for a return of military rule on the assumption that only dictatorial rule will help stem the rot and put Pakistan back on the rails of good governance and economic development.[92] This optimism about the capacity of the armed forces in a vastly changed national and international environment needs second thought. The military itself, perhaps, realizes the problem of international acceptance, and that is the reason it has to take over, preferring to exercise influence over domestic security and critical foreign relations. This complicates civil-military relations, discredits elected governments, and robs them of the autonomy to take important decisions. In spirit, it is an indirect intervention under the assumption that the military is the 'true guardian' of the state. The civilian government of Nawaz Sharif since 2013, and even the Zardari regime (2008-13), accepted encroachment by the military in order to 'save' the democratic system.

Ethnic Elites and Pakistani Nationalism

The provincial elites prefer to define and structure the Pakistani nation in terms of a composite political entity.[93] This implies approximately three things: first, the constituent units have inviolable rights, and these rights must form the basis of a relationship with the central authority. Second, the cultural and political hegemony of the state is impermissible, as it violates the basic sense of being autonomous federating units. Third, the distribution of political power in the system must be rearranged or work such that it satisfies fundamental concerns of majority ethnic groups within the provinces. The political language of this prescription is autonomy, decentralization, participation, and democracy.

In a political community as diverse as Pakistan, nation formation must be regarded, first and foremost, as a political process based on a 'social contract' among member ethnic groups to share political power and material rewards of living together in the nation-state. This is precisely what the ethnic elites or provincial leaders have demanded of the Pakistani state. Most of the provincial parties and ethnic groups have consistently struggled for the preservation of cultural and political rights. Their demands have ranged from greater political autonomy to the recognition of nationalities and national rights but within the framework of a unified Pakistan.[94] The state, the Islamists, and the mainstream political parties have often misrepresented the issue of four nationalities—Punjabi, Baloch, Pashtun, and Sindhi. The recognition of four or more nationalities, as demanded by the Mohajir (Urdu speaking migrants) or Seraiki (southern Punjab), would in no way undermine national solidarity. Rather, voluntary assimilation and inclusionary politics would integrate ethnic interests with the idea of Pakistani nationhood.

In order to understand the question of national identity, it would be necessary to explore the ethnic mix in Pakistan. The existing provincial boundaries of Pakistan as inherited from British India are not ethnic boundaries. Although main ethnic entities form the major clusters in the provinces, most of the ethnic and linguistic groups are interspersed and widely distributed across provincial boundaries. Large concentrations of Pashtuns in Balochistan, Baloch in Sindh and Punjab, Punjabis in Khyber Pakhtunkhwa, and Mohajir in urban areas of Sindh blur the ethnic boundaries. Such a mosaic of ethnicities, and intermixing on a continual basis through migration, carries the potential both for conflict, as well as for integration.

Except for the Mohajir group, all other ethnic transmigrations have occurred over the centuries that have well-defined territorial domains. In the same way, the Mohajir concentration in Karachi and a few other urban areas of Sindh has also acquired the characteristics of local majority. Therefore, the ethnic issue does not lend itself to a clear definition along provincial lines. It is a three-in-one problem: provincial autonomy, preservation of multiple ethnic groups, cultures within the boundaries of each province, and sharing of power. This generates polarizing and contentious politics. Failing to reach power-sharing arrangements with the majority, quite often the minority groups within the provinces align with the national parties from other provinces to offset their weakness. For the last three decades, this has shaped interesting politics of coalition-building at the national level.

The provincial identities are tagged with the identities of the majority ethnic groups due to nativity and historicity of their claim to the region. Therefore, their ethnic evolution has been tied to the regions of their inhabitance, as well as the way they have evolved over thousands of years, and are recognized by others. A sense of separate identity of each group is deeply rooted in a long historical process, in the making of which, an interplay of some common cultural forms have played a great role. Islam didn't displace or dissolve regional identities of the followers; it added a new layer to them with new norms, rituals, and sources of knowledge as well as trans-boundary spiritual connections with West Asia. Communities with a strong regional history have never given up identities. Nor is there any need to do it. We need to recognize that the politics and ideology of identity is primarily about self-preservation as a cultural entity, and about political rights in which, having a common faith doesn't play any role.

Contrary to a common belief, the diversity of the units or their internal compositions do not pose any threat to the state by themselves. As Anwar Syed has noted, it is the repression by the state and its authoritarianism that poses a threat to its territorial integrity.[95] In the case of state formation in the first three decades, the provincial elites, in particular, felt deprived of their due share in power. It was natural for them to look upon the state elites as masters, not friends. Their concerns of autonomy, citizenship rights, and participation in the economic and political process of the state are as justified as the demand for Pakistan itself. It is the absence of democracy and inadequate power sharing arrangements that produce frustration with the state, strengthen group feelings, and may lead to armed struggle for the restoration of rights. The case of NAP, frequently labelled by its detractors as secessionist, illustrates this point. Allowing the party to form governments in Balochistan and the NWFP provinces in 1972 vastly changed its perspective on the national question. The party was the first to adopt Urdu as the provincial language and confined its demand for Pakhtunistan to renaming the Frontier province. But when its Balochistan government was dismissed in February 1973, its Baloch wing took up arms and launched an insurgency that lasted four years.[96] It caused the NAP to split along ethnic lines, brought the military back in power for the third time, with far greater centralization of power than was the case under the Bhutto regime (1972–77).

Provincial Autonomy and Ethnic Cultural Streams

Regional parties and ethnic groups, even with a limited electoral support base, continued to press for democracy and provincial autonomy that they believe would empower them and give them representation, both under the military, as well as in the civilian political arrangements. They have been of the view that devolution without democracy might fail to resolve the broader issue of political power. Their struggle, efforts, and sacrifices haven't gone wasted. Pakistan has learnt some hard lessons, and even under weak democratic governments, the central elites have done a great deal of path correction. They have reoriented the nation formation strategy toward political participation and decentralization. This change rests on the evaluation of centre-province relations and their adverse effects on national solidarity. One of the conclusions political parties have drawn is that the policy of a strong central government combined with authoritarian rule has resulted in a weak Pakistani state; weak in terms of political capacity to integrate ethnic groups or cultivate a sense of strong Pakistani nationalism among them. Building a consensus on creating a federation that must balance the need for an effective centre with adequate autonomy and power for the federating units has not been an easy job because of the long history of centralization. Every federation in the world has tried to obtain this balance, but seldom has any federation succeeded in maintaining the balance at a fixed point. Federalism evolves through experience, and the balance of power shifts back and forth depending on the issues at a given point of time, the capacity of the provinces to deliver, and flexibility of the centre to devolve powers or assume greater responsibilities. Federalism means a cooperative political existence with multiple institutional layers that bind the provinces and the federation together to form a single state and nation. In other words, it is creating unity out of diversity. And since federations like Pakistan represent a complex mixture of ethnic and regional groups, the constitutional arrangement must be flexible and open to dialogue. The other condition is that the political parties and groups must be willing to re-examine powers and autonomy of the provinces by negotiating fresh accords on constitutional matters.

Inflexibility among the ruling politicians of earlier decades on federalism, in fact, caused irreparable damage to the federation through the loss of East Pakistan. The unitary mind-set has changed and has given way to the recognition of provincial autonomy. The passage of the 18th Amendment has granted the provinces far greater powers than any federation in the developing part of the world. This marks a big power shift from the centre to the federating units. The structure of federalism has irreversibly changed, but taking new roots may take longer, until we find the new provincial centres of power by devolving powers further to the districts and creating governing capacity, which appear to be weak at present.

The growth of democracy in Pakistan has created an opportunity for the ethnic and regional media to grow as well. The beginning of the new century has seen a big change in the media policy, which interestingly happened under Pervez Musharraf. New technologies of communication reduced the power of the state to control television broadcasting from foreign locations that made the liberalization of media inevitable. Today, hundreds of television stations compete with each other for viewership. The interesting change is the arrival of ethnic media. The regional languages and cultures have found a space in the media dedicated to specific languages and targeting ethnic clusters of the country. Never have regional cultures found such a wide national or regional space as has been made possible by the development of media in Pakistan. This accommodates the interests of the provinces by offering cultural representation. However, the Urdu media, both in print as well as in the electronic field, remains the most dominant because of the disproportionately greater viewership than the ethnic media can offer. The hegemony of the Urdu language, literature, and the media has become well-established, which is often resented by the sub-nationalist intellectual and political elites; rightly so, because they fear loss of their identity with the fading away of regional languages and cultures.

NOTES

1. Peter H. Wilson, *The Thirty Years War: Europe's Tragedy*. (Cambridge: Harvard University Press, 2009).

2. Thorstein Veblen, 'The Predatory State' in Waldo R. Browne, ed. *Leviathan in Crisis,* (New York: The Viking Press, 1946), 25.

3. Charles Tilly, 'Reflection on the History of European State-Making' in C. Tilly ed. *The Formation of National States in Western Europe,* (Princeton: Princeton University Press, 1975), 15

4. The concept of civil society might be defined as a set of private and autonomous associations of the individuals that exist out of the state. While promoting citizenship rights and interests in wide and different areas, such as economy, culture, and politics, they act as a restraint against the arbitrariness of the state. See: John Keane, 'Despotism and Democracy: The Origin and Development of the Distinction between Civil Society and the State, 1750–8150' in Keane. Ed. *Civil Society and the State: New European Perspectives.* (London: Verso, 1988), 43-48.

5. Wolfgang Mommsen, 'The Varieties of the Nation-State in Modern History: Liberal, Imperialist, Fascist and Contemporary Notions of Nation and Nationality' in Michael Mann ed. *The Rise and Decline of the Nation-State,* (Oxford: Basil Blackwell, 1990).

6. John A. Hall, 'Nationalism: Classified and Explained' *Daedalus* 122/3, (Summer 1993), 2.

7. On Political Ideologies, see: Michael Freeden, Lyman Tower Sargent, and Marc Stears, *The Oxford Handbook of Political Ideologies* (Oxford: Oxford University Press, 2013); Andrew Vincent, *Modern Political Ideologies* (Oxford: Blackwell, 1995); Andrew Heywood, *Political Ideologies: An Introduction* (New York: St. Martin's Press, 1992); Roger Eatwell and Anthony Wright, *Contemporary Political Ideologies* (Boulder: Westview Press, 1993); Lyman Tower Sargent, *Contemporary Political Ideologies: a Comparative Analysis* (Homewood: Dorsey Press, 1969).

8. Christian Reus-Smit, *The Moral Purpose of the State: Culture, Social Identity, and Institutional Rationality in International Relations* (Princeton: Princeton University Press, 1999); Peter B. Evans, Dietrich Rueschemeyer, and Theda Skocpol, *Bringing the State Back In* (Cambridge: Cambridge University Press, 1985); Ha-Joon Chang, *Globalisation, Economic Development, and the Role of the State* (London: Zed Books, 2003).

9. Thomas L. Pangle, *Montesquieu's Philosophy of Liberalism: A Commentary on the Spirit of the Laws* (Chicago: University of Chicago Press, 1973); Destutt De Tracy, et al., *A Commentary and Review of Montesquieu's Spirit of Laws* (New York: B. Franklin, 1969); Melvin Richter, *The Political Theory of Montesquieu* (New York: Cambridge University Press, 1977); Rebecca Kingston, *Montesquieu and His Legacy* (Albany: SUNY Press, 2009). On federalism, see: Melissa V.

Holdstedt, *Federalism: History and Current Issues* (New York: Novinka Books, 2006); Baogang He, Brian Galligan, and Takashi Inoguchi, *Federalism in Asia* (Cheltenham: Edward Elgar, 2007).

10. Ernest Gellner, and John Breuilly, 'Definitions' in Ernest Gellner, ed. *Nations and Nationalism,* (Oxford: Basil Blackwell, 1983), 1–5.

11. Charles Tilly, 'War and State Power' *Middle East Report,* 21 (1991), 38–40

12. John A. Hall, 'Nationalisms: Classified and Explained' *Daedalus* 122, no. 3 (1993), 1–28.

13. Ibid.

14. John Hall, *International Orders* (Oxford: Polity Press, 1994), 80–120. See also: Eric Hobsbawm, *Nations and Nationalism Since 1780* (Chapel Hill: University of North Carolina Press), 7–17.

15. Anthony D. Smith, *The Ethnic Origin of Nations* (Oxford: Basil Blackwell, 1988).

16. See: M. Abel, *Glimpses of Indian National Movement* (Hyderabad: ICFAI University Press, 2005); Philip Oldenburg, *India, Pakistan, and Democracy: Solving the Puzzle of Divergent Paths* (Abingdon: Routledge, 2010); D. Mackenzie Brown, *The Nationalist Movement: Indian Political Thought from Ranade to Bhave* (Berkeley: University of California Press, 1961); Verney Lovett, *A History of the Indian Nationalist Movement,* (Hove: Psychology Press, 1968)

17. Stanley A. Wolpert, *Shameful Flight: The Last Years of the British Empire in India* (Oxford: Oxford University Press, 2006).

18. Imtiaz Ahmad, Partha S. Ghosh, and Helmut Reifeld, *Pluralism and Equality: Values in Indian Society and Politics* (New Delhi: Sage Publications, 2000); M. M. Agrawal, *Ethnicity, Culture, and Nationalism in North-East India* (New Delhi: Indus Pub, 1996); Niraja Gopal Jayal, *Representing India: Ethnic Diversity and the Governance of Public Institutions* (Hampshire: Palgrave Macmillan, 2006).

19. On Muslim nationalism, bringing Muslim Bengal and West Pakistan together, see: Ian Talbot, *Provincial Politics and the Pakistan Movement: The Growth of Muslim League in North-West and North-East India, 1937–1947* (Karachi: Oxford University Press, 1988); Salahuddin Ahmed, *Bangladesh: Past and Present* (New Delhi: A.P.H. Pub, 2004); Kuwajima Sho, *Muslims, Nationalism, and the Partition: 1946 Provincial Elections in India* (New Delhi: Manohar, 1998).

20. Anthony D. Smith, 'State-Making and Nation-Building' in John A. Hall. ed. *States in History,* (Oxford: Basil Blackwell, 1986), 228–63.

21. Robert H. Jackson, *Quasi-states: Sovereignty, International Relations, and the Third World* (Cambridge: Cambridge University Press, 1990).

22. John A. Hall, 'Nationalisms: Classified and Explained' *Daedalus* 122, no. 3 (1993), 1–28.

23. John H. Kautsky, 'Nationalism' in Harvey G. Kebschull, ed. *Politics in Transitional Societies,* (New York: Appleton-Century-Crofts, 1968), 107–20; Micheal F. Lofchie, *State of the Nations* (Berkeley: University of California Press, 1971); S.N. Eisenstadt and Stein Rokkan, *Building States and Nations* (Beverly Hills: Sage Publications, 1973); Karl Deutsch and William Foltz, *Nation-Building* (New York: Atherton Press, 1963); Clifford Greetz, *Old Societies and New States* (New York: Free Press, 1963); Rupert Emerson, *From Empire to Nations: The Rise to Self-Assertion of Asian and African Peoples* (Cambridge: Harvard University Press, 1960).

24. Mohammed Ayoob, 'The Security Problematic of the Third World' *World Politics* 43, no. 2 (January 1991), 265–6. Contrary to Ayoob's view, Caroline Thomas contends that the contemporary international system is benign for state formation as it recognizes the sovereign legitimacy of the new states. But this sovereignty has not immunized the -postcolonial states from adverse external influences like intrusion or intervention. See: Caroline Thomas, 'New Directions in Thinking about Security in the Third World' in Ken Booth, ed. *New Thinking About Strategy and International Security* (London: Harper Collins Academic, 1991), 270.

25. Such an accumulation is primitive in a sense that it is not premediated by the constituent groups. In many Third World countries, it reflects the same trend as witnessed by the European state formation in its early phase. See: Youssef Cohen, Brian R. Brown, and A.F. K. Organski, 'The Paradoxical Nature of State Making: The Violent Creation of Order' *American Political Science Review* 75, no. 4 (1981): 901–10.

26. On the attitudes of the bureaucrats towards politics and politicians, see: Huma Naz, *Bureaucratic Elites & Political Developments in Pakistan, 1947–58* (Islamabad: National Institute of Pakistan Studies, Quaid-i-Azam University, 1990); Asaf Hussain *Elite Politics in an Ideological State: The Case of Pakistan.* (Montreal: Dawson University Press,1979); Robert LaPorte, *Power and Privilege: Influence and Decision-Making in Pakistan.* (California: University of California Press, 1975); Mustafa Chowdury, *Pakistan: Its Politics and Bureaucracy.* (Kansas: Stosius Incorporated/Advent Books Division, 1988)

27. On Bureaucracy's Indictment of Civilian Leaders—Ghulam Mohammad, Iskander Mirza, Ayub Khan, see for instance, Robert LaPorte. 'Pakistan in 1971: The Disintegration of a Nation' *Asian Survey* 12, no. 2 (1972), 97–108; Himmat Sinha, *Babus, Brahmans & Bureaucrats: A Critique of the Administrative System in Pakistan.* (New Dehli: People's Publishing House, 1973); Edward

Feit, *The Armed Bureaucrats: Military-Administrative Regimes and Political Development* (Boston: Houghton Mifflin, 1972).

28. Two bureaucrats, Ghulam Muhammad and Iskandar Mirza, became governor generals. Another bureaucrat, Chaudhary Muhammad Ali got elected as prime minister of the country.

29. Karl Von Vorys, *Political Development in Pakistan* (Princeton: Princeton University Press, 1965); Ziauddin Ahmad Suleri, *Pakistan's Lost Years: Being a Survey of a Decade of Politics, 1948–1958.* (Lahore: Progressive Papers, 1962)

30. See: B. Kemal Yeşilbursa, *The Baghdad Pact: Anglo-American Defence Policies in the Middle East, 1950–1959* (London: Frank Cass, 2005); Magnus Persson, *Great Britain, the United States, and the Security of the Middle East: The Formation of the Baghdad Pact* (Lund: Lund University Press, 1998); N. J. Ashton, 'The Hijacking of a Pact: The Formation of the Baghdad Pact and Anglo-American Tensions in the Middle East, 1955—1958', *Review of International Studies* 19, no.2 (1993), 123–37; Richard L. Jasse, 'The Baghdad Pact: Cold War or Colonialism?' *Middle Eastern Studies* 27, no. 1 (1991), 140–56.

31. Mohammed Ahsen Chaudhri, 'The Principle of Regional Pacts' *Pakistan Horizon* 8, No. 3 (1955), 428–36; B. Kemal Yeşilbursa, *The Baghdad Pact: Anglo-American Defence Policies in the Middle-East, 1950–59* (London: Routledge, 2012), 71–97; Liaquat Ali Khan, *Pakistan, the Heart of Asia: Speeches in the United States and Canada, May and June 1950* (Cambridge: Harvard University Press, 1950).

32. Mohammad Ayub Khan and Nadia Ghani, *Field Marshal Mohammad Ayub Khan: A Selection of Talks and Interviews, 1964–1967* (Karachi: Oxford University Press, 2010).

33. Mohammad Ayub Khan, *Friends Not Masters: A Political Autobiography* (New York: Oxford University Press, 1967).

34. Ibid.

35. Talukder Maniruzzaman, 'Crises in Political Development and the Collapse of the Ayub Regime in Pakistan' *The Journal of Developing Areas* 5, no. 2 (1971), 221–38; Karl Von Vorys, *Political Development in Pakistan.* (Princeton: Princeton University Press, 2015); Lawrence Ziring, *The Ayub Khan Era: Politics in Pakistan, 1958–1969* (Syracuse: Syracuse University Press, 1971)

36. Wayne Ayres Wilcox, 'The Pakistan Coup d'état of 1958' *Pacific Affairs* 38, No. 2 (1965), 142–63; Sumit Ganguly, 'Pakistan's Never–Ending story: Why the October Coup was no Surprise' *Foreign Affairs,* 79, No. 2 (2000), 2–7; Veena Kukreja, *Military Intervention in Politics: A Case Study of Pakistan* (New Dehli: NBO Publisher's Distributors, 1985); Dennis James Doolin, *Pakistan: The 1958 Coup and Its Causes* (Stanford: Department of Political Science, 1960);

Aqil Shah, *The Army and Democracy: Military Politics in Pakistan* (Cambridge: Harvard University Press, 2014); Mazhar Aziz, *Military Control in Pakistan: The Parallel State* (London: Routledge, 2008)

37. Hasan N. Gardezi, 'Neo-colonial Alliances and the Crisis of Pakistan' *Pakistan Forum* Middle East Research and Information Project (MERIP),1/2 (1970), 3–6; S.M. Naseem, 'Economists and Pakistan's Economic Development: Is there a Connection?" *The Pakistan Development Review* 37, No. 4 (1998), 401–29; Mahbub ul Haq, *The Strategy of Economic Planning: A Case Study of Pakistan* (Karachi: Oxford University Press, 1963); Lubna Kanwal, 'Economic Development in Pakistan: A Reflection of Social Division during 1947–1969' *Pakistan Journal of Social Sciences* 35, No. 1 (2015)

38. Morris Janowitz, *Military Institutions and Coercion in the Developing Nations: The Military in the Political Development of New Nations.* (Chicago: University of Chicago Press, 1988); Mary Kaldor, 'The Military in Development', *World Development*, 4/6 (1976), 459–82; A. Bopegamage, 'The Military as a Modernizing Agent in India' *Economic Development and Cultural Change*, 20/1 (1971), 71–9; Hasan Askari Rizvi, *The Military and Politics in Pakistan* (Lahore: Progressive Publishers, 1974); Henry Bienen, *The Military Intervenes: Case Studies in Political Development* (New York: Russell Sage Foundation, 1968)

39. Rizwan Malik, *The Politics of One Unit, 1955–58.* (Lahore: Pakistan Study Centre, University of the Punjab, 1988); Mohammad Ayoob, 'Pakistan's Political Development, 1947 to 1970: Bird's Eye View' *Economic and Political Weekly* 6/3–5 (1971), 199–204; Khalid B. Sayeed, *Politics in Pakistan: The Nature and Direction of Change* (New York: Praeger, 1980).

40. Charles H. Kennedy, 'Policies of Ethnic Preference in Pakistan' *Asian Survey* 24/6 (1984), 688–703; Aftab A. Kazi, 'Ethnic Nationalities, Education, and Problems of National Integration in Pakistan' *Asian Profile*, 16/2 (1988), 147–61; Urmila Phadnis, *Ethnicity and Nation-Building in South Asia* (New Delhi: Sage Publications, 1989).

41. On the negative effects of the military rule see: J. Paul Dunne, 'Economic Effects of Military Expenditure in Developing Countries: A Survey' in N.P. Gleditch, et al, eds., *The Peace Dividend* (Contributions to Economic Analysis, Vol. 235, Emrald Group Publishing Limited,1996), 439–64; Ayesha Jalal, *Democracy and Authoritarianism in South Asia: A Comparative and Historical Perspective.* (Cambridge, Great Britain: Cambridge University Press 1995); Christopher Kingston and Aditya Bhave, 'Military Coups and the Consequences of Durable De Facto Power: The Case of Pakistan', (Master's thesis, Chicago: University of Chicago, 2000).

42. For the new ethnic composition of the military with induction from Balochistan

and Sindh see: Ayesha Sidiqa, 'Pakistan Military—Ethnic Balance in the Armed Forces and Problems of Federalism' *Forum of Federations, Centre for Civic Education—Pakistan*, May 2011.

43. Craig Baxter, 'Pakistan Votes—1970' *Asian Survey* 11/3 (1971), 197–218; Mahmood Monshipouri and Amjad Samuel, 'Development and Democracy in Pakistan: Tenuous or Plausible Nexus?' *Asian Survey* 35/11 (1995), 973–89; David Dunbar, 'Pakistan: The Failure of Political Negotiations' *Asian Survey* 12/5 (1972), 444–61; M. B. Naqvi, *Pakistan at Knife's Edge* (New Delhi: Lotus Collection, 2010).

44. This is the view of Earnest Gellner that John A. Hall has summarized. See John A. Hall, 'Nationalisms: Classified and Explained' Op. Cit., 4.

45. Ali Nawaz Memon, *The Islamic Nation: Status & Future of Muslims in the New World Order* (Beltsville: Writers' International, 1995); Dawn-Marie Gibson, *A History of the Nation of Islam: Race, Islam, and the Quest for Freedom* (Santa Barbara: Praeger, 2012); Vibert L. White, *Inside the Nation of Islam: A Historical and Personal Testimony by a Black Muslim* (Gainesville: University Press of Florida, 2001); Elijah Muhammad, *History of the Nation of Islam* (Atlanta: Secretarius Memps Publications, 1994).

46. Benedict Anderson argues that the 'history of imagining makes nation-building easier'. See: Benedict Anderson, *Imagined Communities* (London: Verso, 1991), 6.

47. Jamil-ud-Din Ahmad, *Speeches and Writings of Mr. Jinnah*, Vol. 1 (Lahore: Sh. Mohammad Ashraf & Sons, 1960), 160.

48. For a detailed account of the controversies, views and development of Muslim nationalism, see, K.K. Aziz, *A History of the Idea of Pakistan* (Lahore: Vanguard, 1987), 4 volumes.

49. S. A. Vahid, *Thoughts and Reflections of Iqbal* (Lahore: Sh. Ashraf & Sons, 1964), 396.

50. Jacob M. Landau, *Pan-Islam: History and Politics* (London: Routledge, 2016); Azmi Özcan, *Pan-Islamism: Indian Muslims, the Ottomans and Britain, 1877–1924* (Leiden: Brill, 1997); John L. Esposito, *Islam and Politics* (Syracuse: Syracuse University Press, 1984); Burjor Avari, *Islamic Civilization in South Asia: A History of Muslim Power and Presence in the Indian Subcontinent* (London: Routledge, 2013).

51. See, for instance, Stanley Wolpert, *Jinnah of Pakistan* (New York: Oxford University Press, 1984).

52. Chaudhary Rehmat Ali, a Punjabi Muslim student at Cambridge University, Britain, coined the name Pakistan out of Punjab, Afghania (KPK), Kashmir, Sindh and Balochistan. Choudhary Raḥmat 'Alī and Khursheed Kamal Aziz,

Complete Works of Rahmat Ali (Islamabad: National Commission on Historical and Cultural Research, 1978).

53. See Abul A'la Maududi, *Islami Riyasat* [Islamic State] (Lahore: Islamic Publications Ltd., 1969).

54. Abul A'la Maududi, *Nationalism and India*, (Pathankot: Maktaba-e-Jamaat-e-Islami, 1967).

55. Pervez Amirali Hoodbhoy and Abdul Hameed Nayyar, 'Rewriting the History of Pakistan' in Asghar Khan, ed. *The Pakistan Experience: State & Religion*, (Lahore: Vanguard, 1985), 164–77.

56. Maulana Hussain Ahmad Madani, *Composite Nationalism and Islam* (New Delhi: Manohar Publ., 2005).

57. Afzal Iqbal, *Select Writings and Speeches of Maulana Mohammed Ali*, (Lahore, 1944), 452.

58. Hafeez Malik, *Moslem Nationalism in India and Pakistan*, (Washington, DC: Public Affairs Press, 1963), 240.

59. Freeland Abbott, 'The Jamaat-e-Islami of Pakistan' *The Middle East Journal* 11 (Winter, 1957), 40.

60. For detail see: Abul A'la Maududi, *Musalman aur Maujuda Siyasi Kashmakash* [Muslims and the present political struggle] Vol. II (Pathankot: Maktaba-i-Jamat-i-Islami, 1938); Maudoodi, *Tehrikh-i-Azadi-i-Hind aur Musalmans* [The Indian independence movement and Muslims] (Lahore: Islamic Publications, 1974).

61. Abul A'la Maududi, *Islamic Law and Constitution*, Khurshid Ahmad trans. and ed., (Lahore: Islamic Publications, 1960), 5–6.

62. This construction is adopted from several works cited in, John T. Jost, Christopher M. Feerico and Jamime L. Napier, 'Political Ideology: Its Structure, Functions, and Elective Affinities' *The Annual Review of Psychology* 60 (2009), 307–37, accessed, July 15, 2016. <https://psych.nyu.edu/jost/Political%20 Ideology Its%20structure,%20functions,%20and%20elective%20a.pdf>.

63. Sarfaraz Ansari, 'Forced Modernization and Public Policy: A Case Study of Ayub Khan Era (1958–69)' *Journal of Political Studies,* 18/1, 45–60.

64. Amir Wasim, 'Senators Question the Existence of Council of Islamic Ideology' *Dawn*, January 13, 2016.

65. Saeeduddin Ahmad Dar, *Ideology of Pakistan* (Islamabad: National Institute of Historical and Cultural Research, 1998).

66. Charles H. Kennedy, *Islamization in Pakistan* (Islamabad: Institute of Policy Research).

67. Sharif al Mujahid, *Quaid-i-Azam Jinnah: Studies in Interpretation* (Karachi: Quaid-i-Azam Academy, 1981).

68. *Quaid-i-Azam Mohammad Ali Jinnah: Speeches as Governor-General of Pakistan 1947–1948* (Karachi: Pakistan Publications, 1948), 65.

69. Ibn Khaldun, *Muqaddima*, Franz Rosenthal, trans. (New York: Pantheon Books, 1958), 393.

70. For Ayub's views, see Mohammad Ayub Khan, *Friends Not Masters* (London: Oxford University Press, 1967).

71. Mohammad Ayub Khan, *Speeches and Statements* (Karachi: n.d.), 57.

72. Hans Speier, 'Preface' to *The Role of the Military in Underdeveloped Countries*, John J. Johnson ed. (Princeton: Princeton University Press, 1962); There is a plethora of literature on this subject. See: S. E. Finer, *The Man on Horseback: The Role of the Military in Politics* (New York: Praeger, 1962); William F. Gutteridge, *Military Institutions and Power in the New States* (New York: Praeger, 1965); Morris Janowitz, *The Military in the Political Development of New Nations* (Chicago: University of Chicago Press, 1964); Samuel P. Huntington, *Political Order in Changing Societies* (New Haven: Yale University Press, 1968).

73. Samuel P. Huntington, *The Third Wave: Democratization in the Late Twentieth Century* (Norman and London: University of Oklahoma Press, 1991).

74. Caroline Thomas explains state strength and weakness in terms of institutional capacities which she differentiates as despotic—arbitrary, and infrastructural—effectively exercised through the institutions. Caroline Thomas, 'Southern Instability, Security and Western Concepts: On an Unhappy Marriage and the Need for a Divorce' in Caroline Thomas and Paikiasothy Saravanamuttu, eds. *The State and Instability in the South*, (New York: St. Martin's Press, 1989), 182–8.

75. Quoted by: Anwar Hussain Syed, *Pakistan: Islam, Politics, and National Solidarity* (New York: Praeger, 1982), 4

76. Mohammed Ayoob, 'The Security Problematic of the Third World' *World Politics* 43/2 (1991), 357–83

77. For a detailed study on the development of Pakistan's bureaucracy see: Charles H. Kennedy, *Bureaucracy in Pakistan* (Karachi: Oxford University Press, 1987)

78. There is no single explanation of praetorians in Pakistan. Hamza Alavi argues that the institutions of the colonial state as transferred to the new state of Pakistan were vastly overdeveloped'. A counterpoint is developed by a prominent Pakistani historian, Ayesha Jalal, who contends that the notion of 'overdeveloped' state is 'ahistorical'. See: Hamza Alavi, 'The State in Postcolonial Societies: Pakistan and Bangladesh' *New Left Review*, (July–August 1974), 59–81; Ayesha Jalal, 'Pakistan's Predicament' *Third World Quarterly* 13/3 (July 1989), 234.

79. See: Ayesha Jalal, *The State of Martial Rule: The Origins of Pakistan's Political Economy of Defence* (Cambridge: Cambridge University Press, 1990), 93–135.

80. On this perspective, see: Hasan Askari Rizvi, *The Military & Politics in Pakistan, 1947–86* (Lahore: Progressive Publishers, 1986).

81. On their manipulations and palace intrigues see: Syed Nur Ahmad, *From Martial Law to Martial Law: Politics in the Punjab, 1919–1958.* Craig Baxter, trans. (Boulder: Westview Press, 1985).

82. *The Muslim* (Islamabad), May 26, 1993.

83. *Dawn*, October 13, 1999.

84. On the military takeover, see: *The News*, October 13, 1999.

85. See the text of General Pervez Musharraf's first speech to the nation on October 18, 1999. *The News*, October 19, 1999.

86. *Dawn*, July 18, 2016.

87. Some of the politicians aligned with the military regimes in the past, like a vocal member of the National Assembly Sheikh Rashid Ahmad from Rawalpindi, media persons and little-known political groups have been asking the military to capture power.

88. Tahir Amin, op. cit.. 77.

89. Lawrence Ziring, *The Ayub Khan Era Politics, 1958–69* (Syracuse: Syracuse University Press, 1971).

90. For an excellent analysis and review of Pakistan's economy under Ayub Khan, see: Gustav F. Papanek, *Pakistan's Development: Social Goals and Private Incentives* (Cambridge: Harvard University Press, 1967).

91. For a critique see: Shahid Kardar, *The Political Economy of Pakistan* (Lahore: Progressive Publishers, 1987).

92. In July 2016, mysteriously, a little known political group, 'Move On Pakistan' put up posters all over the country, imploring the Chief of Army Staff to take over. Imran Khan, Chairman *Tehreek-e-Insaf* referring to the unpopularity of Prime Minister Nawaz Sharif said, 'If military took over, people will celebrate by distributing sweets'. 'People in Pakistan Will Celebrate, Distribute Sweets If Army Takes Over: Imran' *Express Tribune*, July 2016.

93. Anwar H. Syed, 'Political Parties and the Nationality Question in Pakistan; *Journal of South Asian and Middle Eastern Studies* 12/1 (Fall 1988), 42–75.

94. Salam Sabir, *Nawab Khair Bakhsh Murree key interviews*, (Quetta: Mehrdar Institute of Research and Publications, 2011), 27–38.

95. Ibid., 39–54.

96. For details see: Selig S. Harrison, *In Afghanistan's Shadow: Baluch Nationalism and Soviet Temptations* (New York: Carnegie Endowment of International Peace, 1981).

Chapter IV

Ethnicity, Nationalism, and Identity

Pakistan represents one of the most complex multi-ethnic societies at national and provincial levels. Each province of Pakistan contains mixed ethnic groups that have been interacting and intermingling for centuries. This is one of the many results of the pre-colonial free migration, tribal warfare, regional empire-building adventures, and conquests in the region. The different rulers carved out as large states as they could with force or by bringing into subordination the weaker states under their power and influence. They expanded or shrunk, or even disappeared, depending on how weak or powerful they were or how strong their adversaries happened to be. Besides the local power contests, foreigners from Arab lands, Persia, Central Asia, and Afghanistan invaded regions of Pakistan in modern history.

The British were the last foreign powers in the subcontinent to gradually build one of the largest empires in the region. As the British rule expanded towards the regions that comprise Pakistan, many of those states, like Punjab and Sindh, got merged into the *Raj* with provincial status. The British inherited a great mix of linguistic and ethnic groups within these provinces. Whenever they decided to change the boundaries, they did so under administrative considerations, and for extractive objectives in mind. Ethnic or lingual homogeneity of the local populations did not figure in their scheme of provincial demarcations. The British, like other colonial powers, introduced new economies and professions for financial gains. They set up new administrative, military, civil, and educational institutions to make their rule effective. The development of the economy and communication, along with the opening up of new areas for agriculture through canal irrigation under the British rule, increased the physical mobility of regional ethnic groups.[1] Any analysis of Pakistani ethnic groups must take into account the fact that they intersperse across all the provinces, reflecting a long historical pattern of trans-regional migration.

Although there is an accepted notion of a home province in respect of each ethnic group, the same territory is also claimed as a historic homeland by at least one other, and in some instances, more than one ethnic entity. Due to frequent movement of groups in the entire Indus valley basin, a broad mix of ethnic groups has emerged in all provinces of Pakistan. Each province represents the ethnic mosaic of a larger Pakistani society, much like the Sindhi quilt with multiple colours and flowery or geometrical patterns. The inter-provincial migration continues to reshape the size and salience of the ethnic colours throughout the country, which has often produced contentions, rivalry, and contestation over economic and political resources. The local populations, with a deeper sense of nativity, have felt threatened by the inflow of migrants, fearing a loss of power and even demographic balance. For instance, the influx of refugees, first from India after the partition, and then from Afghanistan in the 1980s, seems to have changed the demographic balance between dominant ethnic groups and migrants in Sindh and Balochistan. The native Sindhis have lost their traditional numerical majority in some of the urban areas of their province and resent the capture of their power by the better educated, skilled, and more influential Mohajir groups. The Sindhis and Mohajir together resent the flow of new Pashtun migrants, both from the upper part of the country and from Afghanistan. They consider unchecked migration from KP and Afghanistan as one of the complicating factors for the disorder and instability of Karachi, the largest city in the country.

The historical pattern of migration in and out of Balochistan is very different. Historically, Baloch tribes have been migrating in search of food, grazing lands for animals and productive lands in Punjab and Sindh. They captured most of the areas on the western side of the Indus as a result of internal tribal wars. Tribal wars also pushed some tribes in the direction of the Indus, where they were able to subdue weaker rulers of adjoining districts.[2]

Balochistan has a complex, but interesting, history of evolution from self-governing territorialized tribes to feudal fiefdom and then to an administrative province and federating unit of Pakistan. The history of its evolution is packed with conflicts, struggles, claims, and counter claims to territory and sovereignty by multiple actors. In modern history, the Baloch province has grown out of semi-autonomous princely states of Kalat, Makran, Kharan, and Las Bela, to British Balochistan carved out of Baloch and Pashtun tribes under treaties by the British in the nineteenth century.[3] The proximity to Afghanistan, a region characterized more by conflicts than stability and order has pushed the Pashtun towards Balochistan. The migration of Pashtuns, due more to the great power's interventions and wars, has changed the demographic character of Balochistan to the disadvantage of the Baloch population. Today, more Baloch people live in other provinces than in their home province.[4] Historically, they spilled over into other areas, and similarly, other ethnic groups settled in Balochistan driven by economic and security reasons. The inflow of the Afghan refugees has further complicated ethnic makeup of the province. The Baloch nationalist parties and groups feel greatly insecure about retaining a majority, which by some estimates they have lost to the Pashtuns. The Pashtun nationalists in the Balochistan province have a conflictive history of cooperation, integration, and of seeking separation from Balochistan by demanding that they take their territories and people to join a greater Pashtun province consisting of KP and FATA.[5] The Pashtuns have largely tolerated the Afghan-Pashtun refugees, but they also have an issue with illegal migration, as it adds to competition for jobs, land, businesses, and other forms of economies. Likewise, concentration of Mohajir in urban areas of Sindh along with large groups of Punjabis and Pashtuns threaten to turn Sindhis into a minority in their own province.[6] A fear of losing dominant status by the native groups, and frustrations of the new ones over lack of recognition of their numerical strength, has strained inter-ethnic relations in all provinces. Punjab, the largest one, represents all the ethnic groups of Pakistan, but it has largely been stable in terms of ethnic relations. Its southern part, the Seraiki belt, on account of distinctive language and a narrative of Seraiki sub-nationalism, seeks separation from Punjab by carving out a separate province.[7] Ethnic polarization and regionalism may define ethno-centric politics of Pakistan in the coming years.

All major ethnic groups take their identity from specific cultural traditions. They use language and history to authenticate distinctiveness, separateness, and individuality.[8] Although, there have been overlapping religious and civilization bonds among the peoples of the Indus Valley,[9] they have maintained and asserted separate, individual group consciousness. The question is how distinctive or separate is the identity of each ethnic group and how much it has been tempered by the factors of co-habitation with other ethnic groups for centuries. In my assessment, multi-layered identities that do not seem to come into conflict, have evolved with these groups having shared common homelands for centuries. As a result of social interaction in the market place, ethnic groups, mostly near the borders with other provinces, have become bi-lingual. In this regard, there are two very conflicting patterns of inter-group interaction and adoption of the local language by the settlers. In pre-independence, historical migration patterns, we see the settlers, like the Baloch and the Pashtun or Punjabis, becoming bi-lingual, speaking the language of the majority out of their homes and their group's language within the boundaries of their homes. However, complex social situations of multiple groups interacting never lend themselves to such simple or easy explanations. There are many variations. But overall, we see bi-lingual settled populations.

The post-independence migration that brought a very distinctive language group, the Urdu-speaking migrant from the heart of India, reflects a different pattern. They settled mostly in the urban areas of the country, due to their social background, education, and the professions within the state bureaucracy and businesses. The state of Pakistan adopted Urdu as the national language, which was also the medium of instruction in schools in the Punjab, parts of Sindh, Balochistan, and KP, with some exceptions of instruction in local languages. Urdu language, literature, and culture, associated with the Muslim *ashrafia*, the aristocracy, have left a heavy imprint on the evolving Pakistani culture. Cultures in multiple ethnic and even in modern societies that are characterized by attitudes, beliefs, values, and traditions, reflect a fluid and dynamic process and have a composite character owing to the contribution of regional languages and cultural streams.

Due to constant intermixing and merging, a common Pakistani individual may have an ethnic, caste, tribal, religious, and local identity associated with a place of his origin. However, he can easily shift from one to another, depending on the social and political circumstances, as well as his interests and orientation at a given point in time. This does not, however, diminish his affiliation with, and loyalty to, the major, parent ethnic group that may linger in many cases until urbanization and modernity transforms individual and group identities, which is a long historical process.

Inter-ethnic relations in common homelands and beyond, in urban settings, are mainly the function of two major factors, particularly in the historical context of Pakistan. First, since colonial times, the educational and professional institutions have been concentrated in major cities. They have attracted the young and talented from the villages, remote areas, and other regions to obtain higher education and professional training. The noted trend is that they never go back, and make the new city or any other city where they can find a job their new home. This particular class has shaped the first wave of rural to urban migration. Its economic success and social mobility has served as an example and catalyst for others from similar social backgrounds to migrate to the cities. It was slow in the earlier decades, but with economic transformations in agriculture generating greater income for land-owning families, this type of movement has greatly accelerated, with hundreds of thousands of students from rural areas going to colleges, universities, and boarding schools. As they establish themselves in the cities, close and extended families follow them. However, compared to the new migration of unskilled and semi-skilled workers into the cities, their numbers are much smaller.

The second factor is industrialization and the development of the economy. In the case of Pakistan, it has produced two parallel patterns of ethnic migrations. First, the movement of workers from different provinces into the industrialization hub took place. Karachi was the first, and its earlier lead in industrialization attracted Pashtun, Baloch, and Punjabi migrants. It was not just the jobs in the industry, but the relative affluence of the urban populations that created opportunities for all type of business, service, and domestic sector employment. In recent decades, displacement of peasants from the agricultural sector, and the growth of a new middle class in the rural areas is shaping the new pattern of migration from other provinces, mostly into Sindh and the Punjab. About 3.3% of Pakistan's population is migrating to the urban areas annually, which is the highest rate of urbanization in South Asia.[10] This largely unnoticed wave of migration and urbanization would reshape identities, influence inter-ethnic relations, and have a great impact on national politics. The increasing diversity and pluralism of urban spaces is likely to produce new forms of social, cultural, and political interactions, which can be conflictive or benign. At this stage, it remains conflictive in some of the cities, where diversity is new and more pronounced, like Karachi, Hyderabad, Gilgit, and Quetta.

There are some other important elements that have a great bearing on inter-ethnic relations and the politics of ethnicity. First are state policies, laws, governance, and distributive politics. The state policies have often favoured dominant groups as they are shaped by the patronage politics of local and regional majorities. This has produced many strands of contentious politics and prevented a natural evolution of harmony and accommodation among ethnic groups within the provinces. State policies may have integrative and disintegrative implications. Therefore, they must be considered to be the most crucial variable in understanding ethnicity-driven social movements and politics anywhere.[11]

Democracy itself is not an independent variable in promoting or diffusing ethnicity. It is an integral element of a state-based political system that addresses itself to the larger question of political power. A multi-ethnic political society provides an operational environment for democracy or any other type of political order. Such a society, along with the central elements of general political culture, conditions the functioning of a democratic system. The relationship between democracy and a multi-ethnic political society is interactive, where the influence process flows in both directions. An ethnic character of the society would influence, first and foremost, the political ordering of the community, determine rules of politics, and shape the general patterns of political behaviour. Federalism, in its true sense, offers the best political option to manage diversity. Factors, like the devolution of power, coalition-building, and a degree of democratic maturity of the political system, along with distributive policies of the state and access to power would mitigate or diffuse the ethnic tensions.

An ethnic group claims to have a common language, culture, and distinctive social traits, which differentiate or distinguish it from other similar groups.[12] Ethnic consciousness can grow out of a real or imagined sense of being a separate community.[13] An ethnic identity can be authenticated or established when a group adopts a common identity, and acquires a social label that is recognized as such by others. In societies where social or political integration has been slow, or where the modernization process has not touched the old social divisions, individuals and groups retain ethnic or much narrower identities, like caste, tribe, religious sect, and parochial affiliations. Ethnicity, both in its subjective form of self-characterization, such as Mohajir, and its objectivity with out-group recognition, is determined by political conditions that may keep it dormant or active it, because an ethnic, or any other group identity, itself does not constitute a subject of politics unless such an identity is used as an instrument for a group's political action. The arousing of ethnic sentiments among the members of a group is usually goal-oriented, with a focus on seeking a redistribution of power and national resources to the satisfaction of that group. It is the degree and intensity of demands on the political system by an ethnic group that determines the level of its politicization.

It is the politics of ethnicity that shape political movements in support of common demands. In return, ethnic movements reinforce the political consciousness of the ethnic group. Ethnic movements strengthen group solidarity through political mobilization, which may take the form of an agitation, produce militancy, or involve the community in a democratic process to effect a desired political change.[14] An articulation of the demands that are specific to the needs of an ethnic group separates it further from both the larger national community and from other similar groups. Such distinctions necessitate the setting of criteria according to which we can compare ethnic politics of different groups in Pakistan. One may look at the origins, orientations, and internal group dynamics for explaining their similarities, differences, or uniqueness. A group's ethnicity may be reactive to the rise of the ethnicity of a rival ethnic group with whom it competes for power and resources within the common homeland—the province. One may consider the rise of Mohajir ethnicity as reactive to Sindhi nationalism. Or its origin may be quite autonomous, stimulated exclusively by its own sense of group identity, political demands, or grievances, as is the case of Baloch nationalism. Orientation of an ethnic group may explain whether it desires to radically transform the political order to its advantage, wants some minor adjustments within the system, or wishes to protect the existing distribution of power and resources. Internal group dynamics would show how socially cohesive or fragmented a group is. The level of its social development, such as tribal, feudal, urban, or industrial would provide the basis on which we may compare ethnic social movements, their strengths and weaknesses in Pakistan.

Authoritarianism, Democracy, and Ethnicity

A system choice for ethnically pluralistic societies is of crucial importance. Our central argument is that authoritarianism in any form, but especially the one established by the military regimes with an accumulation of power at the centre, has worked against the spirit of national integration and has promoted the politics of ethnicity. Democracy combined with federalism creates better conditions for diffusing ethnicity and bringing various ethnic groups into the national streams. Having said this, it is important to remember that democracy and ethnicity have a complex relationship.

The problem arises from the fact that democracy as a philosophical idea may have some degree of universality, but the quality and level of democratic institutionalization is conditioned by local social and cultural factors. One must keep the philosophical parts of democracy in the background when recognising how it plays out practically in diverse national circumstances, elite politics, and social consciousness of the people. Let us consider its principles—the theoretical aspects—to measure its impact on ethnicity and ethnic politics in Pakistan, as we explain ethnic nationalisms and their relationship with the Pakistani nationalism and state. Evidently, a democratic system implies a notion of popular sovereignty, which means that the power to form and change a government lies with the citizens who delegate this right to a smaller group through a system of representation.[15] Even at a basic level, democracy allows some freedoms, political participation, and political contest for public offices. Therefore, a political system based on democratic principles would offer opportunities for peaceful political change and help institute a government to serve the public interest, not the interests of persons to promote private ends. The functions and long-term consequences of democracy as a political framework go beyond the organizing politics of the society. It promotes pluralism, a culture of political tolerance, accommodation among conflicting interests, and equal economic and political opportunity for all. However, political legitimacy, representation, recruitment of political elite from all sections of the population, fundamental freedoms, and equal access to political power may be considered to be the core values of democracy.

In exploring their effects on each other, we wish to examine two questions. Does democracy diffuse ethnicity or stimulate it? How does ethnicity strengthen or undermine democracy? Let us start with the first question. Pluralistic and constitutional arrangements of a democratic system politically integrate diverse ethnic communities, both by raising their stakes in the system, and providing them with regular channels of interaction and political communication. In this context, I would like to mention four mechanisms that a democratic process can offer to ethnic groups. First, political participation allows an ethnic group to articulate its demands and enter into a contest for political power. Accommodation of a group's demands would reduce its dissatisfaction and increase its support for the political system. Second, a democratic order offers the best opportunities for political communication among all ethnic groups. Such an order also promotes a political culture of dialogue and tolerance. The ethnic elements, over time, develop strategies of political negotiation and bargaining that often result in the softening of positions and compromises. Third, electoral politics provide another avenue of close cooperation among ethnic groups. The logic of the numbers game in any democratic system compels the ethnic elite to form coalitions with other like-minded groups or with the national political parties, as has always been the case in Pakistan. Political alliances bring about a positive change in the attitudes of ethnic groups, as benefits of political cooperation dilute their extreme positions by generating optimism about empowerment and attainment of rights. The cultural effects of working with others may raise the level of their empathy towards competing groups and the national political forces. Finally, constitutionalism and a higher degree of trust on it may induce the ethnic groups to seek redress for their grievances through peaceful means.

However, every form of politics played out by self-interested political actors—ethnic, regional, and national—makes the political process too complex to lead to any straight or clean and neat consequences. In the initial stage, a democratic system may face turbulence because various ethnic groups may be striving for a political space, or recognition of their status, and for that they may adopt maximal agendas. They may even attempt to elbow out the weaker elements from power structures and attempt to establish their respective dominance. In societies where systemic inequalities exist, democracy invariably stimulates ethnic influence on politics. Opening up the political system to popular participation in traditional societies raises ethnic aspirations, giving rise to demands for autonomy and equitable distribution of power and resources.[16]

The issue is that, in the early stages of nation- and state-building in ethnically pluralistic societies like Pakistan, it is not easy to settle questions of institutional balance, adequate representation of ethnic groups, the equitable distribution of benefits, and rewards of development. It takes time, but what is important is that multi-ethnic nations strictly pursue democracy and true federalism as ideal templates of state- and nation-building. That has not been a persistent path of Pakistan. The country has lapsed into military authoritarianism several times, and its federalism has, in the past, been centre-tilted. Not settling issues pertaining to the rules of the political game—constitution, federalism, provincial autonomy—in the defining decades, Pakistan's nation-building process remained flawed, and produced adverse, tragic consequences. The cases of successful nation- and state-building suggest that they have settled the rules of the political game, including the participation of different ethnic groups in political power and the institutionalization of political change. A consensus on fundamental political values, strong roots of state in civil society, and a democratic political culture are some of the factors that have stabilized the multi-ethnic democracies.

The case of transitional democracies like Pakistan is different. The postcolonial state as inherited by the nationalist elite had to come to grips with the phenomenon of multi-ethnicity that emerged as a very strong force once the sentimentalism of Muslim nationalism began to give way to practical issues of politics. It was a daunting task to politically integrate too many diverse regional and linguistic groups into one state with two separate territorial units. Theoretically, federal, democratic principles provided the best possible solution to the problem of political integration of diverse groups, but the political elites in the contest of power, mainly from West Pakistan, and the rise of the military and bureaucracy placing self-interest before national interests, took the opposite route of centralization and authoritarianism. Centralization of governmental authority, military rule, and dictatorships have only complicated ethnic politics in Pakistan.[17] Pakistan, like many developing democracies, continues to face the challenge of diffusing ethnicity by accommodating, adequately, the interests of the minorities.[18]

Punjab and Pakistani Nationalism

According to the last census in 1998, Punjab constituted more than 55.6% of the population, while the other three provinces together accounted for 44.4%.[19] Also, Punjab is the richest in terms of agricultural and industrial production.[20] Urdu and Muslim nationalism, the two main symbols of Pakistani nationalism, have traditionally received stronger support from the Punjabis than from other provinces. A growing number of Punjabi educated families have adopted Urdu as their first language in urban areas. It is trendy even in small towns and villages to converse with children in Urdu. Ordinary Punjabis feel that Urdu is a superior, decent language and a symbol of literate status. There are historical reasons for what appears to be a 'voluntary' switch to Urdu in the Punjab. Even before the creation of Pakistan, Urdu was the medium of instruction throughout Punjab and in most other areas that now comprise Pakistan. Both the Punjabi intellectuals and elite have patronized Urdu for the past couple of centuries. Today, the best Urdu literature is being produced in the Punjab, where hundreds of popular magazines are published every month. Owing to some of these factors, and the fact that Punjab remains a dominant player in the national politics of the country, the intellectual and political environment of the province has not been congenial to the growth of Punjabi nationalism. The Punjabi intellectuals fear that, over time, they might lose their language. They have consistently campaigned for reverting back to reading, writing, and speaking Punjabi, but to very little effect.[21]

There are material reasons for support of Pakistani nationalism in Punjab as well. Punjabis comprise the largest single ethnic group (60–65%) in the Pakistan Army,[22] which is the largest employer in the country. As an institution, the Pakistan Army has ruled the country for well over three decades. Likewise, the Punjabis have greater representation in the civil services than all the provinces together. They have also made tremendous gains in business, industry, and agriculture. As a whole, the Punjabis have greatly benefitted from the development and modernization process in the post-independence period. For the last two decades, Punjab's economic performance has been far better than all other provinces and regions.[23]

Although it is hard to compare ehtnic groups in terms of energy, motivation, and any other traits, a common self-description among the Punjabis is that they are more enterprising and dynamic than other ethnic groups. This can be seen from their settlement in other provinces where they have developed agricultural lands, and their migration to the Gulf countries for work. It is estimated that, in the 1980s, 85% of the 1.3 million Pakistani workers in the Gulf were Punjabis and Pashtuns, with Punjabis constituting an overwhelming majority.[24] This means that 75% of the remittances in the 80s that were in the neighborhood of $2.5 to $3 billion annually were invested in the Punjab, which have now grown to $16 to 17 billion.[25] Employment opportunities abroad as well as rapid economic growth, particularly due to the effects of the green revolution in the province, and lately the emergence of industrial clusters, and better quality of educational institutions producing a highly qualified and employable professional class are some of the major factors that have prevented the emergence of Punjabi nationalism. As a consequence, the Punjabi language movement and nationalism remain confined to the drawing rooms of a narrow band of Punjabi intellectuals.[26]

Punjab is not an ethnically homogenous province, nor is any other province of Pakistan. It has a large number of Baloch people scattered in its southern and western districts, as well as Pashtuns, and the people of the Potwar region, in the northern districts all of whom don't share the Punjabi identity. Therefore, it would be unfair to claim that all the regions that fall within the territorial confines of the Punjab have a common identity. The peoples in the southern part of the province, comprising three administrative divisions—Multan, Bahawalpur, and Dera Ghazi Khan—speak the Seraiki language and continue to contest Punjabi identity.[27] On the other hand, the Punjabi intellectuals and politicians regard Seraiki as merely a variant of the Punjabi language. There have been two movements in southern Punjab, one political and the other cultural. The people of the (former) Bahawalpur state launched a political agitation in support of a provincial status for Bahawalpur and against its continued merger with Punjab in 1969 after One-Unit was disbanded. The movement evoked a popular response. The demand for a separate province gained so much support that almost all the candidates backed by the *Bahawalpur Mutahida Mahaz* [Bahawalpur United Front] running as independents won more seats than the major political parties in the three districts of the (former) Bahawalpur state.[28] However, a dual policy of repression and co-optation by the PPP regime weakened the movement. The secession of East Pakistan in 1971 also turned the central government and the Punjabi elite more hostile towards regionalist movements.

There are two other factors that work against Bahawalpur as a separate province. First, there is a significant presence of Punjabi settlers in the former Bahawalpur state who dominate business, government jobs, and industry, while the local population comprises of largely Seraiki peasants of mainly land-owning class. The Punjabi settlers who wield considerable administrative and political influence have been mostly against the division of Punjab into smaller units.

They fear that they would lose power to the Seraikis. It is interesting that the Seraiki feudal class that dominates the electoral politics has never given any support to the idea of a separate Bahawalpur or a larger Seraiki province that would include all the three administrative divisions mentioned above. They are comfortably integrated with the power structure of the Punjab. As the Punjabi settlers form a large vote bank in most of the electoral constituencies, the Seraiki political elite prefer to remain silent on the issue, often denouncing those who support regional movements.

The other reason is that the Seraiki nationalists in other parts of the Punjab wish to establish a Seraiki province, generally explained in non-ethnic terms as southern Punjab. Seraiki remains, essentially, a cultural movement, although it is weak and still at the formative stages. The movement emphasizes the learning of the Seraiki language and the promotion of its limited classical and modern literature. The Seraiki consciousness has grown among college and university students both within the Seraiki region and in other areas where Seraikis have settled for jobs. So far, the Seraiki movement remains poorly organized and factionalized.[29] The middle class Seraiki nationalist intellectuals have, for a long time, been promoting the idea of a distinct Seraiki nationality,[30] but have achieved very little in getting any recognition from within or without. They are in a big quandary for two reasons. The rural areas are dominated by the feudals where they cannot dare challenge their traditional power and influence, and the Urdu-speaking migrants from India as well as the Punjabi settlers dominate the urban areas of the Seraiki region.

In fact, the middle class Seraikis have abandoned villages in search of jobs in the main centers of Punjab. There are only a few major towns left in the Seraiki region where the Seraikis can claim a majority. Modernization, development, and the democratic process are more likely to see greater assimilation and integration of the Seraikis with mainstream Punjab, as it has been happening over the past many decades, despite a conflictive narrative of inequity, and inquality among the constituent regions of the Punjab. This is already happening, and is evident from the failure of the Seraiki nationalists to gather any support even among their own constituents. The Seraiki parties and groups have failed to get even a single seat in the past several elections. This is an issue of political conversion of ethnicity or ethnicization, not a question mark on the ethnic identity of the Seraiki people. And that is not the end of the story, as ethnic movements rise, fall, or stay dormant, depending on their interaction with their own community and the pace of the national integration process.

Pashtun Integration

The Khyber Pakhtunkhwa province and the adjoining Federally Administered Tribal Areas (FATA) comprise 15.8% of the total population of the country.[31] The Pashtuns are the predominant ethnic group in these areas. They also form a majority across the Durand-Line in Afghanistan, a country that they founded in the middle of the eighteenth century.[32] They also dominate the northern parts of Balochistan and the Punjab districts adjoining the KP. Since independence, Pashtuns have continued to migrate in larger numbers to Karachi, the troubled metropolis and industrial centre of lower Sindh. There are three other important ethno-linguistic groups in the KP: Baloch, Hindko, and Seraiki. The native people of Peshawar city and its surrounding areas are Hindko speaking and they have a presence in other cities and towns of the province. The main Hindko speaking ethnic group is in the three eastern districts of KP—Abbottabad, Haripur, and Mansehra. A vast majority of the population in district Dera Ismail Khan and Tank speaks Seraiki. Hindko and Seraiki languages are closer to Punjabi than Pashtu. This linguistic divide also marks the political divisions in this province.

Historically, the Seraiki and Hindko speaking people, a minority, have strongly supported centralist elements in Pakistani politics, and they were the main supporters of the Muslim League and its demand for Pakistan in 1947. On the other hand, the Pashtun legendary pacifist leader, Abdul Ghaffar Khan, given his commitment to the ideology of non-violence, began to think of a third option for the Pashtun areas, a country of their own,[33] albeit in vague terms. He also proposed it too late, at a time when the partition plan was already agreed upon.[34] The British, the Congress, and the Muslim League had a consensus on two options, either accession to India or to Pakistan. However, Ghaffar Khan was able to earn a concession from the British to hold a referendum in the then NWFP on the question of accession. He and his party tried to delay the referendum, and later boycotted it for ambiguous reasons, due to which the third option was not recognized.[35] Reaching climax to independence and partition, the Congress abandoned its nationalist allies in the province. The political developments had changed the sentiments in the province. Great numbers of Pashtuns voted to join Pakistan in the referendum, which had become an inevitable political reality looming over the horizon.

Ghaffar Khan and his followers continued to champion the cause of the rights of the Pashtuns, but again in ambiguous terms, demanding a separate state of Pashtunistan that would include the entire province of NWFP and the tribal areas along the Durand-Line. The articulation of Pashtunistan remained vague in terms of status, territories, and an avowed political mission. At the end, as the idea died a natural death, it was nothing more than a trial balloon, perhaps a bargaining chip or just an attempt to pursue Pashtun nationalism for political ends. The demand for Pashtunistan received political support only from Afghanistan where a fellow Pashtun dynasty ruled. There was lukewarm response to the demand from India and the Soviet Union. The Pashtunistan movement couldn't gain strength and never posed a serious threat to the Pakistani state because it did not receive wide support among the Pashtuns. Sadly, the successive Pakistani governments treated Ghaffar Khan quite harshly, putting the old man in prison for a very long time. It was unfortunate, because Ghaffar Khan was an internationally respected leader and had made great contributions to the struggle against British rule in the subcontinent. His great work as a pacifist and his contribution to non-violent struggle, including the founding of social service-oriented Khudai Khidmatgar (servants of God) movement remain unacknowledged.[36]

The Pashtuns present a classic case of integration through economic modernization and political democracy. In the 1960s, the industrial development in Karachi and parts of Punjab attracted Pashtuns to seek work there. And their flow into these areas has continued. They now form roughly 4.2% of Sindh's population, and around 11% of Karachi. A significant portion of the unemployed Pashtuns was absorbed by the new industrial estates in the country. Similarly, the economic and industrial activity in their home province, particularly in the decades of 1970s and 1980s, has provided them with ample opportunity for economic and social mobility. Pashtuns are one of the most dynamic communities of Pakistan and have an entrepreneurial spirit. They have significant economic presence in all areas of Pakistan.

The Pashtuns are the only ethnic group that has disproportionately more representation in the armed forces at 22%.[37] Their numbers in the civil bureaucracy are quite adequate, perhaps more than their proportionate numbers in the populations, particularly at the lower levels, due to their proximity to the capital. The Pashtun elite is very much integrated in the economic and political power structures of Pakistan, and it has happened more rapidly than perhaps the nationalists might have expected. The Pashtun business community owns some of the big industrial houses in the country, specifically in the Punjab and Sindh, besides their home province. Since the 1990s, the Gadoon-Amazai area of the KP has emerged as one of the fastest developing industrial zones in the country, one that the Pashtun business elite dominate. These are some of the positive developments that have gradually dampened Pashtun separatism.

Two other factors also need to be stressed: the Afghan wars and the electoral democracy in the country. Pakistan has been sheltering millions of Afghan Pashtun refugees. Some of the Pashtun nationalists from the KP province have occasionally voiced concerns about providing hospitality to the Afghan Pashtuns and the role of the conservative religious elements in the Afghan war of resistance. Some of them openly supported the communist regime in Kabul and tried to justify Soviet invasion as a defensive move.[38] But a great majority of the Pashtuns supported the war of resistance. The conflict in Afghanistan and Pakistan's supportive role to the Mujahedeen resistance put an end to the Pashtunistan issue. Then, as the state in Afghanistan disintegrated and the Pashtuns in Afghanistan began to depend too heavily on Pakistan to remain as an important political and military factor in their own country, the issue lost its relevance. For the last 38 years, there appears to have been an informal Afghan-Pashtun-Pakistan alliance, which is reflected in Pakistan's support to the Mujahideen and the Taliban over the decades. In fact, Pakistan had played a key role in their resistance to foreign occupations and political survival. This importance is not lost on the Pashtun nationalist elements in Pakistan itself, even though their orientation has consistently remained pro-Kabul, from monarchy to installation of successive governments by Moscow, and since 9/11, by Washington. They genuinely feel for the order, stability, and unity of Afghanistan.

The economic development and democratic process have been the most critical factors in institutionalizing the integration of the Pashtuns into Pakistan. During the past two decades, a broad middle- and a more influential upper-class of industrialists and traders have emerged in the Frontier. Massive investment by the successive governments in the development of infrastructure and industrial estates along with the smuggling of goods from Afghanistan has affected the economic growth of KP consistently over the decades. Another important factor in the economic development of the province is the large number of overseas workers in the Middle East that sends quite a massive amount of remittances. With 13.94% of the share of the national population, KP's foreign remittance share in 2014–15 was 26.67%, which is double the size of its population.[39] Also, over the past two decades, the annual growth of remittances for KP has been much greater than other provinces.[40]

The perceptions of the new middle-class about Pashtun nationalism have changed. The traders, businessmen, industrialists and those working with governments have turned more religious or more concerned with turnovers, profits, and economic opportunities that integrate them with the national market, civil society, and broader politics than with ethnic politics.[41] These transformations have greatly undermined the power and influence of the leaders and political groups that had, at one time, fomented separatism. The National Awami Party, which has been renamed as Awami National Party (ANP), has lost out to both religious and secular national parties in the province. It has been forced to enter into political alliances with national political parties, and on several occasions, has formed a government in coalition with JUI, a religious party with a stronghold in the Pashtun areas of Balochistan and the KP. The ANP has pursued pragmatic politics and has been an effective player in national politics. The party no longer subscribes to any separatism. Like many Pashtuns, they also understand how deeply their community is integrated with Pakistan.

However, the ANP, like other regionalist parties, pursued an alternative course of politics, federalism, provincial autonomy, and devolution of more powers to the provincial governments, but essentially within the framework of Pakistan.[42] One of the demands of the Pashtun nationalists had been the renaming of the NWFP. The peoples of Hazara, Peshawar, and Dera Ismail Khan resisted the move, because they preferred some non-ethnic name for the province, if the name originally coined by the British Indian government (that had a long history and identity of its own) had to be changed after all. In the second tenure of office (1997–99), the PML-N government had reached some understanding with the ANP on this issue but refused to accept this demand, fearing that such a concession would erode its support in the Punjab as well as among its traditional constituents, like Hindko, Hazara, and the Seraiki-speaking populations of NWFP. Renaming of the province became such a major issue that it finally brought to an end a decade of political coalition between the ANP and PML-N.[43] The latter, however, has been more sensitive to the concerns of the ANP about the construction of Kalabagh Dam—a massive water reservoir and hydro-electric power project that has been shelved for decades due to opposition from Sindh and KP. This is one of the cases where emotive nationalist politics has trumped economic rationalism and prudence. Placed in a more positive light, Pakistani parties and leaders have grown more pragmatic, realistic, and open to listening to the other side. I do not consider it a sign of weakness—as the absence of strong leaders—rather as an indication of political maturity in seeking a middle ground on which all the political stakeholders would agree.

It is a reflection of pragmatic politics that the political parties have changed the structure of federalism by devolving greater powers to the provinces through the 18th Amendment. Some might argue that the powers and responsibilities given to the provinces in some areas are beyond their capacity to deliver. The fact that it was done with unanimity among the regional, nationalist, religious, and national political parties together in a historic compact, marks progress in redefining federalism in Pakistan. In the bargain, the ANP got what it had always wanted: an ethnic name for the province—Khyber Pakhtunkhwa. It was not without controversy, and sadly it erased history, but then, in the end, it is the demand-driven, pragmatic politics and the relative power of the players that determines the outcome. The ANP made a hard bargain, and won.

Baloch Fears and Nationalism

In no other province are the basic facts about history, ethnicity, and identity as contested as in Balochistan. The reason is that the Baloch have some real and some imagined fears about becoming a minority in their 'own' province. And nowhere has ethnic demography become as distorted and controversial as in the case of Balochistan. With two contending ethnic groups—the Baloch and Pashtun—and with an unceasing flow of the Afghans into the upper parts of the province, the question of which of these constitute a majority has become murky. It started with the British reporting on ethnic and religious groups in the censuses. Every British *Report on the Administration of Balochistan* from the beginning of the twentieth century to 1946 begins with the following introductory paragraph: 'The Baloch though giving their name to the whole country, are not the most numerous people in it, being exceeded in numbers by both the Brahuis and Afghans.'[44] The 1941 decennial census, which we should consider an authentic document about the base of each ethnic group in Balochistan and other provinces, shows 857,835 as the total population of the province.[45] Compared to the previous census, the province lost 10,000 of its population 'mainly due to the continued mass migration of Brahuis from Kalat State into Sind'.[46] The total population of the states (Kalat, Lasbela, and Kharan) is shown as 356,204 against 463,508 in the 1931 census.[47] During this period, while we see an outflow of Baloch tribes into Sindh, we also see Afghans, both Hazara and Pashtun, moving in from Afghanistan. This historical pattern might be responsible for greatly reduced Baloch numbers, which the Baloch leaders fear is the presence of Afghan refugees and an uninterrupted movement of Afghans into the province.

The second important fact is that a wide range of languages are spoken in Balochistan, which have historically been overshadowed by the Baloch-Pashtun ethnicities and ethnic rivalry. The administrative report referred to above mentions the following languages in this particular order: 'Pashtu, Brahui, Eastern and Western Baluchi, Jatki or Siraiki, Jagdali, or Sindhi, Khetrani, and Lasi.'[48] Modern scholarship and current political discourses hardly go beyond counting two indigenous languages of Balochistan—Balochi and Pashtu.

There is yet another fact about Balochistan that needs to be seen in its proper historical context. This is about the administrative entities and how, and when, they came to form a unified province of Balochistan. Among these entities, what is well documented and without any controversy, is the British Balochistan. It consisted of three different regions, which, before the British conquest, were ruled by Afghanistan or by the tribal chiefs. First, it included within it all the Pashtun territories, acquired by force by the British Indian Empire and under a treaty from Afghanistan toward the end of the nineteenth century. The second category of people and territories consisted of the Baloch areas of the Bugti and Marri tribes. Third are the tribes from the Jhalawan region. Fourth, Quetta, which was leased out of the Kalat State and became a military base and administrative centre of the British, close to Persia and Afghanistan.

The third element in the consolidation of Balochistan is the princely states of Kalat, Lasbela, Kharan, and Makran. In the last decades of colonial rule, the British claimed these states as princely states, appointed advisors in each of the states and never dealt with them through the agency of the largest state, Kalat. For instance, the 1909–10 Administrative Report states that, 'Mir Muhammad Yakub Khan (Kharan) signed an agreement in which he accepted the boundary laid down by Major Whyte.'[49] Having said this, there is, however, inconsistency in British reporting about the status of the Balochistan states. In some of the reports, it clearly mentions that there are only two states—Kalat and Lasbela. In the early period, they talk of Makran as a fiduciary of the Kalat state. However, in the successive decades, they regard all of them as princely states of India.[50] For each year, and in every report, the British documented every minute detail from crimes to crops, yields, revenues, feuds, and general conditions of the people and relations of the states with the British authority. Balochistan, in the British strategic planning for the defence of its Empire in India, had acquired major significance towards the later part of the nineteenth century, in the 'great game'.[51] The British carefully planned and took the hazardous and most difficult task of extending the railways from the core of the Empire through the entire vastness of Balochistan to the periphery of Afghanistan. This feat remains unparalleled in the history of infrastructure development, from surveys and land settlement, to its costly and painful execution. It was accompanied by the introduction of state institutions, security arrangements, laws, rules and regulations, and the sowing of the seeds of modernization through the establishment of a modern school system in the province. However, due to its vastness, low density of population, and tribal social structure, the integration of the province with the rest of the Empire was relatively weaker than other regions. This represented a typical colonial problem between the centre and the periphery—the more removed a region from the centre of governance, the lesser attention was paid to it. Like the peripheries of all empires, Balochistan remained more of a security concern under the British than a zone of economic opportunity and progress.

Balochistan is ethnically plural, diverse, and fragmented along many dimensions, and has been in such a state throughout history because of its social tribal formation. Even within tribes, there are variations, and some areas of Balochistan are even non-tribal. The case in point is the social character of the Baloch in Makran coast, which stands out in a remarkable contrast to other regions. The population here is varied and divided between those who seem to be of Africa in origins and share hardly anything with the rest of tribal Balochistan. There are indigenous Baloch social groups in this part of the province that have no tribal affiliations. All Baloch tribes have separate territorial domains and are governed by tribal chiefs. The story of emerging towns and cities, very few at the moment, is very different, however, where populations are tribal identities, but share new common citizenship of the towns—a modernizing urban trend that will define the future of this province. In contrast to the towns, the tribes and sub-tribes have deeper parochial attitudes, and mostly live on subsistence agriculture or pastoralism. Ethnically and politically, Balochistan is much more fragmented than has been realized by outside observers. Despite inter-tribal feuds and localism of the sub-tribes, Baloch nationalism has been alive throughout the last seven decades, and on several occasions, it has generated conflict with the central state. The demands of the nationalists have varied and changed over time, from Baloch rights, identity and autonomy to some groups demanding a separate 'greater Balochistan' state that would also include Iran's Balochistan-Sistan province.[52]

Trouble began at the time of Partition. Balochistan's joining of Pakistan should not have been controversial, and its continued troubles with the federation would not have been so consistent, had the geopolitics of the region been more benign for Pakistan or had this vast province been fully integrated with the British Empire. Balochistan was on the outer fringes of the British rule and at the cross-roads of Afghanistan and the NWFP. Some Baloch nationalists, only a few, at the time of partition, saw an opportunity to separate Balochistan from the new, unstable state of Pakistan that faced chaos internally, and conflicts on the borders with Afghanistan and India. These two factors, in fact, have consistently influenced the Baloch nationalist aspirations. There is a third factor influencing the contemporary rise of Baloch ethnicity—the vast natural resources base, the long sea coast, and prospects of integration through infrastructural development—that we should not miss out in assessing what drives the Baloch sentiment and why certain foreign powers have been backing insurgency.

More than the history of individual tribes and khanates (the prototype, tribal states still in the making), in our view, it was prospective geopolitics that played a key role in generating a controversy over the status of Kalat and other princely states while joining Pakistan in 1947. It was this geopolitical thought: why can Baloch people, with so much land and resources in the modern age of nationalism, not be a nation in their own right? It is an important question in the sub-national narratives of all kinds, and in communities that have similar characteristics anywhere in the world. Although the Shahi Jirga, the official consultative assembly of the Baloch tribes that was established by the British, decided to accede to Pakistan, the Khan of Kalat, a ruler of a princely state in the province, hesitated, wanting to negotiate a special status, and then declared 'independence'. As this action was against the declared principles of the partition plan, and since it could pose a serious threat to the integrity of the new state, the central government sent a limited force to put pressure on the Khan to sign an accession document on 1 April 1948.[53] The Khan offered no resistance and signed the document of accession to Pakistan.[54] He was taken to Karachi and sent abroad as a member of the Pakistani delegation to the UN; there, he retracted his statement of 'independence'.[55] However, some elements within the Kalat state began to organize resistance with support from Afghanistan, but they were too weak to make any impact against a weak, incipient state of Pakistan.[56] That didn't end the estrangement of Balochistan from the centre, as politics of federalism and democracy began to falter in the first decade of independence—formation of one unit and military takeover, for example. The first conflict took place in 1958–59 under the first military regime, over the allotment of lands to the Punjabi settlers in the areas close to Sindh.[57] These areas were to be irrigated by a new canal called the Pat Feeder that was then under construction from the Guddu barrage in upper Sindh. These clashes were limited, and did not provoke any coordinated or centralized Baloch response. The issue was resolved when the local Baloch tribes were also allotted lands in the area. But this, and many other episodes indicate fear among the Baloch of being turned into a minority and losing control over natural resources of the province.

Balochistan has been through two serious insurgencies, including the one that began around 2006, and continues to trouble the security and stability of some parts of the province.[58] Each of the two insurgencies has one common context—Baloch separatism—but very differently triggering national circumstances. Another common factor between the current and the 1974–77 insurgencies is the role of the foreign powers and sanctuaries in Afghanistan.[59] The current insurgency has been at a very low and localized level, but has lasted longer and has been a festering political wound that poses a challenge to the development and integration of the province through the development of the Gwadar Port and the China-Pakistan Economic Corridor (CPEC).

The first round of Baloch insurgency was far more serious than the present one, which is somewhat alive but fast withering away. It began in February 1973 when the central government of Zulfikar Ali Bhutto dismissed the provincial government of Balochistan on the flimsy grounds that it was violating the Constitution and raising Baloch armies to secede from Pakistan. Bhutto simply wanted to remove an opposition government that was acting more autonomously than his autocratic character would allow. In disbanding the elected government of Balochistan, Bhutto had the blessings of the Shah of Iran, who feared that Baloch nationalism would spread to Iranian Balochistan and destabilize his rule there. However, Bhutto misread the political situation in Balochistan. The anti-Ayub movement and the restoration of political activity leading to the 1970 elections had changed the political landscape of Balochistan. The most significant change was that the new Baloch intelligentsia, which was the product of post-independence modernization, and the tribal chiefs, worked out a broader coalition between the two. Another change was that the Baloch coalition led by the first generation of nationalists, forged close political alliances with the Pashtun nationalists from the NWFP, which also helped them win political support of the Pashtuns in the Balochistan province. A common interest in, and struggle for, seeking provincial autonomy brought the two ethnic groups together.

The Baloch were outraged over the dismissal of their first elected government.[60] They waged an intensive guerrilla war for four years until Bhutto was thrown out of power by the military. The military regime released the Pashtun and Baloch leaders who had been incarcerated for more than four years and were facing treason charges before a special court that Bhutto had established for hearing cases against them in the Hyderabad prison, in Sindh. In 1978, the government granted amnesty to the Baloch guerrillas, allocated funds for their resettlement, released thousands of the remaining prisoners and started a reconciliation process.[61] The Baloch guerrillas had considerable support from Afghanistan where they had been given sanctuary. The Baloch nationalists might have emerged stronger if the Soviet Union had consolidated its hold over Afghanistan. But amnesty by the government of Pakistan and growing troubles for the Soviets in Afghanistan dimmed their hope for external support.

The revival of democracy in Pakistan brought about a fundamental change in the political attitudes of the Baloch leaders. They have grown more pragmatic and realistic about their options owing to changes within Pakistani politics and in the strategic environment of the adjacent region. Today, the Baloch nationalist movement is fragmented. The first generation of the nationalist leaders have either passed away or have left the stage because of old age. The new insurgency of 2006–16 is very different. It has new players (the educated youth from colleges and universities) who are more radical than those leading the previous one. Besides Afghanistan, the insurgency also has support from India and other neighbouring countries for their rivalry and their opposition to the prospects of Pakistan succeeding with integrating Balochistan through development projects. The problem with the new insurgency is that it has failed to garner support even among the factions that have taken up arms against the Pakistani state. The biggest weakness of the insurgents is that they are isolated from mainstream Baloch politics. Most of the tribes and the political parties have joined the national politics and have secured autonomy and major development projects that are likely to transform the economy and society of the region.[62] The Baloch nationalist parties have consistently endorsed this view. The important development in the context of Baloch ethnicity is that the Baloch nationalist parties have adopted a democratic, peaceful path for their rights, and the centre has been more prudent in bringing them into national and Balochistan-centered coalition politics.

Balochistan is no longer a main political reserve of the nationalists. The religious parties, like the JUI, and the mainstream national parties, PPP and PML-N, have increased their support in the province. The Baloch nationalists have become divided and fragmented over time. A vast majority of tribal leaders, traditional political families, and dominant Baloch elite factions pursue constitutional and participatory paths to solving problems. However, some sections of Baloch college graduates, the lower middle classes and dissidents within the tribal elites support militancy.[63] The Pashtuns are no more aligned with the Baloch. With the inflow of the Afghan refugees to Balochistan, the interests of the Pashtuns and the Baloch have come into conflict. The Baloch fear that the Afghan refugees are going to tilt the demographic balance in favour of the Pashtuns, who want to carve out a separate province from Balochistan and demand a greater recognition of their numbers in economic and political structures of the region.[64]

Balochistan, much like Sindh, has experienced competition, rivalry, and confrontation among the ethnic communities within the provinces. The Baloch elites continue to voice concern about the distribution of financial resources between the central government and their province. They want greater share of royalties from the sale of natural gas, a better deal in the allocation of finances for development, and a greater say in the development of the Gwadar Port and the routing of the CPEC. It is precisely the prospects of success of these ongoing and very promising projects that make the Baloch militants feel that they might lose the battle of separating Balochistan.[65]

Balochistan—with its vast mineral wealth, the development of the Gwadar Port, and its connectivity through motorways and planned railways with other provinces as well as China—has acquired far greater economic, secure, and strategic significance than ever before. Its emerging pivotal role in national and regional commerce, trade, industry, and economic activities has produced two dialectical trends. One is towards its deeper integration with the rest of the country through development, mainly focusing on infrastructural projects in the present phase. The development paradigm is premised on the idea that CPEC and the Gwadar port will open up economic opportunities for the ethnic Baloch populations that have been left behind, and also increase their economic and political participation. There are other major changes that may positively impact federalism by increasing autonomy and providing greater administrative and fiscal space to the provinces, including Balochistan. The most remarkable one is the passage of the 18th constitutional amendment that has substantially changed the structures of power between the centre and the provinces. However, from the point of view of Baloch nationalists, the powers, concessions, and allocation of resources granted so far fall short of their expectations. They continue to promote a narrative of serious grievances against the centre and the Punjab, focusing on a denial of national rights, the usurpation of natural resources and manipulation of the electoral process. They are greatly upset by the military operations against the insurgents, the disappearance of Baloch 'activists', and bullet-ridden bodies of militants found along the roads.[66] While a majority of them would seek a political settlement, accommodation, and reconciliation, the extreme fringe of the Baloch nationalists would like to pursue a dream of an 'independent' Balochistan.

Ethnic Polarization in Sindh

Ethnic diversity today in Sindh is as complex as in any other part of the country, but compared to other provinces, the power struggle appears to be deadlier with militant wings of the ethnic, and some mainstream, religious parties. It is complex for three reasons. First, constant migration of Pashtuns from Balochistan, KP, and Afghanistan over the decades has transformed the ethnic landscape of Karachi. Other ethnic groups, such as those from the Seraiki regions of the Punjab, Balochistan, and Sindh, have continued to settle in Karachi. The city has become an ethnic mix, a microcosm of Pakistan, but in the absence of the rule of law and effective state and political institutions, it has turned into a fierce battleground for resources, power, and domination. A no-holds-barred politics continues to produce violence and a criminal economy. The second factor that has changed the demography of Karachi and urban Sindh is the mass exodus of the Hindu population and its replacement by Muslim migrants, the Mohajir from India. The third element adding to the complexity of Karachi and Sindh is the emerging issue of religious-sectarian identity. With the rise of religious groups and parties, the identity issue is no longer confined to language and culture. Sectarian identity has rather transcended ethnic boundaries by bonding groups together along religious lines.

The best way to understand the ethnic transformation of Sindh and Karachi is by exploring answers to two questions about them. First, what was the distribution of ethnicity in Sindh at the time of partition? Was Karachi then a Sindhi city, as the Sindhi nationalists have often claimed it to be? We can get a clear answer from the 1941 India census, which is the closest we have to the time Pakistan became independent. The total population of Sindh was 4,535,008. The Muslim population of Sindh, then, was 71% while the Hindus, including the scheduled classes, comprised 27%. The rest were Sikhs, Jains, and others. Karachi district in the 1940s, which was a much larger territorial unit than it is today, had a population of 67,963 people. Close to 50% of the population of Karachi was Hindu. The census provides a breakdown of the populations according to religious communities. But within the two main communities, it provides a further distribution along tribes and castes. Among the Muslims, the Baloch in Sindh comprised a significant segment, which are divided into every tribe and sub-tribe that live today. The Baloch population in Sindh surged by 32% between 1931 and 1941 due to the canal networks constructed by the British. The Baloch population of Karachi was quite significant at 18%, excluding Makranis. The number of Jains was 3,687 in the city.[67]

In seventy years, the demography of Karachi and Sindh has completely changed. The main polarization in Sindh is between the Mohajirs who came to Karachi in large numbers at the time of partition and the native Sindhis. The settlement of Mohajirs in Karachi and other major towns of Sindh gained momentum with the making of Karachi as the capital city and carving it out of Sindh as a federal territory. The Sindhis protested this move because they feared that more refugees from India would be brought in. This is precisely what happened. In the early years of Pakistan, from 1947 to

1951, one million Mohajirs were settled in Sindh. Liaquat Ali Khan, the first Prime Minister of the country, and himself a Mohajir, had a generous policy towards the newcomers in the allotment of prime urban properties to them through the Evacuee Property Trust.[68] In 1951, within four years of Pakistan's creation, Mohajirs constituted about 50% of the population of the urban areas in Sindh. They gained majorities in major towns—Karachi, Hyderabad, Mirpur Khas, and Nawabshah.[69] More significantly, the Mohajirs dominated the newly established central government of Pakistan, which the Sindhis complain they used to the benefit of their community, ignoring the genuine interests of the local populations.[70] The Sindhis from the very beginning appeared to be uncomfortable with the concentration of Mohajirs in their province.[71] That marked the beginning of ethnic tensions which simmered for decades, and that have produced a reactive Mohajir ethnicity.

The root of the troubles is not in the proliferation of ethnic groups, migration, or the diversity of Sindh because the story of other provinces of Pakistan or how the populations in South Asia are shifting and being shuffled is no different. The cause is a lack of development of an appropriate institutional architecture and political institutions to handle this diversity. Political contestation without requisite institutions produces confrontational politics as it has in Sindh, and elsewhere in the country. Three main ethnic groups—Mohajir, Sindhis, and the Pashtuns, along with as many sectarian movements, are locked into a struggle for power, with every group retaining a militant wing. For this reason, Sindh has witnessed more ethnic polarization and violence in recent years than any other province in Pakistan. Most of the violence has, however, been confined to Karachi, the port city of Sindh and the financial and industrial centre of the country.

Karachi represents all nationalities of Pakistan, which are its strength as well as its weakness. It is a weakness that the politics of the city, in contrast to the first few decades of independence, has degenerated into ethnic and sectarian fragmentation. Today, there is no party, leader, or ideology capable of generating a common politics of citizenship that would bring diverse ethnic groups together. The old parties and ideas have died out, and the new ones have yet to emerge and gain traction.

More ethnic groups have settled in Karachi for economic reasons. According to the 1998 census, Sindhis made up 59.7% of the population of the province. Mohajirs constituted the second largest group at 21.1%. Punjabis were 7%, Pashtuns 4.2%, and Baloch 2.1%.[72] Most of these ethnic groups have taken up jobs and businesses in Karachi or in other urban areas. The flow of the Mohajirs and other ethnic groups from the neighbouring provinces has continued, mostly comprised of Pashtuns from KP, Balochistan, and Afghanistan. Sindhis fear that they may be reduced to a minority. For decades, Sindhi nationalist sentiment has run very high, which is directed both against the Mohajirs as well as the central government of Pakistan.

Bhutto started to redress some of the grievances of the Sindhis in the early 1970s. As a native Sindhi, he understood the feeling of hurt and neglect among his people. To compensate for past deprivation, Bhutto decided to fix a quota for the rural Sindhis in provincial and federal jobs on the basis of their population. Similar quotas for other provinces were also set according to their ratios of population. The job quotas were not a new concept. They had been practiced in many forms as a tool of affirmative action to bring up the disadvantaged groups of the society since the British times. But it was applied differently in Sindh; the government created urban and rural categories and allocated jobs according to their numbers. The quota stipulated that 10% of the jobs in the government would be filled on the basis of all-Pakistan merit, 50% allocated to the Punjab, 11.5% to the NWFP, 7.6% to urban Sindh, 11.4% to rural Sindh, and 3.5%

to Balochistan.[73] This was obviously meant to protect the interests of the Sindhis, who otherwise might have lost positions to the Mohajirs in an open competition. Another difference was that provincial jobs were also allocated on this pattern. To complicate the matters further, quota was not confined to jobs only; it was extended to admissions in professional institutions, like engineering and medical colleges. Such a policy had long-term effects on the inter-ethnic relations in the province, as it institutionalized the urban-rural divide, which in ethnic terms, translated into Mohajirs and Sindhis having conflicting interests. While addressing the problem of Sindhi backwardness, the quota system ran counter to the objectives of national integration, and in particular, counter to the political cohesion of Sindh.

Bhutto's policies of empowering Sindhis did not stop at increasing and maintaining adequate representation in the provincial and federal bureaucracies, educational institutions, and autonomous financial and industrial corporations run by the state. The provincial government that was headed by Mumtaz Ali Bhutto took a drastic step in July 1972 by getting a law passed by the provincial assembly to make Sindhi the official language of the province and a compulsory language from fourth to twelfth grade.[74] This provoked widespread riots by the Urdu-speaking Mohajirs in urban areas, who wanted Urdu to be made one of the official languages of the province. On the intervention of the federal government later, a compromise was struck, and Urdu was also made one of the provincial languages. Bhutto's apparently pro-Sindhi policies alienated the Mohajirs and sowed the seeds of enduring bitterness. Even after about half a century since that episode, the relations between the two communities continue to be marred by antagonism, mistrust, and rivalry.[75]

The question that remains is: why does the Pakistan Peoples Party (PPP) adopt a clearly ethnic agenda in Sindh? The answer lies in the growth of Sindhi nationalism. Although the PPP had emerged as the largest national party on the political scene and had been critical of regional nationalism of different groups, it skilfully appropriated the program of the Sindhi nationalists. In the election campaign of 1970, it did not question the grievances of Sindh that were articulated by nationalists like late G. M. Syed and his party, but questioned their credibility and leadership to deliver anything. The Sindhi voters overwhelmingly voted for the PPP, defeating all the candidates of the Sindhi Awami Mahaz of Syed who had appealed to the Sindhi ethnicity. Since then, the PPP of Bhutto has dominated the politics of rural Sindh. The Sindhi nationalist groups continue to be an important voice and have some following in the educational institutions, but lack mass following. Their electoral constituency is still too weak to challenge the power of traditional land-owning elites who continue to form a solid electoral slate of the PPP. In the last seven elections, since 1988, the nationalist groups have done very poorly. They hardly have any representation in the provincial or national legislature. The PPP, which emerged as left of the centre progressive national party, has been reduced to a regional party of rural Sindh where it still maintains considerable support.

In contrast to the Sindhi nationalists, the MQM, which is the driving force behind the Mohajir ethnicity, has dominated elections in Karachi and Hyderabad for the past three decades, winning an overwhelming majority of the seats. The MQM has been riding the strong waves of Mohajir identity and the issue of ethnic rights. The politics of the Mohajir community of urban Sindh has witnessed a radical change since the mid-1980s. This is a community that supported the demand for Pakistan on the basis of Muslim nationalism and rejected all forms of provincialism and ethnic separatism for decades. In the first four decades, it aligned with the mainstream religious and secular political parties that advocated centralization and Islam. Today, it wants Mohajirs to be recognized as a fifth nationality, and does not hide its ambitions to separate Karachi from Sindh.[76]

How can one explain the transformation of Mohajirs into an emerging distinctive ethnic category in Pakistan? The answer is in the relative decline of the power structure of the country. First, the change of self-perception as a separate ethnic group has occurred over a long period of time. Mohajir nationalism did not gain acceptance or currency immediately after the enforcement of the quota system in 1972. However, the political lines were drawn between the Mohajirs and the PPP at that point, and the two have often continued to remain confrontational punctuated with some periods as uneasy coalition partners. But over time, the quota system has significantly reduced the representation of the Mohajirs in the federal and provincial civil services, which they had rightly feared, the rescinding of which constitutes one of their major demands. In 1973, the Mohajirs had 30.29% share of the top jobs in the federal bureaucracy, far higher than their less than 8% share of the entire population of the country. At this time, Sindhis had only 2.5%.[77]

According to the 1989 statistics of District Management Group officers in the federal government, the representation of rural Sindhis rose to 8.5%, while that of Mohajirs declined to 7.1%.[78] During the last quarter of the century, the representation of rural Sindhis and urban areas (Mohajirs) in the federal bureaucracy has become equal at 6.5% and 6.6% respectively.[79] These statistics do not show representation in other services. Although the representation of the Sindhis and other ethnic groups has significantly increased, thanks to the quota system, the Mohajirs still enjoy a numerical advantage in federal jobs if we include Pakistanis with Urdu as a mother tongue from other provinces of Pakistan. In some of the institutions, like broadcasting (PTV, Radio Pakistan), their numbers, for historical reasons, remain higher than their ratio of the populations. Even in these places, the Mohajir representation has been on the decline. It is the relative decline of their representation, as the natives have gradually come up, and not under-representation, that explains the frustration of the Mohajirs. One has to address a general question of political power here. At the time of independence, the Mohajirs dominated both the bureaucratic as well as the political structure of the new state of Pakistan. Most of the top leadership of the Muslim League, the party that formed the government after independence, came from the Muslim minority provinces of India. The natives had far less power than their numbers. But the question of distribution of power did not attract much attention at the time, as the country faced numerous problems of resettlement and readjustment. It has been argued that it was partly the fear of losing out power to the natives that the Mohajir-dominated Muslim League did not conduct any elections.[80]

Since the first general elections of 1970, the native political leaders have dominated the national political scene. The political parties like JI and the Muslim League factions that the Mohajirs had supported also lost out to the PPP, which in the context of Sindh was seen as anti-Mohajir. The Mohajir community in urban Sindh found itself in a political vacuum. The Mohajir youth in particular resented the quota system because it restricted their entry into government jobs and professional educational institutions, which also explains their rise as the salaried Muslim class of undivided India.[81] The lower middle- and working-class of the Mohajirs faced growing competition for jobs in the industries as Pashtuns, the Baloch, and Punjabis began to seek employment in Karachi. Likewise, the Mohajir industrial elite that dominated the modern sectors of the economy like banking, services and manufacturing also faced competition from new and old industrial houses of NWFP and Punjab and new social classes of these regions that emerged with post-independence educational opportunities. All these factors contributed to the alienation of the Mohajirs. Old Mohajir generation and their leaders had faded out of the public life by the eighties, and the traditional political parties that had following in the urban areas of Sindh showed reluctance to convert to the politics of ethnicity and regionalism.

Karachi, as a big sprawling city, has been facing other troubles. Various governments deprived it of local self-government and did not invest in the development of amenities from the bulk of the resources that the city generated. The financial resources of Karachi were appropriated by the centre and the provincial governments, with very little left in the kitty to be used in the further development of the city. Utility services failed to deliver as the bureaucrats placed in key positions by the provincial government continued to rob them, increasing inefficiency and cost, and consequently public anger. There is another factor, which is generally overlooked but I have repeatedly brought into discussion in this work: the role of military regimes in ethnic fragmentation and confrontation. Under the 1977–78 military rule, Karachi, like the entire country, went through de-politicization. Suffocating natural democratic politics in Pakistan has generated narrow identities, parochial commitment, and loyalties. It is no surprise that ethnic groups of Karachi haven't been able to form a single political community with common interests in civic life: rather they have sought political refuge in ethnic silos.[82]

Mohajirs, like others, created a silo of their own. A political ground well existed, which the All Pakistan Mohajir Students Organization exploited skilfully, first by founding the MQM and then silencing old political groups in Karachi, often violently. The emergence of the Mohajir ethnicity and its violent expression in the 1990s may also be seen in the context of the rise of Sindhi national sentiment in the early years of the 1980s, Pakistan's defining decade in shaping ethnic, religious, and sectarian lineages for the successive decades. Z.A. Bhutto, venerated as a hero by most of the Sindhis, was executed by the military regime in April 1979 on the basis of a controversial court decision.[83] In the Sindhi social and political narrative, it was a murder committed by the army dominated by the Punjabis. Bhutto, in the estimation of the Sindhis, was not a convict, but a martyr. The Bhutto family, understanding this political undercurrent, has constructed a mausoleum over his grave, symbolizing his transcendence to 'sainthood'. In Sindh, people protested Bhutto's execution widely. This provided new political ammunition to the Sindhi nationalists to attack the military regime. The nationalists used the Movement for the Restoration of Democracy (MRD) in 1983 very effectively to stir up mass agitation. Although the MRD was a coalition of national political parties, and had representation from all the provinces, it failed to attract much attention in any other province except in rural Sindh. There were violent clashes between the agitating mobs and the security forces. Also, some well-armed groups sporadically attacked police and military units. Given the persistence and intensity of these attacks, the military regime became convinced that there was a link between the Sindhi nationalists and the Indian intelligence agencies.[84] It feared that the Sindhi militants supported by India would seek a separatist path. Before the Sindhi militancy could get out of control, the military authorities crushed it through an extensive operation.[85]

The military regime did not confine its strategy of countering Sindhi militant nationalism to military means. It encouraged, financed, and organized the MQM as a counterweight to the Sindhi separatism.[86] It is ironic that the state functionaries would sponsor an ethnic organization, and even for some time, and still manage to ignore its violence against political rivals. The MQM used all legal and illegal means to establish itself firmly in Hyderabad and Karachi, the two cities that have considerable numbers of the Mohajir community. However, it would be unfair to attribute the rising power of the MQM to the Pakistani state intelligence agencies. Except initial funding and patronization, the state did not support beyond a certain level. There was some misunderstanding of the Mohajir phenomenon on the part of the military regime of Zia ul-Haq. It thought, like in the past, that the Mohajirs would continue to support the central government because they had a local rival. Precisely for this reason, the regime fanned the climate of rivalry between Mohajirs and Sindhis. Contrary to the expectation of the military, the MQM took quite an independent course. It has vigorously pursued a militant, nationalist ethnic agenda, perhaps, more rigid and dangerous than the Sindhi separatism, which has faded.

Although the MQM has continued to enjoy a mass following among the working and lower middle classes, allegations of extortion, torture, and killings of political opponents have begun to erode its support base.[87] Persistent allegations of target killings, including the members of the Mohajir community, have gravely damaged the national standing of the MQM.[88] There are now serious political divisions within the Mohajir community of Sindh, as the grip of Mr Altaf Husain has loosened. The factors of age, illness, and exile in London, from where he is facing a murder investigation and scores of criminal cases if he returns to Pakistan, have emboldened old and new rivals, like the Pak Sarzamin Party, to challenge his leadership. There is a three-way split within the MQM—Haqiqi, London, and Pakistan. However, it is too early to suggest a major shift in the politics of the Mohajir community. Mohajir nationalism is a reality in the urban areas of Sindh, one that, even with splits and political fragmentation, is not likely to disappear.

Notes

1. Imran Ali, *Canal Colonization in Punjab*, (Princeton: Princeton University Press, 1982)
2. This is the story of all Baloch tribes that now straddle the Indus river from Dera Ismail Khan in KP to Dadu in Sindh. It is no coincidence that the biggest landlords are tribal chiefs that occupied lands from the native chieftains. These lands were granted as personal property by the British for their loyalty and support to the Empire. This note is based on the author's field work in the districts adjoining the Indus.
3. The Khan of Kalat signed treaties with British India in 1841 and 1876. The second treaty (1876) leased out Quetta for Rs. 25,000 per annum. See: Sneh

Mahajan, *British Foreign Policy, 1874–1914: The Role of India* (London: Routledge, 2002), 52–60.

4. The population of Balochistan, according to the Census of 1998, was 6,566,000 people. *Population and Housing Census of Pakistan 1998,* (Islamabad: Punjab Government, 2000).

5. This is the position of the Pakhtunkhwa Milli Party of Balochistan, spelled out in their manifesto: 'Aims and Objectives' Pashtoonkhwa Milli Awami Party, accessed November 10, 2016, <http://pmap.info/contact-us.html>.

6. Author's interviews with Sindhi intellectuals, Hyderabad, June 2012.

7. Nukhbah Taj Langah, 'Call for Siraiki Province' (Ottawa and Islamabad: Forum of Federations and Centre for Civic Education Pakistan, 2011); Muhammad Mushtaq, 'Regional Identities in Quest of Separate Provinces: A New Challenge for the Pakistani Federation', *Journal of Political Studies* 23, no. 1 (2016):289; Aisha Shahzad, 'Relative Deprivation in Pakistan: An Analysis of the Seraiki Movement', *Pakistan Perspective* 20, no. 1 (2015):69; Hussain Ahmad Khan and Samina Choonara, *Re-thinking Punjab: The Construction of Siraiki Identity* (Lahore: Research and Publication Centre, 2004).

8. Tariq Rahman, *Language and Politics in Pakistan* (Karachi: Oxford University Press, 1996).

9. On this theme, see: Aitzas Ahsan, *The Indus Saga and the Making of Pakistan* (Lahore: Nahr Ghar Publications, 2013).

10. Aadil Nkhoda, 'Rural to Urban Areas: Migration Increases with Drop in Agri-income Levels' *The Express Tribune,* August 28, 2016; Michael Kugelman, *Urbanization in Pakistan: Causes and Consequences* (Oslo: Norwegian Peace Building Resource Centre, January 2013).

11. Neil Nevitte and Charles H. Kennedy, *Ethnic Preference and Public Policy in Developing States* (Boulder: Lynee Rienner Publishers, Inc., 1986)

12. On the question of definition, see: Red W. Riggs, *Ethnicity: Concepts and Terms Used in Ethnicity Research* (Honolulu: International Social Science Council, 1985).

13. Benedict R. O' G. Anderson, *Imagined Communities: Reflections on the Origins and Spread of Nationalism* (London: Verso, 1983)

14. C. Inayatullah, 'Democracy, Ethnonationalism and the Emerging World Order,' in Sushil Kumar ed. *Gorbachev's Reforms and International Change* (New Delhi: Lancers Books, 1993), 201–23.

15. James L. Hyland, *Democratic Theory: The Philosophical Foundations* (Manchester: Manchester University Press, 1995); Carole Pateman, *Participation and Democratic Theory* (Cambridge: Cambridge University Press, 1970); Ian Shapiro, *The State of Democratic Theory* (Princeton: Princeton University Press,

2003); Graeme Campbell Duncan, *Democratic Theory and Practice* (Cambridge: Cambridge University Press, 1983)gah, "Call for Siraiki Province.60.ith the tan and Afghanistan12. of populationsakistanl fragmentation is not likely to disappea

16. See, for instance, Robert Melson and Howard Wolpe, 'Modernization and Politics of Ethnic Communalism: A Theoretical Perspective' *American Political Science Review* 64 (December 1970), 1112–1130.

17. Hasan-Askari Rizvi, 'The Legacy of Military Rule in Pakistan' *Survival*, 31/3, May–June 1989, 255–68.

18. Partha S Ghosh, *Ethnic Conflict and Conflict Management: The Indian Case*, ICES Pamphlet Series–2 (Kandy, Sri Lanka: International Centre for Ethnic Studies, 1996), 34–5.

19. *Population and Housing Census of Pakistan, 1998* (Islamabad: Population Census Organization, Statistics Division, Govt. of Pakistan, 1998).

20. Sohail Jehangir Malik, Safiya Aftab, and Nargis Sultana, *Pakistan's Economic Performance, 1947 to 1993: A Descriptive Analysis* (Lahore: Sure Publishers, 1994); 'Highlights Pakistan Economic Survey 2014–15' Government of Pakistan, Finance Division. <http://finance.gov.pk/survey/chapters_15/Highlights.pdf>. Accessed October 12, 2016; Hafiz Pasha, 'Growth of the Provincial Economies' *Institute for Policy Reforms*, 2015.

21. Sara Kazmi, 'Mind Your Language—The Movement for the Preservation of Punjabi' *Dawn*, August 4, 2016.

22. Charles H. Kennedy, 'The Politics of Ethnicity in Sindh' *Asian Survey* 31/10 (October, 1991), 946.

23. Mubarik Ali and Derek Byerlee, *Productivity Growth and Resource Degradation in Pakistan's Punjab: A Decomposition Analysis* (Washington: World Bank, Rural Development Dept., 2000); *Pakistan's Provinces* (Mumbai: Strategic Foresight Group, 2004); *Punjab Growth Strategy 2018: Accelerating Economic Growth and Improving Social Outcomes* (Lahore: Government of the Punjab, 2015).

24. Charles H. Kennedy, 'Rural Groups and the Zia Regime' in Craig Baxter ed. *Zia's Pakistan: Politics in a Frontline State*(Boulder: Westview Press, 1985)

25. The available data from 2014 and 2015 recorded an inflow of the remittances for the period of July–April 2014–15 at $14,969.66 million compared to $12,897.91 million during the corresponding period the previous year. There was an increase of 16.06% over the previous year. The share of remittances province-wise was as follows: KP 13.9%, Punjab 55.19%, Sindh 24.74%, Balochistan 6.13%. Labour Force Survey, 2014–15, Ministry of Labour and Manpower, Government of Pakistan, 2015.

26. Yunas Samad, 'Pakistan or Punjabistan: Crisis of National Identity' *International*

Journal of Punjab Studies 2/1 (1995), 23–42; Alyssa Ayres, *Speaking like a State: Language and Nationalism in Pakistan* (Cambridge: Cambridge University Press, 2009), 67–78; Imran Ali, ed. 'The Punjab and the Retardation of Nationalism' *The Political Inheritance of Pakistan*, (New York: St. Martin's Press 1991), 29–52; Muhammad Fateh Malik, *Punjabi Identity* (Lahore: Sang-e-Meel Publications, 1989).

27. Professor Christopher Shackle is of the view that Seraiki language has many variants. Some are close to Sindhi, while others are close to Punjabi and other regional languages. See: *The Siraiki Language of Central Pakistan: A Reference Grammar* (London: School of Oriental and African Studies, 1976).

28. Most seats went to the supporters of the Mahaz whether they stood as independents or as part of any political parties. Umbreen Javaid, 'Movement for Bahawalpur Province' *Journal of Political Studies,* 15 (2009), 41–57.

29. In the eighties, they set up Seraiki Lok Sanjh, an organization that aimed at promoting Seraiki cultural consciousness. It did good work for a few years but later fell victim to personal rivalries and intrigues.

30. Zaman Jafery, *Saraiki, Sind, Balochistan: S.S.B. and National Question* (Multan: Melluha Publications, 1986).

31. *1998 Census Report of Khyber Agency* (Islamabad: Population Census Organization, Statistics Division, Govt. of Pakistan, 2000).

32. This refers to the international boundary between Afghanistan and Pakistan that was drawn by an agreement between the Afghan King and the British Indian Empire in 1893.

33. O.K. Caroe, the last Governor of NWFP, in a confidential letter of 22 May 1947 to Sir John Colville, Acting Viceroy and Governor General of India says the following: 'My ministry and Abdul Ghaffar Khan have started propaganda on a theme which I advised them to take up some months ago: that a Pathan national province under a coalition if possible, and making its own alliances as may suit it…The switch over has probably come too late.' Letter No. GH–58, Governor Camp, NWFP (Parachinar), 22 May 1947. I.OR/L/PJ/5/304. The British Library, London.

34. Abdul Ghaffar Khan, *Khan Abdul Ghaffar Khan: A Centennial Tribute* (New Delhi: Har-Anand Publications, 1995); Rajeshwari Krishna, *Khan Abdul Ghaffar Khan* (Bangalore: Sapna Book House, 2002).

35. E. Janson, *India, Pakistan or Pakhtunistan?* (Uppsala: Act Universitatis Upsaliensis, 1981)

36. Mohammad Raqib, 'The Muslim Pashtun Movement of the North-West Frontier of India, 1930–1934', in M. Stephen, ed. *Civilian Jihads* (New York: Palgrave Macmillan, 2009), 107-118; Abdul Ghaffar Khan and P.S. Ramu,

Khudai Khidmatgar and National Movement: Momentous Speeches of Badshah Khan (Delhi: S.S. Publishers, 1992); Mukulika Banerjee, *The Pathan Unarmed: Opposition & Memory in the North West Frontier* (Santa Fe: School of American Research Press, 2000); Mukulika Banerjee, *A Study of the Khudai Khidmatgar Movement, 1930–1947, N.W.F.P., British India* (Oxford: Oxford University Press, 1994); Sruti Bala, 'Waging Nonviolence: Reflections on the History Writing of the Pashtun Nonviolent Movement, Khudai Khidmatgar' *Peace & Change* 38/2 (2013), 131–54.

37. On Ethnic breakdowns and trends on the recruits in Pakistan Army, Christine Fair and Shuja Nawaz mention the following trends: In 2005, Punjab accounted for slightly less than 60% of all new officers. Punjab's recent contribution to officer intake is similar to the Punjab's 56% share of Pakistan's population (as per the 1998 census). A dramatic change can also be observed for the market share for NWFP which roughly doubled, from 10% in 1971 to over 22% in 2005. According to the 1998 Census, NWFP only accounted for 13% of Pakistan's overall population, suggesting considerable overrepresentation of new officers. Recruits from FATA remained somewhat stable and were roughly proportional to their population distribution in Pakistan. Balochistan, which accounts for about 5% of Pakistan's population, by 2005 accounted for about 5% or more of new officer recruits. Christine Fair and Shuja Nawaz. 'The Changing Pakistan Army Officer Corps' *The Journal of Strategic Studies* 34/1 (2011), 63–94.

38. A good number of Pashtun nationalists had fled to Afghanistan in the middle of the 1970s, when the National Awami Party, later banned by the Federal Government, had launched insurgency and engaged in subversion. They supported the Soviet-installed governments though only through statements. The public sentiment in the Pakistan Pashtun territories was pro-Mujahideen, in the making and strengthening of which, the military regime had played a major role. These developments weakened Pashtun nationalism considerably.

39. *Labour Force Survey 2014–2015*, Ministry of Labour and Manpower, Government of Pakistan.

40. Rashid Amjad, Ghulam Mohammad Arif, and Muhammad Irfan, 'Preliminary Study: Explaining the Ten-fold Increase in Remittances to Pakistan 2001–2012' *Working Papers & Research Reports* (Islamabad: Pakistan Institute of Development Economics, 2012).

41. Sartaj Khan and Riaz Ahmed, 'The Changing Face of Pashtun Nationalism' *The News*, The Political Economy Section, July 2, 2000.

42. See the speech of President of ANP Ajmal Khatak in *The Nation*, January 22, 1998.

43. 'A Collapsing House of Cards' (editorial), *The Nation*, February 4, 1998.

44. *Report on the Administration of Balochistan Agency for 1908–09* (Calcutta: Superintendent Government Prenting, India, 1909), 1.

45. *Administration Report of the Balochistan Agency for the Year 1st April 1940 to the 31st March 1941* (Calcutta: Government Printing, India, 1941), 5

46. Ibid.

47. Ibid.

48. *Administration Report of the Balochistan Agency for the Year 1st April 1940 to the 31st March 1941*, 27.

49. *Administration Report of the Balochistan Agency for the Year 1909–10* (Calcutta: Superintendent Government Printing: 1910)

50. R. Hughes-Buller, *Balochistan: Administrative Report of Census Operations* (Quetta: Directorate of Archives, Government of Balochistan, 1989).

51. T.A. Heathcote, *Balochistan, British and the Great Game: The Struggle for the Bolan Pass, Gateway to India* (London: C. Hurst & Company, 2016).

52. Inayatullah Baloch, *The Problem of 'Greater Balochistan: A Study of Baluch Nationalism* (Stuttgart: Steiner Verlag Wiesbaden, 1987)

53. Martin Axmann, *Back to the Future: The Khanate of Kalat and the Genesis of Baluch Nationalism, 1915–1955*. (Oxford: Oxford University Press, 2012); 'How Balochistan Became a Part of Pakistan—A Historical Perspective' *The Nation*, (Islamabad) 2015.

54. Ian Copland, 'The Princely States, the Muslim League, and the Partition of India in 1947' *The International History Review* 13/1 (1991), 38–69; Paul Titus and Nina Swidler, 'Knights, Not Pawns: Ethnic Nationalism and Regional Dynamics in Postcolonial Balochistan', *International Journal of Middle East Studies*, Vol. 32, No. 1 (Feb. 2000), 47–69; Imtiaz Ali, 'The Balochistan Problem' *Pakistan Horizon*, 58/2 (2005), 41–62.

55. Naheed Anjum Chisti, 'Jinnah's Balochistan: At Cross Road' *Journal of South Asian Development Studies* 2/2 (June 2013), 71–6; Naseer Dashti, *The Baloch and Balochistan: A Historical Account from the Beginning to the Fall of Baloch State* (New York: Trafford Publishing, 2012).

56. Malik Siraj Akbar, *The Redefined Dimensions of Baloch Nationalist Movement* (New York: Xlibris, 2011), 292; Roger D. Long et al., *State and Nation-Building in Pakistan: Beyond Islam and Security* (London: Routledge/Taylor & Francis Group, 2016), 129–40.

57. Nasreen Akhtar, 'Balochistan Nationalist Movement and Unrest in Pakistan' *South Asian Survey* 18/1 (2011), 121–35.

58. Saleem Shahid, 'Bugti Killed in Operation: Six Officers among 21 Security Personnel Dead' *Dawn*, August 27, 2016.

59. Tahir Amin, *Ethno-National Movements of Pakistan: Domestic and International Factors* (Islamabad: Institute of Policy Studies, 1988).

60. Rafiulllah Kakar, 'The Baloch Question after the Eighteenth Amendment' in Ishtiaq Ahmad and Adnan Rafiq ed. *Pakistan's Democratic Transition: Change and Persistence* (London and New York: Routledge, 2017), 172.

61. Shaikh Aziz, 'A Leaf from History: Reclaiming Balochistan Peacefully' *Dawn*, October 5, 2014.

62. Zofeen T. Ebrahim, 'China-Pakistan Economic Corridor: A Boon for the Economy and Bane for the Locals' *Dawn*, May 12, 2016.

63. Author's interview with Hasil Bizenjo, Karachi.

64. Saleem Shahid, 'Census Unacceptable in Refugees's Presence, says NP' *Dawn*, January 30, 2017.

65. Banari Mengal, 'Will the Baloch be Victim of Pakistani State's Deceitful Tactics Again?' *Express Tribune* (blog), January 24, 2016.

66. Author's interviews with Baloch leaders, Quetta (April 2015) Karachi (February 2015).

67. *Census of India, Sind*, Vol. xii, Tables by H. T. Lambrick, I.C.S (Delhi: Manager of Publications, Government of India), 22–24, 27–28, 35.

68. Policy of allotting land to the Mohahirs discriminated against the Sindhis. Almost all immigrants got something, with most of them showing no records of their properties in India. A simple affidavit was enough to claim property in Pakistan as a compensation for leaving India.

69. Shahid Kardar, 'Polarizations in the Regions and Prospects for Integration' in S.A. Zaidi, ed. *Regional Imbalances and the National Question in Pakistan* (Lahore: Vanguard, 1992).

70. Author's interviews with the Sindhi nationalists, Hyderabad, June, 2012.

71. Ibid.

72. *1998 Census Report of Pakistan* (Islamabad: Population Census Organization, Statistics Division, Government of Pakistan, 1990).

73. Charles H. Kennedy, *Bureaucracy in Pakistan* (Karachi: Oxford University Press, 1987), 181–208.

74. *Dawn,* July 8, 1972.

75. Author's interviews with the Sindhi nationalists, Hyderabad, June, 2012.

76. Feroz Ahmed, 'Ethnicity and Politics: The Rise of Mohajir Separatism' *South Asia Bulletin*, 8 (1988), 32–45; Farhat Haq, 'Rise of the MQM in Pakistan: Politics of Ethnic Mobilization' *Asian Survey,* 35/11 (1995), 990–1004; Iftikhar H. Malik, 'Ethno-nationalism in Pakistan: A Commentary on Mohajir Qaumi Mahaz (MQM) in Sindh' *South Asia: Journal of South Asian Studies* 18/2 (1995), 49–72; Christopher O. Hurst, 'Pakistan's Ethnic Divide' *Studies in Conflict & Terrorism* 19/2 (1996), 179–98; Laurent Gayer, *Karachi: Ordered Disorder and the Struggle for the City* (New York: Oxford University Press, 2014).

77. *Thirteenth Triennial Census of Central Government Employees, 1973* (Islamabad: Cabinet Division, Government of Pakistan, 1973).

78. Tariq Rahman, *Language and Politics in Pakistan* (Karachi: Oxford University Press, 1996), 130.

79. Islamabad: Cabinet Division, Government of Pakistan, April 2013. <http://202.83.164.29/estab/userfiles1/file/Establishment/publication /04-2013%20Final%20STATISTICS%202012-2013.pdf>

80. Mohammad Waseem, *State and Politics in Pakistan* (Lahore: Progressive Publishers, 1988)

81. Hamza Alavi, 'Social forces and Ideology in the Making of Pakistan' *Economic and Political Weekly*, 37/51 (2002), 5119–124.

82. 'War on Three Fronts' *Dawn* (editorial), November 5, 1998.

83. Adeel Khan, 'Pakistan's Sindhi Ethnic Nationalism: Migration, Marginalization, and the Threat of "Indianization"' *Asian Survey* 42/2 (2002), 213–29; Amir Ali Chandio and Shahida Amir Chandio, 'The Execution of Zulfiqar Ali Bhutto: Its Impacts on the Politics of Sindh' *The Government-Annual Research Journal of Political Science* 2/2 (2013), 27–36; Amir Ali Chandio, 'Politics Of Sindh Under Zia Government: An Analysis Of Nationalists Vs Federalists Orientations' PhD diss. (Bahauddin Zakariya University, Multan, 2009); Zulfikar Ali Bhutto, *If I Am Assassinated …* (New Delhi: Vikas, 1979).

84. Khalid Bin Sayeed, 'Pakistan in 1983: Internal Stresses More Serious than External Problems' *Asian Survey. A Survey of Asia in 1983: Part II* 24/2 (1983), 219–28; Sayed Mushahid Hussain, *Pakistan's Politics The Zia Years* (Lahore: Progressive Publishers, 1990), 118; Charles H. Kennedy, 'The Politics of Ethnicity in Sindh' *Asian Survey* 31/10 (1991), 938–55.

85. Tahir Amin, *Ethno-National Movements of Pakistan*, op. cit., 198.

86. Author's interviews with the Sindhi nationalists, Hyderabad, June, 2012.

87. Idrees Bakhtiar, 'Shock after Shock' *Herald*, (August, 1997), 47–49; *The First 10 General Elections of Pakistan: A Story of Pakistan's Transition from Democracy above Rule of Law to Democracy under Rule of Law: 1970–2013* (Islamabad: Pakistan Institute of Legislative Development and Transparency, 2013).

88. These are general views of Sindhis and Punjabis. Even a significant section of the Mohajir elite thinks that the MQM is a fascist set up and blame the military regime of Zia ul-Haq for its emergence. Owen Bennet-Jones, 'Altaf Hussain: the Notorious MQM Leader who Swapped Pakistan for London' *The Guardian*, (July 29, 2013), accessed, February 8, 2017. <https://www.theguardian.com/world/2013/jul/29/altaf-hussain-mqm-leader-pakistan-london>. See also: Azhar Abbas, 'Eyeball to Eyeball' *Herald*, (July 1997), 37.

Chapter V

Political Islam and National Identity

In the reconstruction of postcolonial states and societies in the Muslim majority states, political Islam has been, and may continue to remain, one of the more strident voices. The primary objective and motivation of those associated with political Islam is to transform the constitution, laws, policies, and social practices of their respective societies and states according to the fundamental principles of Islam.[1] They believe that Islam is not just a religion, as the way other religions are understood and practiced; for them, it is a perfect religion, superior to all others, the final choice of God for mankind and a complete code of life to answer any question man may face in any age, anywhere in the world.[2] From this point of view, Islam is not a private matter, but instead, a public issue; it is not individual piety, but a collective striving for a pure Islamic society; it cannot be seen in parts but as a whole, covering all aspects of private, public, and collective life of a community.[3] In this sense, Islam is about power— the political power of the state and its use to transform society. These are some of the common points among the Islamist movements throughout the world of Islam.[4] They all emerged roughly around the same time, in the waning years of European empires and the post-independence national reconstruction phase, as too many diverse plans, ideas, and beliefs competed in the shaping of national states. The ideological competition over the soul of the state was, however, not confined to the Muslim majority states—it was universal in the competitive world of ideas and ideologies in the inter–wars period

(1921–45), and more specifically in the post-World War II era, as various themes of nationalism, indigenous social reform movements, socialism, democracy, and capitalism began to attract the imagination of the leaders, intellectuals, and reformers in the postcolonial world.[5]

Choosing an Ideology

The activists and intellectuals with Islamic orientation faced a challenging question within themselves: what could be an appropriate choice for Muslims, as some hoped to take control of their people and territories from empires? Unequivocally, the answer was Islam itself, as later Imam Khomeini and the Islamic revolution of Iran popularized.[6] Before I focus on the national context and issues of political Islam in Pakistan, let me point out some common themes of political Islam, which are also embedded into the Islamic movement in this country. First, it is the critique of colonialism and colonial powers, as disruptive, divisive, and exploitative. They believe that the western ideas, institutions, and practices in the name of reforms and modernization have produced adverse consequences in Islamic societies, resulting in alienating Muslim populations from their civilization, cultures, and values.[7] Second, while they are not averse to learning from western experience and borrow what is good in modernity and progress, their essential criteria in doing so is compatibility with Islam. On this point, the traditionalist and modernist Muslims differ greatly, as the latter, impressed by scientific and material achievements of the modern world, apply fresh and rational approaches to the interpretation of Islam.[8] Is liberal democracy, the essential framework of the modern world, acceptable to the Islamists? Yes, it is, but with many questions, deviations, and conditions.[9] They question the sovereignty of the Parliament, place conditions on it of supremacy of the Islamic law, and would wish to subordinate it to the supervision of learned, Islamic theologians.[10] Finally, they want to enforce sharia (Islamic law) in its entirety, without any exception and change to the character of the state from republics to Islamic republics.

Pakistan is one of three Islamic republics, along with Afghanistan and Iran, and interestingly, all are contiguous and all are non-Arab. But it is not an Islamic republic in the image of political Islam as represented and interpreted by the religious parties of Pakistan.[11] It is an Islamic republic as a result of the secular elite's concession to Islamic parties, a political compromise and accommodation to settle issues and defuse the power and influence of the religious groups.[12] The elites thought that minor concessions wouldn't amount to surrendering on the fundamental character of the state and the constitution; instead, they thought it would take the wind out of the sails of the religious groups. This was apparent in their defending of the passage of the Objective Resolution in 1949, the formative phase of the history of constitutionalism. In answering reservations expressed by the members of the Hindu minority, all from erstwhile East Pakistan, the League stalwarts argued that the Resolution was in the preamble, referring to the non-operative part of the constitution, that it wouldn't have any impact on the parliamentary-democratic character of the constitution, and that it would never hurt the rights of the minorities.[13] The minority members of the Constituent Assembly raised pertinent questions about the sovereignty, rights of the religious minorities, and separation of religion from public affairs of the state.[14] One of them, Kumar Datta, lamented that had this Resolution been presented in its current form during the lifetime of Quaid-i-Azam, he would have opposed it.[15] They were assured that Pakistan would be an Islamic state as other Muslim countries (Turkey, Iran, and Afghanistan) were—that Pakistan would be no different from them, and that the rights of the minorities would be protected as equal citizens.[16] The Hindu members persisted in their opposition in an eloquent, soft, and persistent manner. They made references to writings of Maulana Abul A'la Maududi, citing him as saying, 'Non-Muslims wouldn't be entrusted with positions of high responsibility in an Islamic state—head of the state, commander-in-chief of the armed forces'.[17] Maulana Shabbir Ahmad Usmani, the force behind the Objective Resolution, who had, it is believed, collaborated with Maulana Maududi, was very straight forward in his defence of the Resolution. In his view, the Muslim majority had the right to shape its laws and constitution as other majorities around the world have done, and that, in an Islamic state, minorities would be guaranteed the rights under Islam, as they have always been.[18]

The passage of the Objective Resolution marks the first phase of political Islam, which may be termed as indirect influence over the making of the constitution. Religious parties had no representation in the first Constituent Assembly, born out of the 1946 general elections in undivided India. Their strategy was two-fold during this period. First, they aimed to create a common consensual agenda among all shades of religious opinion on the Islamic character of the constitution of the new state. It came in the form of the Ulema Committee Report to the Basic Principles Committee that was given the task of setting principles for the writing of the constitution. Second, they used the familiar forum of the mosque, delivering sermons and threats of agitation, if their concerns about the future constitution of the country were not accommodated. A state struggling to establish itself in the midst of so many crises was not willing to open another front against the religious parties. There was a leadership issue as well. Weak leaders without a strong social support base, and lacking a vision, made expedient political choices; the pushing of the Objective Resolution was one of them. Some also genuinely wanted to oblige the religious lobby that had, in the final years of the struggle for Pakistan, played a pivotal role in mobilizing the masses in support of the demand for Pakistan.[19] The ruling party members thought the Resolution would not conflict with the central purpose of creating a democratic, parliamentary, federal form of government.

The Objective Resolution was the first major success of political Islam, which those who had moved it in the Constitutional Assembly interpreted very differently, and continue to do so. They believe it settled the issue of the idea of Pakistan as an Islamic state.[20] Placing the Resolution at the centre of their political mobilization, they demanded practical manifestation of it by pressing demands for the enforcement of Islamic laws and a transformation of the state according to their ideas of an Islamic state.[21] Among the various groups, the *Jamaat-i-Islami* (JI) was the most organized, with training of its cadre from modern educational institutions, preaching to the literate, urban middle class, and producing an impressive amount of literature in the form of magazines, pamphlets, and journals.[22] The focus of every activity of the JI was to establish a dedicated constituency throughout the country and mobilize it for demanding the establishment of an Islamic state, which Maududi argued was a 'religious obligation of Muslims' in Muslim majority states.[23] The Jamiat Ulema-i-Islam (JUI) devoted itself to establishing madrassas, the traditional institutions of Islamic learning on the pattern of Dar-ul-Aloom, Deoband of India. They were pushing equally for enforcement of Islamic laws, but differed greatly with the JI and with other religious groups on theological issues, as they do even today.

Who is a Muslim?

One thing that brought the religious parties and several of the groups together on one platform was the demand that the individuals belonging to the Ahmadi sect, who claimed to be Muslims, be declared non-Muslims. Pakistan inherited this religious controversy from the early twentieth century when one of the religious scholars, Mirza Ghulam Ahmad (1835–1908), from Qadian in the Punjab, declared himself to be a prophet, but within the religious lineage of Islam.[24] All other sects had declared the Ahmadis as non-Muslims in their religious decrees and had produced voluminous literature proving Ghulam Ahmad as a false prophet, and thus, its followers as having committed apostasy.[25] The Majlis-e-Ahrar had led the campaign against the Ahmadi sect for decades, and found a fresh opportunity in the new state of Pakistan, which it believed, like other religious parties, was created 'in the name of Islam'.[26] One of their propaganda plank was that the Ahmadi sect was created by the imperial British to divide Muslims, and they being 'non-Muslims' couldn't be trusted with power of the state. The Majlis, JI, and other parties targeted Ahmadi persons in high positions in the government. Their particular focus was on Sir Zafarullah Khan, a highly accomplished, outstanding Foreign Minister of Pakistan.[27] They wanted all the Ahmadis removed from their bureaucratic, military, and government positions. The religious parties mobilized people in support of their demand that led to bloody riots in Lahore in which scores of members of the Ahmadi community were killed. Pakistan imposed its first Martial law in the city of Lahore in 1953 to suppress the riots that erupted on the familiar pattern of pre-partition communal violence.[28]

The state suppressed the agitation, restored order and put all the leaders of the movement on trial, some of whom were given the death sentence, including Maulana Maududi. It was the first major confrontation between the Pakistani state and the religious groups. It is difficult to say which side of the confrontation won and which side lost, but the important thing is that the state, even in the face of political instability, refused to surrender to the demands of religious parties. The issue of declaring the Ahmadis as non-Muslims was suppressed, but not resolved. It remained a burning controversy, a popular subject of sermons in the mosque, and religious polemics that today might be interpreted as hate-speech.[29]

The *Report of the Court of Inquiry Constituted under Punjab Act II of 1954 to Enquire into the Punjab Disturbances of 1953*, better known as the 'Justice Munir Report' (named after the chairman of the Court of Inquiry), held the prime minister Khawaja Nizamuddin largely responsible for not taking a timely decision on rejecting the demands of the ulema, which, if conceded, would have tarnished the image of Pakistan and would have been a clear violation of fundamental rights under the constitution.[30] The Justice Munir Report held the religious parties and groups responsible for the attacks against the persons and properties of the Ahmadi community. Their literature, speeches, and protest marches were provocative and led to the disorder and collapse of the state's authority. The report countered the claims of the religious groups and that any community could be declared as non-Muslim(s) by any other—because in the past, some elements within Islam had declared others as non-Muslim(s)—which didn't bode well for the coherence, stability, and peace of the community, nor could any state, in the name of an Islamic state do so.[31] It argued that no two Muslim clerics could agree on the definition of who a Muslim was. To ensure religious peace and social order, the Report made some bold arguments regarding faith being a private matter, and that no sect or faction could be declared non-Muslim as long as it claimed to be Muslim; no other person or religious figure could sit in judgment over the conduct of others or hold an inquisition of another persons' faith, beliefs, or creed.[32] The Report analyses how and why religious factions became possessed with the idea of an Islamic state and why they wanted to enforce their will on the majority. The answer it gave was the confusion in the minds of religious leaders about reliving the past glory of Islam in the modern world by enacting the same state of early Islam, which couldn't be done in the circumstances of their time. This inability culminates into a state of helplessness, with the Musalman waiting for someone to come and help him come out of this morass of uncertainty and confusion. And he will go on waiting without anything happening. Nothing but a bold re-orientation of Islam to separate the vital from the lifeless can preserve it as a world idea and convert the Musalman into a citizen of the present and the future world from the archaic incongruity that he is today.[33]

Naturally, the Report did not do well with the religious constituency that was obsessed with declaring the Ahmadis as non-Muslims, disregarding the fact that the demand conflicted with the principles of the prevailing law and constitution. The JI and other parties reviewed the Report very harshly in their publications and speeches.

While the anti-Ahmadi rhetoric continued mainly in the form of literature production and speeches, the religious parties and groups engaged in low-politics of organizing themselves, creating their respective constituencies and paying attention to the recruitment of workers and their training. They appeared to be competing more than working together in the 1950s, even questioning the true credentials, legitimacy, or appropriateness of the approach to realize the objective of Islamizing state and society. Among all of them, the JI attempted to rise above the sectarian divide, and presented Islam as an ideology, thinking that the best strategy to make Pakistan Islamic would be through politics. Despite the fact that JI questioned the Western form of democracy, and insisted on Islam as a complete system, it still accepted it, as did the other parties. For this reason, the religious parties of Pakistan may be termed as institutionalists, and not revolutionary in their struggle for the supremacy of Islam and its central place in the affairs of the state.

Ayub Regime—Muslim Modernism

Like other parties and groups, the religious parties found limited opportunity under the first military regime of Ayub Khan (1958–69), which placed harsh limits on freedom of speech, assembly, and political activities. The interesting thing is that while mainstream politics was banned or constrained, religious politics remained relatively free. The parties and groups continued demanding Islamization, presenting Islamic ideas as alternatives to the modernist, reform agenda of Ayub Khan. They wanted to build an Islamic state with an Islamic law and constitution, which they would define.

Ayub Khan had different plans for the state—a modern, development-oriented, security driven, stable country. He thought that, neither the parliamentary system, nor the social structures and composition of the elite classes, was good for the progress of the society. He argued that the parliamentary system had failed, that it was chaotic and caused divisions within the society.[34] Like many military rulers popular at that time, Ayub emerged as a modernist-reformist. He believed that religious politics and traditional interpretations of Islam and its practices were out-of-date, and that the ulema couldn't be allowed to exercise monopoly over the meanings of religious beliefs and laws. Ayub was very critical of those sections of the ulema that were nationalists in the 1940s and supported the All India Congress, as well as those who had been opposed to any territorial notions of the state, which Pakistan was going to be. It was a clear reference to the writings of Maulana Maududi, about whom, he derisively says 'this venerable man migrated to Pakistan…'[35]

Interestingly, Ayub was not oblivious to the role of Islam in the society, and he viewed it as a positive force and energy, but only if it were liberated from the religious orthodoxy and interpreted to use its principles for national unity, public service, and social virtue.[36] In his note of 1959, which he copies in his biography, he talks of Islam as an ideology with its internal principles that had to be interpreted in the context of the time we live in.[37] For this reason, he created new institutions, including the Advisory Council of Islamic Ideology and Islamic Research Institute that would be staffed with scholars that were knowledgeable of Islam as well as of the modern sciences to guide the legislature. After delving in some detail on the question of interpretation of Islam in modern times, he believed, like modernist Muslims, that it could be done by the legislature, which, as a representative body, was sovereign and democratic as an embodiment of the will of the people. No council of Islamic scholars could act above the legislature and judiciary in this regard. One finds similarities between his views and those of Fazlur Rahman whom he employed as the Director of the Islamic Research Institute.[38] This was a line of thinking in concurrence with the Muslim modernists. He wished to encourage and support reformist-rationalist interpreters of Islam to counter religious orthodoxy and re-orient the society towards progressive, rationalist Islam.[39]

His political program for reconstruction of the state was radical, as he exercised absolute power in promulgating a new constitution in 1962, ordering a presidential form of government. He believed that democracy, as a system, had to be cultivated from the lower tier—the basic democracy or local councils. He established a controlled or guided democracy and co-opted significant numbers of the tribal and landed elite into a new political hierarchy.[40] His declared goal was development first, and an appropriate democracy, according to the 'genius of the people', which only Ayub Khan knew.[41] He wanted a strong executive in the form of the President, a post that he filled first as a result of a referendum, and then elections, to control and guide the development of Pakistan. For him, centralization of power was necessary for national coherence, stability, and progress. Many of his ideas did not take flight beyond the co-opted elites; rather, they provoked resistance, and anti-centre feelings in the provinces with diverse cultures, which he wished to harmonize with the centralization process. He thought his economic development model and the perceived positive gains for society would settle issues of national integration.

Ayub had a much larger agenda of reform, and he carried it through for almost a decade very effectively. Quite a few of his reformist actions annoyed the religious groups and parties. First, he dropped the prefix Islamic from the Republic of Pakistan when the constitutional commission set up by him proposed a draft of the new constitution. That stirred the hornet's nest. The parties reacted very sharply to Ayub Khan's 'secularization' effort. Even when riding high on the horse of power, the military ruler stumbled on it, quickly reversing his position, which became a major state elite concession to the religious lobby. Part I (1) of the 1962 Constitution reads: 'The state of Pakistan shall be a republic under the name of the Islamic Republic of Pakistan.'[42] As always, this was meant to take an issue out of the hands of clamorous religious opposition, defuse political tensions, and focus on reforms. Like the passage of the Objective Resolution, this was also done without much conviction. Political expediency, more than any other principle, took precedence for the ruler. By conceding a retreat, Ayub Khan, in a way, acknowledged the influence of the religious right, which he thought would be smothered over time as his reforms began to produce good results. His popularity among the masses in the first few years gave him this confidence. It was not just his top position in the military alone that gave so much power to this first military ruler of the country; rather it was a great degree of political support in the first seven years, elite co-optation, political stability, and the highest economic growth in the region.

Ayub Khan's modernization program over-extended to social and cultural spheres, which he believed must tag along with economic development and reinforce it. Never in Pakistan's history has any ruler been so bold or remotely effective on two vital social issues—women's rights and family planning to contain the growth of the population. There has long been a controversy between the religious orthodoxy and the modernist Muslims, since the later part of the nineteenth century, in fact, about whether to separate civil matters and laws from Islamic laws.[43] Ayub Khan took a big leap in this respect and promulgated the famous Family Laws Ordinance 1961, giving legal rights to women to seek divorce through courts, placing limits on polygamy, prescribing a minimum age for marriage, and allowing women right to maintenance when divorced.[44] It was a historic stride forward, that has been hailed as the most progressive piece of social legislation.[45] Equally impressive was the campaign for curtailing the growth of the population with massive publicity and a provision of services, as well as incentives for sterilization of couples with multiple children.[46]

While the literate and progressive sections of the society hailed Ayub Khan's reforms in these two vital areas of national life, the religious groups opposed them, terming them to be against the spirit of Islam.[47] They judged the law and the population control measures according to their notion of Islam and its interpretation, which they thought ran contrary to what religion stood for. Even after many decades, and a general acceptance of the two reforms, conservative religious sections continue to resist and even condemn them. They turned their sermons, speeches, and religious print media against Ayub Khan. While there was not much they could do about the family laws which were implemented by the state, in the case of family planning, the JI advocated more children among Muslims, to increase the Muslim population in the world. They condemned every theory and concept of population growth and its relationship with the natural resources, targeting Malthus's theory of population, economic growth and social structure.[48] Their slogan was 'man is born with one mouth, but two hands'.[49] The clerics ridiculed the programs, poked fun, and advised people not to follow them, as they stood against Islam.

The religious parties found Ayub to be promoting secularization in the name of social reforms and modernization, and working against their conception of an Islamic state. They similarly condemned his patronage of the rationalist, modernist scholars and intellectuals who occupied positions in the Islamic Advisory Council and the Islamic Research Institute. They even issued fatwas (religious decrees) against the views that they believed were not conforming with Islam.[50] But Ayub was to be blamed for all this, as he was the one responsible for promoting a brand of reformist Islam that was very different from the dominant religious tradition in the subcontinent and the Middle East.

The religious opposition was generally isolated from mainstream politics until the anti-Ayub agitation around 1966–67, confined mainly to the speeches, statements, and publications against the regime. The religious parties had limited constituency, limited resources, and limited influence as individual organizations, but when united on any single issue, they could bring their workers out onto the streets. This is what has bothered all mainstream political parties and leaders, and their collective strength equally perturbed Ayub Khan. Even in the anti-Ayub agitation, it was not the religious parties, but a charismatic Zulfikar Ali Bhutto, who challenged the military regime when he came out of the regime in 1966. His electric personality, energy, and fresh ideas for social justice, equality, economic reform, and people's power brought hundreds of thousands into the streets of Pakistan. At that time, the religious parties were just the appendage of the movement for democracy, never the drivers of it. Rather they benefitted from the political opening that Bhutto's challenge to Ayub Khan created.

Neither Ayub Khan nor any other ruler, military or civilian, has been secular or liberal in the western sense of these concepts. They have not been averse to the Islamic identity of Pakistan. All constitutions of the country, from 1956 to 1973 contain Islamic provisions. The 1962 Constitution under the 'Principles of Policy' states: 'No law shall be repugnant to the teachings and requirements of Islam as set in the Holy Qur'an and Sunnah and all existing laws shall be brought in conformity with the Holy Qur'an and Sunnah.' It also recommends teaching of the Holy Qur'an and *Islamiat* (Islamic studies) to the Muslims as compulsory.[51] Pakistan's doctrine of repugnancy has held for decades, and it remains the defining feature of the relationship of

Islam with the constitution, laws, and policies. Unlike Iran, Pakistan has not granted the theologians the power to sit above the legislature, constitution, or judiciary and have a final word on what is Islamic and what is not. They may have opinions, as they do on contentious issues, laws, and policies in the democratic framework, but have never been in a position to get anything accepted outside the constitution.

The influence and popularity of the religious parties committed to Islamism and Islamic ideology was tested for the first time at the popular level in the 1970 general elections. About four to five parties contested independently and they badly lost both in East and West Pakistan. The JI was able to secure only four seats in the National Assembly; the JUI fared much better and became part of a coalition government in the North-West Frontier Province, now KP. Pakistan's first general elections saw three ideologies competing for political space and popular appeal—Islam, ethnic nationalism, and socialism. Political Islam didn't get the support of the people; rather, its popular base has continuously shrunk. In terms of the popular vote, the 1970 elections represented the best showing for political Islam. The general elections punctured the balloon of the coming Islamic revolution through the ballot box. The religious parties were shocked by the power of the traditional elites in West Pakistan, and the far greater influence of ideas and ideologies—socialism and ethnic nationalism in East Pakistan—that they considered against the spirit of Islam, Islamic nationalism, and national solidarity.[52]

Rise of Secular Alternatives

The rise of Bhutto on the slogan of social justice, equality, and welfare state packed in his socialist theory, and likewise, popularity of the Awami League of Sheikh Mujeebur Rahman in East Pakistan, put into question national identity narratives woven around the two-nation theory and Islamic ideology. The elections, results proved that religion was not an issue; it was rights, entitlements, material and pragmatic interests that have always defined electoral behaviour of ordinary people. They are divorced from the obtuse ideological debates and more focused on what worldly good would happen if they voted or not for some party. The fact is that Islam as an alternative system of governance presented by the JI and other religious parties did not convince the electorates that their economic conditions, ethnic rights, and personal opportunities for progress would improve under the rule of these parties. But such reckoning has never dissuaded the ideological parties of any persuasion to abandon their projects. Their ideological self-certitude, particularly of those founded in Islam or, for that matter, in any other religion, provides them different lenses to analyse the world and political facts. Since they never put their ideas under serious questioning—faith—they reach the conclusion that the society is not yet ready to accept what they stand for. That is exactly what is divorcing them from political reality—idealism and a perceptual gap between the self-styled reformers and the society. Never does such politics succeed if it is not capable of taking the masses along, or if it fails to respond to what they believe in or aspire for. The problem with ideology is that it wants to change the reality, and in the case of Islam and politics that is yet to happen.

Islamic nationalism and national identity based on the one that the Pakistani elite and the religious parties, in their own separate ways, had created to bring unity, solidary, and one nation out of diverse ethnic elements—and integrate the distant land of the Muslim Bengal, then East Pakistan—suffered the severest crisis of its efficacy in 1970–71. There are many post-facto explanations of what caused the disintegration of Pakistan that the first generation had known about and lived through: from perceived and real grievances, inequality and exploitation by the West Pakistani elites, neglect of development and exclusion of East Pakistanis, military rule, and denial of democratic rights and representation in the structures of power.[53] In addition, the refusal to allow the Awami League—which secured absolute mandate in East Pakistan and had the majority to form the government at the centre—the right to form its government. Terming demands of autonomy—which were negotiable—as treason, the military regime decided to suppress agitation by military action, which spiralled into chaos, civil war, atrocities, and Indian military intervention.[54] Nothing could save Pakistan from the self-destructive path that its leaders had taken for the previous two decades in designing the template of state- and nation-building, which rested on untested, whimsical assumptions.[55]

The sentiment of Muslim nationalism, Islamic solidarity, and consensus clubbed into the two-nation theory had served its purpose in winning independence for Pakistan, including Muslim Bengal in the federation of Pakistan. The union between two ethnically very diverse, remote states, separated by hostile India in the middle, required a pragmatic geopolitical vision, an inclusive political order and a federal system with maximum autonomy for East Pakistan. Pakistani elites made quite the opposite choices in each of these respects. Islam—the essential binding force—and Bengali nationalism came into direct conflict in 1971, one that had been in the making for a long time, and ultimately, Bengali nationalism won.[56] What actually went wrong in the making of a humiliating defeat, surrender, national disintegration, and the lowest, darkest point in the history of Pakistan has never been a subject of critical soul-searching in Pakistan. Those who have ruled the country, and continue to do so, have sought an easy escape in the familiar conspiracy theories— Agartala conspiracy, involvement of Indian intelligence, and Bengali nationalists as enemies of Pakistan.[57] A more serious thought should have been given to creating a symbiotic relationship between Islamic nationalism and ethnic pluralism. They are not inherently in conflict, as layered identities and regional interests could be addressed through a politics of inclusion, representation, and adequate autonomy within the context of an effective central government.

The East Pakistan debacle demonstrated the practical limits of Muslim nationalism making any sense within a state that comprises of Muslim majority areas; it was another matter when these regions were struggling against Indian nationalism for the justification of creating an independent Pakistan. The essential ingredients of national solidarity, cohesion, and nationalism comprise a complex set of myths, narratives, ideas, a unique reading and understanding of history, and, of course, a self-imagining.[58] Pakistan had all of them encapsulated in the grand idea of Muslim nationalism that earned a historic success in creating a state in India's Muslim majority areas. The failure in East Pakistan lies in a lack of understanding of the practical aspects of this or any other brand of nationalism that is driven by a vision of enduring common interests. In all human affairs, from the smallest unit of family to simple structures of the tribe as well as the more complex character of the state, it is always the primacy of what one would get out of it that determines the bonds, the cohesion, and peace and order. Pakistan was unable to translate emotive Muslim nationalism into a concrete social contract, which would have been broad and open, and flexible enough to provide room for the accommodation of interests. It is on the ashes of frustration, anger, and disappointments that sub-nationalism and ethnicisation are born, and they obtain the power to empty the best of ideas and ideologies of any promise. There is a great deal to learn from the East Pakistan tragedy, and the main lesson is that national integration occurs by integrating interests, creating inter-dependencies, building dense networks of political, cultural and social institutions, and more importantly, by employing forces of economic development and modernization. Only in such a fertile soil, will any idea of nationalism, Muslim, secular, or composite nationalism, grow, flourish, and blossom.

Islamic Socialism

In popularizing the politics of economic reform and restructuring, Zulfikar Ali Bhutto could not escape the placing of Islam in the service of socialism. Like Islamic democracy, Islamic economics, and the formulation of Islamic socialism as one of the four electoral planks of the Pakistan Peoples Party manifesto in the 1970 elections was meant to give religious meanings and significance to socialism. Arab reformist regimes have used the appellation of Arab socialism. In the national, cultural climate, ideas that had foreign roots and could be seen (as they have been) as alien and conflicting with tradition and religion have been baptized by religious prefixes. In a nutshell, it was a brand of socialism which Bhutto promised and implemented, that had a mixture of limited land reforms, and extensive nationalization of industries, banks, schools, and colleges. He rode to popularity and power on account of his personal charisma and opposition to Ayub Khan, once his political mentor, and promise of the redistribution of wealth concentrated in industrial and business families with people-centred approach—socialism. It was a combination of all these factors that brought Bhutto into power. Also, the first of the four slogans was: Islam is our religion, democracy is our politics, and the people are the source of power.[59]

Bhutto was a liberal, progressive politician, and quite opposed to the Islamist political parties and their obscurantism. Why would he then employ Islam in his politics? It appears to be consistent with the pattern established by the national elites from the independence movement to present-day politics, which employs the Islamic idiom for popular effect. It is a recognition of Islam as a social force, and reflects a careful reading of the society as conservative, traditional in its habit of comparing ideas, institutions, and practices with the Islamic injunctions. Bhutto's choice of the Islamic prefix in socialism illustrates this point.

Pakistan lived through a political and social climate of intense ideological debate, discussion, and controversies for almost two-decades beginning with the anti-Ayub movement. Bhutto knew well how and on what grounds his economic reform agenda would be opposed by the religious parties and that socialism is against Islam. This is exactly what they did. The JI in particular churned out a series of pamphlets and publications terming socialism synonymous with atheism and thus, a heretical innovation in Islam, which, it argued, was a complete system in itself and did not need any such tags.[60] In response, Bhutto's party justified socialism as an embodiment of the economic spirit of Islam, signifying its social justice system, equality, and collective ownership of the wealth of the society.[61] In a bitter, often toxic, ideological controversy, Bhutto's ideas of Islamic Socialism attracted far greater public support than the manifestoes of the religious parties. The Islamic rationalization of socialism, as an idea to end inequality and support for the poor proved an effective way of neutralizing the Islamist critique. The religious parties were, thus, down, but never out of the political arena of Pakistan. They would wait for more work and better times to get their ideas of Islamization of the state and society implemented.

The national religious parties even with smaller numbers in the national legislature (1972–77), were able to get their demands of Islamic provisions accommodated in the 1973 Constitution, which stipulates that in the Islamic Republic, Objective Resolution, no legislation is to be in conflict with Islam, and that the heads of the state and government are to be Muslim persons only. This is not to suggest that the mainstream national elites were opposed to these requirements that were carried over from the previous constitutions. This template has evolved over time through bargaining and negotiations within the legislature and outside, and it is considered to be a middle ground reached between an Islamist view of the state and a secular-liberal polity.

One very important controversy, lingering since independence—the declaration of the Ahmadi community as non-Muslim—found some unexpected supporters in the liberal-secular Zulfikar Ali Bhutto. It was in early 1974 that he brought the issue before the National Assembly. In the meantime, there were demands, low profile agitation by the anti-Ahmadi clerics, and frequent rallies pressing the demand that the Parliament of Pakistan declare them as non-Muslims; it did so by amending the constitution. What the pressures, motivations, or political incentives were for Bhutto to take a position on such a controversial issue are questions, answers to which raise even more questions. For one thing, he feared nothing from this community, which is well-organized, largely belonging to the middle-class, urban, and highly literate in bureaucracy, business, and other professions. It is also non-political, essentially devoted to the care of its own community and its own affairs. The religious parties had three concerns that might have weighed on the thinking of Bhutto. First, they thought they had significant numbers in important government positions, more than their communal strength would justify, and this was, they alleged, because of illegal patronage and nepotism. Second, they argued that they were engaged in proselytizing their 'un-Islamic' faith in the name of Islam, confusing ordinary Muslims and converting them. Third, that all other sects of Islam throughout the Islamic world had a consensus on the Ahmadi being out of the essential order of Islam because it rejected the finality of the prophethood of the Prophet Muhammad.[62]

Bhutto's style of leadership is partially responsible for the decision that he took against the Ahmadi community—his populism. On the ground, in the general public throughout the Islamic world and within Pakistan, the Ahmadis were never accepted as Muslims. Second, Saudi Arabia, a few months earlier, had declared this community as non-Muslims, and it was one of the countries Bhutto was looking towards to build the base of his Muslim diplomacy. Finally, he aspired to take the leadership of the Muslim world, bringing Pakistan out of isolation and the trauma of East Pakistan. His better credentials as a champion of Muslim causes would give power and influence to play a bigger role for him and the country.[63] All parties— religious, secular, regional, and mainstream—voted together to amend the constitution to declare the Ahmadis as non-Muslims.[64] Both, the consensus on a religious issue and the Parliament passing a judgment on the faith of a community, were unprecedented. But this didn't bring the religious parties anywhere close to Bhutto or earn him their respect, let alone any support.

In the intense religious climate that Pakistan has been through for decades, it appears that hushing up one controversy produces many more. They have run in a string of one demand leading to another. The religious parties found an opening in the nationwide agitation launched by the Pakistan National Alliance (PNA), a coalition of nine parties of which they are a part, that contested the 1977 elections and lost, allegedly due to massive rigging by Bhutto's government.[65] In writing a consensual manifesto, the PNA conceded to the demand of enforcement of the Islamic system, which was labelled as 'Nizam-i-Mustafa' (Prophet's system).[66] This became the main slogan in the agitation identified with holding fresh rounds of elections, and ensuring transparency and fairness. The agitation paralyzed Bhutto's government in the summer of 1977, leading to the military taking over major cities to control the unrest. Bhutto played one last major political gambit, hoping to regain control of the streets, control that had slipped into the hands of the religious parties; he announced an Islamization package. He banned the sale of alcohol and its consumption, and declared Friday as a weekly holiday.[67] These rather symbolic measures didn't get him any respite from the political crisis, leading to his fall, arrest, and trial under the military rule, his subsequent conviction for a murder, and his tragic execution—generally believed to be a 'judicial' murder.[68]

State Sponsored Islamization

It was the third military regime under general Zia ul-Haq (1977–88) that went after Zulfikar Ali Bhutto with a vengeance—politics and survival became closely personal. The general took over power, apparently to end the political stalemate, which by some accounts, was only resolved when he took the fateful decision to impose Martial law on 5 July 1977.[69] General Haq pledged to the nation that he would devote all his energies to conduct free and fair elections after restoring order and stability, disturbed by the confrontation between the previous government and the political opposition. He also committed to handing over power to the civilians. He kept himself in power for more than eleven-years when he died along with some of his top-ranking military officers and the American ambassador to Pakistan in a plane crash in August 1988. He cancelled scheduled re-run of the elections a few weeks before they were to take place in November 1977, for the reasons that the country was unstable and required reforms and restructuring—a ploy every military regime in the country has used.[70] Unlike the three other military rulers, two before him, and one after him, he adopted an Islamist line in promoting Pakistan's national identity. He embraced the Islamist narrative about the rationale behind the creation of the country as an Islamic state, and set himself the task of enforcing Islamic laws, though selectively. In his first speech to the nation, General Haq made his intention very clear: 'Pakistan was made in the name of Islam and will continue to survive only if it sticks to Islam. This is why I consider the introduction of an Islamic system as an essential prerequisite for the country'.[71] He praised the Islamic spirit behind the Nizam-i-Mustafa movement, the anti-Bhutto agitation, just before making this meaningful comment.[72]

That was construed as an obvious hint of encouragement to the Islamist constituency as well as a message to the nation and the political parties about what was on Zia ul-Haq's mind. After cancelling elections, he went on to announce Islamization measures, covering culture, laws, education, judiciary, and the economy. He went beyond the elite consensus on the relationship of Islam and state that rested on the doctrine of repugnancy. In the realm of culture, women news presenters on Pakistan Television, at the time the only channel people watched, were required to cover their heads. They ended the news bulletins with 'Allah Hafiz' instead of 'Khuda Hafiz', a centuries old tradition of saying goodbye in the region. The impact of this change is so deeply ingrained that hundreds of TV channels in contemporary Pakistan end the bulletins with 'Allah Hafiz'. This change is at the societal level now; rarely do we hear people saying 'Khuda Hafiz'. Some of the intellectuals have rightly argued that it was a wilful attempt to re-orient Pakistani culture away from its very strong Indo-Persian base to the Arabian stream, in which Wahhabi beliefs of the ruler and his constituency played a major role.[73] The government issued orders to private and public institutions, factories, and all workplaces to create space and make arrangements for prayers during office timings.

For the first time, adultery and fornication were criminalized and added to the Pakistan Penal Code through the Hudood Ordinance in 1979. The Ordinance carried 'Islamic' punishments: whipping, stoning to death, and amputation of hands in cases of theft and robbery.[74] When challenged, the apex judiciary declared these punishments, as un-Islamic.[75] Ambiguities in these laws and their flawed application resulted in the wrongful conviction of women as adulterers who were actually victims of rape. A new law of evidence was introduced, which made the evidence of two women (in financial matters) equal to one man's evidence. The law of *Diyyat* and *Qisas*—relating to blood money or compensation for murdered persons—halved the compensation paid for women victims of murder compared to that of men. Another equally troublesome part of these laws was that homicide was no longer a crime against society (a universal tradition), but an offence against an individual and family only. The members of the family, for compensation, can forgive a convict and get him released. In most of the cases of honour-killings, as they take place within the family, the family members forgive murderers and the killers of women. They are promptly released after a 'settlement', even those who have been awarded death sentences. This deep legacy of Zia's Islamization continues to take a heavy toll on women, as the state has left the blood-money settlements to the heirs of murdered women, which actually sanctions and allows the participation in such murders.

For a very long time, the Islamist parties had been demanding an end of interest-based economy and its conversion into an Islamic economy to implement the 'principles of policy' provisions of the 1956 and 1962 constitutions, which set a goal of ending riba (interest).[76] Since the principles of policy were considered non-operative, no government took any steps towards ending riba because that would require changing the basic structure of the economy, writing new laws, and establishing regulatory institutions. What is riba and what is not riba in modern economies is a question that does not lend to an easy or unanimous answer. Zia was the first ruler to take big initiatives to Islamize the economy with a primary focus on the elimination of riba. In order to set the country on this path, he reconstituted the Council of Islamic Ideology within three months in power. He changed its composition with the placement of conservative religious figures for deliberations and advice to restructure the economy according to Islamic principles.[77] While the Council got busy in commissioning and writing reports on Islamic reforms, the Zia government directed the banks to open profit and loss accounts parallel to interest bearing accounts. It required the banks to establish Islamic banking counters and open separate branches for this purpose.[78] Three instruments began to Islamize the economy—executive orders, laws, and court decisions that came as a way of challenges to the executive orders and laws.[79] The above-mentioned measure came as executive orders and instructions from the State Bank of Pakistan in the shaping of which ministries of law and commerce were involved.

A major legal initiative came in the form of Zakat and Ushr Ordinance in 1980, which required the deduction of 2.5% on savings accounts, government securities, corporate shares, and annuities of insurance companies.[80] The government established zakat funds at federal, provincial, and district levels that distributed the zakat collected to welfare programs for the poor, living below the poverty line. The system has survived with some changes; it is no longer a compulsory deduction from the savings accounts. First, the Shia members of the community revolted against this tax, until they were exempted from zakat, which now required filing an application in the banks for this purpose. But harm in terms of divisions in the society had been already caused, creating an atmosphere of sectarian tensions in the country. To further support the Islamization of the economy, Zia promulgated the Shari'at Ordinance in June 1988, which established a Permanent Commission for this purpose. However, the Ordinance expired within six months, as Zia died. His successor, president Ghulam Ishaq Khan, re-issued the Ordinance but it died a natural death, as the next legislature did not endorse it.

A major shift towards the Islamization of the economy came due to a decision of the Supreme Court of Pakistan in December 1999, in the famous Aslam Khaki or 'riba' case. The SC upheld the decision of the Shari'at Court that had struck down eight economic laws that were written between 1839 (the Interest Act) to 1965 as being in conflict with Islamic injunctions.[81] These laws were to become null and void with effect from March 2000. While delivering the judgment, the SC gave a detailed outline to the government to re-enact laws and restructure the economy according to the Islamic principles. The government had no option but to prepare for reforms to comply with the judgment.

While the government began to set up a legal and institutional mechanism to amend laws and seek professional advice on how to go about transforming banking and financial systems without disrupting economic life, relief came from the SC in a review petition filed by the United Bank. The plea of the Bank was that the decision of the Supreme Court was not enforceable because the changes and the path to follow that the court had suggested in its order would take too much time and many changes in the laws. It pleaded to the Court to suspend the judgment, extend time until 2002 to help prepare the Federal Government for changes, and to maintain the status quo. In its judgment on 24 June, the Court squashed its riba judgment, and sent the case back to the Federal Shari'at Court for review and re-examination 'after thorough research and comparative study of the financial systems prevalent in the contemporary Muslim countries of the world.'[82] With the change in the government and re-constitution of both the Federal Shari'at Court and the Supreme Court of Pakistan under Pervez Musharraf, the court-driven Islamization of the economy failed to make any further progress.

The impact of the reforms initiated by Zia ul-Haq has been very profound on the attitudes of the public, as a section of the society is genuinely interested in riba-free business transactions. Today, Islamic banking, and Islamic mutual funds and shareholding in companies have become popular. All major banks have Islamic banking branches, dedicated counters within their mainstream banking, and Islamic business products.

A few comments on what motivated Zia to undertake Islamization of the state and society and how one may judge his deep legacy are in order. As it is apparent from his first speech, especially the last part of it, delivered on 5 July 1977, Zia wanted to cultivate the Islamist constituency, and the religious groups and parties to counter the popularity and influence of the PPP and other political parties.[83] The military has always been the main source of strength and institutional support for the military rulers, but all have required, and found, political allies—as a public facade. Why draw on the religious parties, particularly the JI as a political partner, when the traditional elite families were willing to change loyalties, as they did? It was Zia's ideological preference for Islam as a political ideology, and so the religious parties were natural allies in this respect. They also shared his contempt and hostility towards the PPP and its leader. Two major events transformed the relationship between Zia and political Islam. The first was the Islamic revolution in Iran in February 1979, and second, the Soviet military occupation of Afghanistan in December 1980. The Islamic revolution of Iran was seen essentially as a mark of Shia revival and the power of the clergy to restructure the Iranian state and society. It revived the dream of a Sunni Islamic state in Pakistan. The difference here was that the Sunni clerical establishment was fragmented and divided in too many groups and parties. Neither could they bring about a revolution on the pattern of Iran by confronting the state, nor did they enjoy any broad political support. It was convenient for them to align with Zia ul-Haq in pursuit of their Islamization goals. In contrast to the religious parties, Zia ul-Haq was a pragmatic political man, a shrewd tactician with his own political interests, and his vision of a secure, strong, and integrated Pakistan took precedence over ideological issues. He was willing to travel some distance with the religious parties, but beyond a point, he appeared to be constrained.

Afghan Jihad and Religious Politics

The Afghan-Soviet war (1980–88) further brought the religious groups and the Zia regime closer. They supported jihad in Afghanistan by sheltering the Afghan Mujahedeen parties, hosting millions of refugees and offering all possible sources—weapons, cash, and volunteers—to defeat the Soviet forces in Afghanistan. The second wave of the Cold War between the superpowers and the election of President Ronald Reagan brought four diverse elements together—The United States, the army, Afghan Mujahedeen, and the Islamists—from every part of the Muslim world. All of them had different motivations and diverse interests, and even conflicting priorities. However, they had a shared interest in defeating the Soviet power and end its occupation of Afghanistan.[84] Zia ul-Haq played a masterly role in shaping the anti-Soviet coalition, and remained a driving spirit behind it until his death in August 1988. Pakistan's strategy of raising the cost of the Soviet occupation by supporting the Afghan resistance worked, forcing the Soviet Union to negotiate a withdrawal deal and withdraw, which it did under the Geneva Accords of 1988.[85] It would take more sober moments and many years of reflection to count the costs and consequences for the two states—Afghanistan and Pakistan—their societies and people.

The Islamist legacy of Zia ul-Haq has proven to be deep, complex, and very troublesome for Pakistan. The forces of radical, militant Islam that Pakistan confronts today and that threaten its internal security and societal cohesion have risen out of the debris of the Afghan wars. They present themselves in the form of jihad sentiment and transnational terror networks. The links among the volunteers recruited in the Middle East, Afghanistan, and Pakistan to fight against the Soviet forces morphed into a broader agenda of Islamic radicalism. The objective of Islamic radicals is to wage jihad against their national states, capture power, and establish a universal Islamic state. Pakistan has been in the 'eye of the storm' for almost a decade now, paying a heavy price for its past strategic choices.[86] The use of religion and jihad in support of domestic and foreign policy objectives has created three negative consequences for the state and society. The first is the rise of religious divisions within the society, like sectarianism. The rise of, and power of, one stream of faith within Islam has given rise to fears and insecurity among others. Just as the Islamic revolution of Iran with Shia revivalism began to create a sense of empowerment among the Shias, some sections of the Sunni religious activism sensed a growing Iranian influence. In the same way, Islamization by Zia created resentment among the Shias because they would like to have their own sect-base Islamic studies and would like to be exempted from zakat and ushr laws. By becoming the frontline state of jihad in the Afghan-Soviet war, Pakistan became porous to all the external influences of sectarianism and power rivalries of Iran and the Arab states.

Second, with jihad being sponsored by the state of Pakistan in Afghanistan and Kashmir, Jihadist groups began to proliferate. A youth bulge and the availability of foreign funding to train and equip them, generated a political economy of conflict with a deep interest exhibited by Jihadi leaders and their organizations to continue fights by picking a front of their own choice—sectarian, anti-minority, or against foreign foes. Their concentration in the border regions actually resulted in the retreat of the state and its traditionally weak governing infrastructure. The Jihadi militants, later organizing themselves into several Taliban groups, used their tribal links to create their Islamic fiefdoms at local levels and wage a war against the Pakistani state and society. Finally, extremism, religious intolerance, and radical ideas and ideologies are now on the rise. As a result, Pakistan's pluralistic culture and religious diversity have been strained and placed under stress. Zia's legacies have endured longer because the national and regional climate of conflict that his politics and policies created continues to be a source of troubles.

The Shadow of Troubled Legacies

Post-Zia politics have been too chaotic and unstable, and have been marred by fierce contestations for power to steer the country away from the Islamist-Jihadi path on which the General and his religious allies had set the country. There was no national party, ideology, vision, or leadership left to orient the country away from the deadly choices the military regime had made. Even after more than a quarter of a century after Zia's death, the country has not been able to return to normalcy, reconstruction, and reforms. It has been struggling just to survive. However, it is an incorrect assumption that everything in Pakistan was going well when Zia took over. The country was divided along political lines, facing major confrontation between Bhutto and his political opposition; the nationalization program had ruined the economy and an insurgency was raging in Balochistan. But Zia was neither a visionary nor a healer of a wounded society, gravely damaged by the East Pakistan trauma and political conflicts of the Bhutto era (1972–77). His person and politics were tempered by political interest, contempt for Bhutto and his politics, and an amorphous religious zeal. The American embrace to fight against a 'common' foe—the Soviet Union in Afghanistan—further clouded his political decision-making. A decade of conflict and dangerous alliance between the state and Jihadi forces from within and outside veered the country away from its modernist moorings.

The succeeding governments, unstable and locked in no-holds-barred politics had too much of a mess, institutional decay, and disrupted political and institutional development left to be confronted. Pakistan needed statesmen and visionaries to regenerate itself as a state and get rid of the turmoil of the past. The repeated military regimes stunted the natural growth of parties, and leadership, and prevented the flourishing of fresh ideas to rethink some of Pakistan's choices. It had none; its fate came to be determined by self-seeking, corrupt, dynastic leaders with the military playing political games in the shadows, pulling strings, changing sets of political actors to suit its interests, and pushing them to do things that it deemed good for Pakistan. The PPP and PML-N, the two major parties with allies in the religious and regional parties played the musical-chairs game, engaged more in ousting the other than working together to consolidate democracy, stabilize the country, and deal with the troubled legacy of the Zia years. Instability and political conflict have been the catalyst in Pakistan for reproducing themselves. Pakistan had four general elections between 1988 and 1997, with the two parties having exchanged their positions of power four times. The military was neither neutralized from politics nor a non-partisan state institution; rather, it played an activist role to destabilize and bring into power an alternate set of political actors. With the institutional energies so wasted, attention was focused on political survival and the vital task of national security was left to the military to settle, which was more of the same continued, in terms of declining state institutions, the rise of radical Islam, and rising frustrations of the large sections of the society.

Out of the chaos of politics, arose the personal ambition of General Pervez Musharraf and the latent power of the military as an institution, resulting in Pakistan's fourth military regime (1999–2008), and another eleven years of political disruption. Just as Zia had presented himself in the image of a 'just' and 'pious' Islamic ruler by donning a skull cap and exhibiting a personal demeanour of modesty, humility, and simplicity, Musharraf projected himself as a 'liberal' with pictures of his puppies under his arms, partying with the social liberals and talking endlessly of reforms that were limited and revolved around his politics of legitimacy and survival. Imagine how a nuclear power state got mired into pettiness, personal vendettas, hate, and revenge at the highest levels. Not new though, Musharraf pushed it to the extremes. He took over power with the use of military forces when Prime Minister Nawaz Sharif sacked him as the Chief of Army Staff on 11 October 1999, fearing he was already planning a coup. Just as Zia revived a dead murder case against

Bhutto, Musharraf framed Sharif in a plane-hijacking case, carrying the same punishment—death sentence. He was saved for political banishment, but when the fortunes of the two men changed, Nawaz in his third tenure (2013–July 2017) did everything to humiliate and persecute Musharraf. Thanks to the military and his foreign friends, he got an exit route to exile after staying confined to his home for two and a half years.

There is no end to the chaotic politics of Pakistan. It is personalized and myopic, which keeps the society fragmented and the centres of political power divided along party, regional, and institutional lines. It is the same political template of jostling for power, institutional manipulation, massive corruption, and very little to get the country back in good institutional health. The only saving grace is that democracy remains a preferred form of politics among the political elites even when their own behaviour may not be entirely democratic. The liberal sections of Pakistan, a narrow band, assumes that bad democracy is better than military dictatorship, and live on the hope that bad democracy practiced over time will produce better democracy. I tend to endorse this view, because the alternative of military rule—even one more time—will lead Pakistan to a blind alley. The issue with dysfunctional democracy is that it creates capacity issues that leave civilians unable to address the legacy issues of extremism, terrorism, and Jihadi networks on their own, and according to their own sense of how the state and society can be normalized. Because of institutional imbalance—the problematic civil-military relations—and their own weaknesses, they have lost the autonomy to think creatively, set domestic and international priorities, and act as independent actors. Functioning in a constrained environment, they have to manoeuvre their space between international pressure to 'do more' and the power of the military to dictate terms. That incapacitates the political parties and their leaders to set a clear agenda for structural changes or getting Pakistan back on the modernist-liberal track.

With all its failings and failures, Pakistan appears to be an unlikely candidate for an Islamic state in the image of revivalist, political Islam. There are at least four factors that have protected Pakistan against radical Islam and radical Islamization. First, Pakistan has one the most robust framework of the state—its military, state, and political institutions. For this reason, the country has endured many of the self-inflicted crises, and in the last one decade has been able to withstand the challenge of Islamic militancy.

Second, democracy with all its flaws and problems has presented the most formidable challenge to political Islam. By forcing them to compete with the other parties, their claims of 'popular' support have been repeatedly exposed. A conception of democracy that rests on sound ideas, if not consistency of constitutionalism, political participation, free media, and the rise of civil society are all positive factors that contribute to political alternatives. The difference from other Muslim countries is that Pakistan has been an open social and political space for all; thus, it never suffocated itself to the extent that the Islamists would gain critical strength.

Third, the Pakistani elites have negotiated amicably a middle ground between Islam and liberal-secularism in inserting Islamic provisions in all constitutions. This middle ground settles three fundamental issues: no law will be made that is in conflict with Islam; the state will create an enabling environment for Muslims, and people of other faith to live their lives according to their religions; efforts will be made to adapt existing laws according to the spirit of Islam. These provisions do not compromise the essential framework of a democratic, constitutional state, representative government or equal rights.

Fourth, the religious political parties continue to have a distinctive voice on national and regional issues, but they are integrated into the political system. A reverse is true in Iran, Egypt and other Middle Eastern states. Finally, the people of Pakistan do not seek their Islamic authenticity through an Islamic state, as visualized by the religious parties. They believe in separating the two spheres of politics and religion, leaving the latter to the individual and society. This view competes effectively with the strong proclivity of religious groups towards Islamic laws and a romanticized view of the early years of Islam as a perfect Islamic state, and then strive for it.

NOTES

1. Mohammed Ayoob, *The Many Faces of Political Islam: Religion and Politics in the Muslim World* (Ann Arbor: University of Michigan Press, 2008); Frédéric Volpi, *Political Islam Observed: Disciplinary Perspectives* (New York: Columbia University Press, 2010); Shahram Akbarzadeh, *Routledge Handbook of Political Islam* (Abingdon: Routledge, 2012); Olivier Roy, *The Failure of Political Islam* (Cambridge: Harvard University Press, 1994); Muhammad Saïd Al Ashmawy, *Islam and the Political Order* (Washington: Council for Research in Values and Philosophies, 1994); Frédéric Volpi, *Political Islam: A Critical Reader* (London: Routledge, 2011).

2. On Islam as a complete code of life and an answer to all questions, see: Muhammad Ali Alkhuli, *Need for Islam* (Jordan: Dar Al-Falah Publishing, 2006); Sayyid Abul A'la Maududi, *The Islamic Way of Life* (Islamabad: Islamic Dawah Centre International, 1980); S. A. Khulusi, *Islam Our Choice* (Woking: Woking Muslim Mission & Literary Trust, 1961); Akhtaruddin Ahmad, *Why Islam?* (Cairo: Islamic Inc. Publishing and Distribution, 1997).

3. Philip Khuri Hitti, *Islam: A Way of Life*, (Minnesota: University of Minnesota Press, 1970); Turgul Keskin, *The Sociology of Islam*, (Reading: Ithaca Press, 2012); Nilufer Gole, 'Islam in Public: New Visibilities and New Imaginaries' *Public Culture* 14/1 (2002),173–90; Duncan Black Macdonald, *The Religious Attitude and Life in Islam: Being the Haskell Lectures on Comparative Religion Delivered Before the University of Chicago in 1906.* (Chicago: University of Chicago Press, 1909); Abdul Aziz Sachedina, 'The Role of Islam in the Public Square: Guidance or Governance?' *Islamic Democratic Discourse: Theory, Debates, and Philosophical Perspectives* 12/2 (2006),173–92; William A. Graham, 'Traditionalism in Islam: An Essay in Interpretation' *The Journal of Interdisciplinary History* 23/3 (1993), 495–522.

4. Barry M. Rubin, *Guide to Islamist Movements* (Armonk: M.E. Sharpe, 2010); Jon Armajani, *Modern Islamist Movements: History, Religion, and Politics* (Chichester:

Wiley-Blackwell, 2012); Ḍiyā' Rašwān and Muḥammad Fāyiz Faraḥāt, *The Spectrum of Islamist Movements* (Berlin: H. Schiler, 2007); Frank Peter, *Islamic Movements of Europe* (London: Tauris, 2013); Shaukat Ali, *Dimensions and Dilemmas of Islamist Movements* (Lahore: Sang-e-Meel Publications, 1998).

5. Sheri Berman, *The Social Democratic Moment: Ideas and Politics in the Making of Interwar Europe.* (Cambridge: Harvard University Press, 1998); C. Ernest Dawn, 'The Formation of Pan-Arab Ideology in the Interwar Years' *International Journal of Middle East Studies* 20/1 (1988), 67–91; Roberta Garner, 'Post War Perspectives' in Roberta Garner, ed. *Social Theory: Power and Identity in the Global Era* (Toronto: University of Toronto Press, 2010), 323–37; Michael Freeden, *Reassessing Political Ideologies: The Durability of Dissent* (London: Routledge, 2001), 117; John R. Lampe and Mark Mazower, *Ideologies and National Identities: The Case of Twentieth-century South-eastern Europe* (Budapest: Central European University Press, 2004); M. A. Riff, *Dictionary of Modern Political Ideologies* (New York: St. Martin's Press, 1987).

6. Ervand Abrahamian, *Khomeinism: Essays on the Islamic Republic* (Berkeley: University of California Press, 1993); Arshin Adib-Moghaddam, *A Critical Introduction to Khomeini* (Cambridge: Cambridge University Press, 2014); Jahangir Amuzegar, 'Islamic Fundamentalism in Action: The Case of Iran' *Middle East Policy* 4/1–2 (1995), 22–33.

7. Sani Muhammad Umar, *Islam and Colonialism: Intellectual Responses of Muslims of Northern Nigeria to British Colonial Rule* (Amsterdam: Brill, 2006); Hamid Dabashi, *Islamic Liberation Theology: Resisting the Empire* (London: Routledge, 2008); Marcel Maussen, Veit-Michael Bader, and Annelies Moors, *Colonial and -Postcolonial Governance of Islam: Continuities and Ruptures* (Amsterdam: Amsterdam University Press, 2011); Michael R. Anderson, 'Islamic Law and the Colonial Encounter in British India' *Institutions and Ideologies: A SOAS South Asia Reader* 10/3 (1993), 165–85; David Gilmartin, *Empire and Islam: Punjab and the Making of Pakistan*, (Berkeley: University of California Press, 1988); Rudolph Peters, *Islam and Colonialism: The Doctrine of Jihad in Modern History* (The Hague: Mouton, 1979).

8. Fazlur Rahman, 'Muslim Modernism in the Indo-Pakistan Subcontinent' *Bulletin of the School of Oriental and African Studies* 21/1 (1958), 82–99; Mazheruddin Siddiqi, 'General Characteristics of Muslim Modernism' *Islamic Studies* 9/1 (1970), 33–68; Mazheruddin Siddiqi, 'Intellectual Bases of Muslim Modernism—I' *Islamic Studies* 9/2 (1970), 149–71; Fazlur Rahman, 'Islamic Modernism: Its Scope, Method and Alternatives' *International Journal of Middle East Studies* 1/4 (1970), 317–33; Mansoor Moaddel, *Islamic Modernism, Nationalism, and Fundamentalism: Episode and Discourse* (Chicago: University

of Chicago Press, 2005); Fazlur Rahman, *Islam and Modernity: Transformation of an Intellectual Tradition* (Chicago: University of Chicago Press, 1982).

9. John L Esposito, and John Obert Voll. *Islam and Democracy* (New York: Oxford University Press, 1996); Martin Kramer, 'Islam vs. Democracy' *Commentary* 95/1 (1993), 35; Asef Bayat, *Islam and Democracy: What Is the Real Question?* (Leiden: Amsterdam University Press, 2007); Timothy D. Sisk, *Islam and Democracy: Religion, Politics, and Power in the Middle East* (Washington, DC: United States Institute of Peace, 1992); Fatima Mernissi, *Islam and Democracy: Fear of the Modern World* (Reading: Addison-Wesley Publishers, 1992); Shireen Hunter and Huma Malik, *Modernization, Democracy, and Islam* (Westport: Praeger Publishers, 2005); Hussin Mutalib, *Islam and Democracy: The Southeast Asian Experience* (Singapore: Konrad-Adenauer-Stiftung Singapore, 2004).

10. Iran has instituted a Council of the Guardians, which scrutinizes legislation by the Majlis and may reject it if it is found to be conflicting with Islamic law. In the same way, the religious parties in Pakistan would like the Council of Islamic Ideology to be supreme over the Parliament, a status that they have failed to get, and which is not likely to happen in the present day context of Pakistan.

11. Pakistan is not an Islamic republic as imagined by the religious parties in Pakistan. See for instance, Seyyed Vali Reza Nasr, *The Vanguard of the Islamic Revolution: The Jama'at-i Islami of Pakistan* (Berkeley: University of California Press, 1994); Freeland Abbott, 'The Jama'at-i-Islami of Pakistan' *Middle East Journal* 11/1 (1957), 37–51.

12. Muqarab Akbar, 'Pakistan: An Islamic State or a State for Muslims? A Critical Appraisal of Islam's Role in Pakistan' *Pakistan Journal of Islamic Research*, Vol. 15 (2015), 24–85.

13. See speech of Abdul Rab Nishter, *The National Assembly of Pakistan Debates: Official Report,* (Government of Pakistan, 1956).

14. Pakistan Constituent Assembly, *Debates: Official Report 9; 12* (Government of Pakistan Press, 1951); Rizwan Ullah Kokab, 'Constitution Making in Pakistan and East Bengal's Demand for Provincial Autonomy (1947–58)' *Pakistan Vision* 12/2 (2011), 165. For the text of speeches by Hindu members see: Sharif al Mujahid, ed. *Ideological Orientation of Pakistan*, (Karachi: National Committee for Birth Centenary Celebrations of Quaid-i-Azam, 1976), 9–31.

15. One of the minority members said that the Quaid would have opposed the Objective Resolution. See, text of speech of Mr Sris Chandra Chattopadhya in G. W. Choudhury, *Documents and Speeches on the Constitution of Pakistan* (Dacca: Green Book House, 1967); I. A. Rehman, 'Objectives Resolution Bade Farewell to Quaid's Ideals' *The News*, (Karachi: January 25, 2015); Kausar

Parveen, 'The Role of Opposition in Constitution Making: Debate on the Objectives Resolution' *Pakistan Vision* 1/11.

16. Objectives Resolution was strongly supported by Dr Ishtiaq Hussain Qureshi, Maulana Shabbir Ahmad Usmani, Sardar Abdurrab Nishtar, Noor Ahmad, Begam Shaista, Muhammad Hussain and others. G. W. Choudhury, *Documents and Speeches on the Constitution of Pakistan* (Dacca: Green Book House, 1967).

17. Syed Abul A'la Maududi and Khurshid Ahmad, *The Islamic Law and Constitution* (Lahore: Islamic Publications, 1960).

18. See speech of Maulana Shabbir Ahmad Usmani, 'Constituent Assembly of Pakistan', *Constitutional Debates* 5/3, (March 9, 1949), 43–6.

19. Ishtiaq Husain Qureshi, *Perspectives of Islam and Pakistan* (Karachi: Ma'aref, 1979).

20. 'Objectives Resolution Protects Minorities' *The Nation*, (March 13, 2015); Asaf Hussain. 'Ethnicity, National Identity and Praetorianism: The Case of Pakistan' *Asian Survey* 16/10 (1976), 918–30; Sayed Riaz Ahmad, *Maulana Maududi and the Islamic State*. (People's Publishing House, 1976).

21. Syed Abul A'la Maududi and Khurshid Ahmad, *The Islamic Law and Constitution* (Lahore: Islamic Publications, 1960).

22. *Jamaat-e-Islami* publishes a daily newspaper *Jisarat* and a monthly journal *Tarjamanul Qur'an*. The *Jamaat* and its subsidiary groups have at least 22 media publications that promote an Islamic worldview. For a list of publications see Amir Rana, 'Jihadi Print Media in Pakistan: An Overview' *Conflict and Peace Studies* 1/1 (2008), 1–18.

23. Abul A'la Maududi and Khurshid Ahmad, *Political Theory of Islam* (Lahore: Islamic Publications, 1980).

24. Yohanan Friedmann, *Prophecy Continuous: Aspects of Ahmadi Religious Thought and its Medieval Background* (Oxford: Oxford University Press, 2003); Zahid Aziz, *A Survey of the Lahore Ahmadiyya Movement: History, Beliefs, Aims and Work* (Lahore: Ahmadiyya Anjuman Lahore Publications, 2008); Simon Rose Valentine, *Islam and the Ahmadiyya Jama'at: History, Belief, Practice* (London: Hurst, 2008); Spencer Lavan, *The Ahmadiyah Movement: A History and Perspective*. (New Dehli: Manohar Book Service, 1974)

25. Surendranath Kaushik, 'Anti-Ahmadiya Movement in Pakistan', *South Asian Studies* 20/1 (1985), 16–40; Sadia Saeed, 'Pakistani Nationalism and the State Marginalisation of the Ahmadiyya Community in Pakistan' *Studies in Ethnicity and Nationalism* 7/3 (2007), 132–52; Zainab Rahman, 'State Restrictions on the Ahmadiyya Sect in Indonesia and Pakistan: Islam or Political Survival?' *Australian Journal of Political Science* 49/3 (2014), 408–22; Mahmood Amjad Khan, 'Persecution of the Ahmadiyya Community in Pakistan: An Analysis

Under International Law and International Relations' *Harvard Human Rights Journal* 16/3 (2003), 217; Iftikhar H. Malik, *Religious Minorities in Pakistan*, 6 (London: Minority Rights Group International, 2002).

26. Samina Awan, *Political Islam in Colonial Punjab: Majlis -i-Ahrar 1929–49* (Karachi: Oxford University Press, 2010).

27. Ali Usman Qasmi, *The Ahmadis and the Politics of Religious Exclusion in Pakistan*, (Delhi: Anthem Press, Reprint edition 2015); Arif Humayun, *Connivance by Silence: How the Majority's Failure to Challenge Politically Motivated Interpretation of the Qur'an Empowered Radicals to Propagate Extremism* (Philadelphia: Xlibris, 2010), 54–64.

28. See the *Report of the Court Inquiry Constituted Under Punjab Act II to Enquire into the Punjab Disturbances of 1953* (Lahore: Printed by the Superintendent, Government Printing, 1954).

29. Fatima Z. Rahman, 'Pakistan: A Conducive Setting for Islamist Violence Against Ahmadis' in Jawad Syed, et el. eds. *Faith-Based Violence and Deobandi Militancy in Pakistan*, (London: Palgrave Macmillan, 2016), 209–30; Waris Awan, Rizwan Ullah Kokab, and Rehana Iqbal, 'Jama'at-i-Islami: Movement for Islamic Constitution and Anti-Ahmadiyah Campaign' *Asian Culture and History* 5/2 (2013), 181–210.

30. The *Report of the Court of Inquiry constituted under Punjab Act II of 1954 to Enquire into the Punjab Disturbances of 1953* (Lahore: Government Printing Press, 1954), 231–3.

31. Ibid. 235

32. Ibid.

33. Ibid. 298

34. Mohammad Ayub Khan, *Friends Not Masters: A Political Autobiography* (New York: Oxford University Press, 1967).

35. Ibid.

36. Ibid.

37. Ibid.

38. Fazlur Rahman, *Islamic Methodology in History* (Karachi: Central Institute of Islamic Research, 1965).

39. Ali Usman Qasmi, 'God's Kingdom on Earth? Politics of Islam in Pakistan, 1947–1969' *Modern Asian Studies* 44/6, (November 2010), 1197–253.

40. Lawrence Ziring, *The Ayub Khan Era: Politics in Pakistan, 1958–1969* (Syracuse: Syracuse University Press, 1971).

41. Mohammad Ayub Khan, 'Pakistan Perspective', *Foreign Affairs* 38/4 (1960), 547–56.

42. Aziz Ahmad and G. E. Von Grunebaum, eds., *Muslim Self-Statement in India and Pakistan, 1857–968* (Lahore: Suhail Academy, 2004), 219.

43. Anita Weiss, *Interpreting Islam, Modernity and Women's Rights in Pakistan* (New York: Palgrave Macmillan, 2014).

44. *The Muslim Family Laws Ordinance 1961* (Islamabad: Legislative and Parliamentary Affairs Division, Ministry of Law, Justice and Parliamentary Affairs, 2010).

45. Howard Wriggins, *Pakistan in Transition* (Islamabad: University of Islamabad Press, 1975), 36–8.

46. Lee L. Bean and A. D. Bhatti, 'Pakistan's Population in 1970s: Problems and Prospects' in J. Henry Korson, ed. *Contemporary Problems of Pakistan,* (Leiden: E. J. Brill, 1974), 81–8.

47. Sarfraz Husain Ansari, 'Forced Modernization and Public Policy: A Case Study of Ayub Khan Era, 1958–69' *Journal of Political Studies* 18/1, 45–60.

48. Thomas Robert Malthus, *An Essay on the Principle of Population*, 1 (New York: Cosimo Classics, 2007).

49. The JI chalked the walls all over Pakistan with this slogan in the 1960s. Author's observations.

50. Fazalur Rahman had his book *Islam* published in 1966, which provoked agitation by the JI and other religious parties. He was forced to resign in 1968. Fazalur Rahman, *Islam* (Chicago: University of Chicago Press, 1966).

51. On Islamic provisions in the Constitution of 1962 see articles 199–204. *Constitutional Documents Pakistan* V, (Karachi: Ministry of Publications, 1962).

52. Craig Baxter, 'Pakistan Votes—1970', *Asian Survey* 11/3 (1971), 197–218; Iftikhar Ahmad, *Pakistan General Elections, 1970* (Lahore: South Asian Institute, Punjab University, 1976); *First 10 General Elections of Pakistan: A Story of Pakistan Transition from above Rule of Law to under Rule of Law, 1970–2013*, (Islamabad: PILDAT, May 2013).

53. Rounaq Jahan, *Pakistan: Failure in National Integration* (New York: Columbia University Press, 1972).

54. Richard Sisson and Leo E. Rose, *War and Secession: Pakistan, India, and the Creation of Bangladesh* (Berkeley: University of California Press, 1990).

55. Aftab A. Kazi, *Ethnicity and Education in Nation-Building in Pakistan* (Lahore: Vanguard, 1994); Roger D. Long et al., *State and Nation-Building in Pakistan: Beyond Islam and Security* (London: Routledge 2016); Ashok K. Behuria, *State versus Nations in Pakistan: Sindhi, Baloch and Pakhtun Responses to Nation-Building* (New Delhi: Institute for Defence Studies & Analyses, 2015); Khalid Bin Sayeed, 'Religion and Nation-Building in Pakistan' *Middle East Journal* 17/3

(1963), 279–91; Christophe Jaffrelot, *Pakistan: Nationalism without a Nation?* (New Delhi: Manohar, 2002).

56. M. Abdul. Hafiz and Abdur Rob Khan, *Nation-Building in Bangladesh: Retrospect and Prospect* (Dhaka: Bangladesh Institute of International and Strategic Studies, 1986); Samaren Roy, *The Bengalees: Glimpses of History and Culture* (New Delhi: Allied Publishers, 1999); Badruddin Umar, *The Emergence of Bangladesh: Rise of Bengali Nationalism, 1958–1971* (New York: Oxford University Press, 2006); Śekhara Bandyopādhyāẏa, *Bengal, Rethinking History: Essays in Historiography* (New Delhi: Manohar Publishers & Distributors, 2001).

57. Syed Badrul Ahsan, 'Agartala Conspiracy Case and its Ramifications' *The Daily Observer* (Dhaka), (June 19, 2015); *The All Pakistan Legal Decisions* 26/2, (1974), 140–60.

58. Kamal Khursheed Aziz, *The Making of Pakistan: A Study in Nationalism* (Lahore: Sang-E-Meel Publication, 2002); Adeel Khan, *Politics of Identity: Ethnic Nationalism and the State in Pakistan* (New Delhi: Sage Publishers, 2005).

59. *Manifestos of Pakistan Peoples Party 1970 and 1977*, reproduced by Sani Husain Panhwar, member Sindh Council, PPP. <http://bhutto.org/Acrobat/Manifestos%20of%20Pakistan%20Peoples%20Party.pdf>. Accessed on January 18, 2017.

60. The Jamaat-e-Islami launched a big propaganda campaign against socialism during the 1970 elections. The JI publications, like the daily Urdu newspaper *Jasarat* and several magazines and journals carried anti-socialism articles. It published a series of pamphlets terming socialism to be against the spirit of Islam.

61. Nadeem Paracha, 'Islamic Socialism: A History from left to right' *Dawn*, February 21, 2013; Shahid Javed Burki, *Pakistan Under Bhutto: 1971–1977* (New York: St. Martins Press, 1980); John L. Esposito and John Obert Voll, *Islam and Democracy* (New York: Oxford University Press, 1996), 107.

62. Farahnaz Ispahani, *Purifying the Land of the Pure: Pakistan's Religious Minorities* (New Delhi: HarperCollins India, 2015), 15; *A Response to the Article Entitled The Qadiyanies, a Non-Muslim Minority in Pakistan* (Washington: Ahmadiyya Movement in Islam, 1975); Roy Jackson, *Mawlana Maududi and Political Islam: Authority and the Islamic State* (London: Routledge, 2011).

63. On why Bhutto took the decision to declare Ahmadis as non-Muslims, see: Antonio R. Gualtieri, *The Ahmadis: Community, Gender, and Politics in a Muslim Society* (Montreal: McGill-Queen's University Press, 2004); Farhan Mujahid Chak, *Islam and Pakistan's Political Culture* (New York: Routledge, 2015), 129.

64. National Assembly of Pakistan, *Proceedings of the Special Committee of the Whole House Held in Camera to Consider the Qadiani Issue* Special Report. (Islamabad:

Printing Corporation of Pakistan, August 5, 1974); Mahboob Husain, 'Establishing Constitutional Status of Qadianies: A Study of Parliamentary Debates, 1974' *Pakistan Vision* 14/2 (2012), 76–93.

65. *A Dispassionate Analysis of How Elections Are Stolen & Will of the People Is Defeated: Reflection on the Electoral History of Pakistan (1970–2008)* (Islamabad: Pakistan Institute of Legislative Development and Transparency, 2008).

66. Nadeem Paracha, 'Pakistan's Contrary Years (1971–77): A Cultural History of the Bhutto Era' *Dawn Sunday Magazine*, (December 4, 2015); John L. Esposito, *Islam and Politics* (Syracuse, NY: Syracuse University Press, 1984), 176; Rafi Ullah Shehab, *Fifty Years of Pakistan* (Lahore: Maqbool Academy, 1990), 287.

67. Charles H. Kennedy, 'Islamization and Legal Reform in Pakistan, 1979–1989' *Pacific Affairs,* 15/12 (1990), 62–77.

68. Victoria Schofield, *Bhutto: Trial and Execution* (London: Cassell, 1979); Jagdish Chandra Batra, *The Trial and Execution of Bhutto* (Berkeley: University of California Press, 1979).

69. 'Martial Law is Proclaimed: Elections in October Next' *Dawn,* (July 6, 1977). For the audio of the speech, go to <http://www.dailymotion.com/video/x20tvci_general-zia-ul-Haq-full-martial-declaration-speech-july-5-1977_news>.

70. Anthony Hyman, Muhammed Ghayur, and Naresh Kaushik, *Pakistan, Zia and After,* (New Delhi: Abhinav Publications, 1989), 17; Shahid Javed Burki, 'Pakistan under Zia, 1977–1988' *Asian Survey* 28/10 (1988), 1082–1100.

71. <http://www.dailymotion.com/video/x20tvci_general-zia-ul-Haq-full-martial-declaration-speech-july-5-1977_news>. Accessed, June 30, 2016.

72. Ibid.

73. Saroosh Irfani, 'Pakistan's Sectarian Violence: Between the Arabist Shift and Indo-Persian Culture' in Sathu Limaye, Mohan Malik & Robert Wirsing, eds. *Religious Radicalism and Security in South Asia,* (Honolulu, Hawaii: Asia-Pacific Center for Security Studies, 2004), 147–70.

74. Martin Lau, 'Twenty-Five Years of Hudood Ordinances—A Review' *Washington and Lee Law Review,* 64/4, (September 2007), 1292–96.

75. Ibid.

76. Article 38 (f), 'Principles of Policy', Constitution of 1973; Article 29 (f), 'The State shall endeavor to-eliminate *riba* as early as possible', 1956 Constitution; Principle 18 of 'Principles of Policy', Constitution of 1962.

77. Muhammad Akram Khan, *An Introduction to Islamic Economics* (Islamabad: The International Institute of Islamic Thought and Institute for Policy Studies, 1994), 83.

78. Ibid., 138–40.

79. For details, see, Aurangzeb Mehmood, 'Islamisation of Economy in Pakistan: Past, Present and Future', *Islamic Studies* 41, no. 4 (2002): 675–704.

80. See details in *Zakat and* Ushr *Ordinance of 1980.* <http://www.zakat.gop.pk/system/files/zakatushr1980.pdf>. Accessed, July 1, 2016.

81. *Dr M. Aslam Khaki and Others vs. Syed Muhammad Hashim and others*, PLD, 2000, SC, 225.

82. *United Bank Limited vs M/S Farooq Brothers etc.*, PLD 2002, SC, 815–16.

83. Op. cit., (five ref no)

84. Barnett R. Rubin, *The Fragmentation of Afghanistan: State Formation and Collapse in the International System* (New Haven: Yale University Press, 2002).

85. Riaz M. Khan, *Untying the Afghan Knot: Negotiating Soviet Withdrawal* (Durham: Duke University Press, 1991).

86. Owen Bennett Jones, *Pakistan: In the Eye of the Storm* (New Haven, CT: Yale University Press, 2002).

Chapter VI

Culture and Cultural Politics

S ocial life in every society everywhere, disregarding the level of
development, location, religion, language, or civilization, is
defined by values, institutions, and beliefs people hold, as well as
heroes they remember and celebrate, festivals they organize, the dress
code they prefer, music and arts that they enjoy—all of which shape
and sustain their culture. Contrary to common misconceptions,
culture is not confined to art forms, literature, or creative expression;
it is how people live their lives at the present, how they have lived
in the past, and how they have evolved distinctive cultural patterns
that are specific to their community. Each part of the world, be it
a nation, a country, or even ethnic and religious communities in
a state exhibit individualistic cultural traits. The reason is that the
cultural character of a community evolves with it in an unending
process of continuity, change, and refinement. Therefore, culture is
variable and changes over time, depending on the material progress
of the society, industrialization, urbanization, and interactions among
different cultural communities within the nation or with other states
and countries through, what is now known as a dominant influence,
or globalization.

Broadly defined, culture is a combination of attitudes, values, social
institutions, beliefs, and system of thought, civilizational heritage,
and entire ways of living of a community or a nation. Culture is
the most authentic source of identity of a nation or a state and the
marker of a difference among nations. It is not just the boundaries

and sovereignties of each state that distinguish them from one another, but the culture, identity, and nationalism also differentiate them. Otherwise, structurally, all states are similar and perform analogous functions. In order to promote individuality, states promote their culture, and heritage, including literature, languages, history, struggles, and unique national characteristics. Even nations that speak the same language, and may have similar civilizational roots—like many English speaking countries—differentiate themselves with reference to history, geography, heritage, and the unique political and social experiences of their people.

Politics of Culture

Cultural narratives have been connected with aggressive nationalism with myths of national superiority. Historically, and even in modern times, states have used national culture in broader terms as a means of promoting ideology, expanding political influence, and competing with rival nations. American hegemony in the larger part of the twentieth century and its Cold War-related international politics appear to have a strong cultural component, which more visible objects, like nuclear weapons, deterrence, and military and economic power, keep out of intellectual consideration.[1] Culture, in fact, was employed as a tool in the justification of the colonization of (perceived as) weak people and societies—the 'civilizing' of the 'uncivilized'.[2] In the eighteenth century, the European empire builders, particularly the British, thought of imperialism as doing good to the subject societies. They articulated it as a positive force, contributing to the development and civilization of the colonized by introducing democracy, liberal ideas, education, literacy, and social reforms.[3]

In promoting imperialism mainly through force and military conquest, the imperialist powers and their intellectual apologists manufactured a myth of Western culture—philosophy, ideas, institutions, and post-renaissance modernity—being superior to the rest. The imperial struggle among nations, and particularly between the colonizer and the colonized was, first and foremost, a struggle for power, resources, domination, and exploitation. It was supported by the myth of cultural superiority, used essentially to eliminate local cultures as a potential source of resistance. India as a whole as well as every region and parts, boasted of cultures more ancient, authentic, philosophically richer, and organic to the people than the alien culture the British introduced. The English were too self-assured of their own cultural superiority to bother studying and appreciating the rich Indian civilizations, cultures, social institutions, and philosophies.[4] They assigned themselves a messianic mission of converting and transforming India according to their image of a 'good', 'civilized' society. In 1833, Thomas Babington Macaulay, a member of the British Parliament, while arguing in support of changing the Charter of the East India Company said the following about the Company's rule over India:

> I see a government anxiously bent on the public good. Even in its errors I recognize a paternal feeling towards the great people committed to its charge. I see toleration strictly maintained. Yet I see bloody and degrading superstitions gradually losing their power. I see the morality, the philosophy, the taste of Europe, beginning to produce a salutary effect on the hearts and understandings of our subjects. I see the public mind of India, that public mind which we found debased and contracted by the worst forms of political and religious tyranny, expanding itself to just and noble views of the ends of government and of the social duties of man.[5]

To further promote such objectives, William Bentinck, the Governor-General of India constituted a committee in 1834 of which Thomas Macaulay was one of the influential members. It was mandated to decide whether to introduce the English educational system or retain the native, oriental systems. In the 'minutes' of this committee, Macaulay wrote that a 'single shelf of a good European library was worth the whole literature of India and Arabic' arguing that the Indians be taught English.[6] It was a reflection of sheer hubris, as well as that of an imperial resolve to change Indian society for the better through education. Arrogance and ignorance about the Indian and Islamic civilizations apart, the British policy to reform and reconstruct the social and political life of the subcontinent became tied with every aspect of the imperial mission. Imperialism was in many ways the brainchild of the European Enlightenment project, both in the positive sense of liberal values, as well as in the rise of European powers and their territorial expansion in the form of establishing colonies. It demonstrates two important dimensions of the relationship of culture with power whether colonial or national. First, the British, being the first hegemonic power, pursued a policy of spreading liberal values mainly through education but also by introducing reformist laws and policies. Such a policy also supported the political objective of cultivating an indigenous, intermediary class that would be converted to English 'tastes' and 'manners'.[7] The postcolonial states and elites have largely been more conscious of the national heritage and more sensitive to local cultures, but they have also embraced the Western paradigm of modernity under the rubric of development. Often, they have failed to keep the balance between appropriate development that is relevant to the needs of the society and based on national resources, as well as the national culture. Actually, as it was during the colonial era, national culture remains dependent on politics, public policy, and level and scope of modernity in a society.

Second, contrary to the conservative view that the culture of a nation would determine progress and success of a society, culture is not an independent force to impede or accelerate positive change. It is an old intellectual and policy debate, and we find strong opinions on both sides.[8] From a liberalist point of view, it is the power and politics, and to which ends they work, that would determine progress, positive social change, and development. The most important comment on the relationship of culture to the idea of progress is by Daniel Patrick Moynihan: 'The central conservative truth is that it is culture, not politics, that determines the success of a society. The central liberal truth is that politics can change a culture and save it from itself.'[9] Pakistan and many other postcolonial states have never considered their cultures to be barriers to national development. For them, it has been colonial legacies—institutional imbalance, underdevelopment of resources, low level of human development, conflicts and political instability—that have been the real problems impeding progress. They have relied on politics as an instrument—for example, public policy and economic planning—to help achieve progress. The issue of progress is linked to the larger issue of state and nation-building, and the impediments are familiar, like weak institutions, social disorder, corrupt elite, poor governance, and a weak rule-of-law tradition. The question is whether these issues relate to culture or politics. They are the subject matter of politics, and when politics addresses these issues successfully, it contributes to the positive influence on culture by strengthening values that facilitate development.

An understanding of culture and how it can be useful in terms of its linkages with democracy, modernity, human rights, and the general progress of society is important for another reason as well. This is its relationship with the construction of national identity. Culture and national identity travel together, reinforce each other, and are two sides of the same coin. Both of them have been important political enterprises in the multicultural, multi-ethnic context of most of the postcolonial states. Pakistan has many unifying strands of its nationalism, which include common history, religion, geography, and intermingling of ethnic populations for centuries around the Indus plain, rich for its agriculture and livelihood. Above all, a common political struggle for an independent Muslim majority homeland—a historical achievement of Muslim nationalism and political struggle inspired by this idea—has formalized and cemented the historical bonds. However, the intermingling of ethnic groups even for centuries has not diminished their individual ethnic characters. This makes Pakistan a multicultural society with a great variety of sub-cultures of the constituent provinces and regions. Even in each region, one may find many different cultural groups with distinctive linguistic identities.

Narrative of Muslim Culture

Among the many challenges that Pakistan confronted as a new state constituted out of linguistically diverse Muslim majority regions, were the twin issues of identity and national culture. The issue was not that cultures and identities didn't exist in the regions that became Pakistan; they were an organic, social part of the diverse people and ethnic groups. It was the diversity of cultures and identities, and each group's desire for recognition and acknowledgement of its culture. The challenge the early state builders of Pakistan faced was imagining, framing, and constructing a narrative about the Pakistani culture. In the background of multiculturalism of the regions with an overlay of Islam, Islamic thought and institutions, was the problem of constructing a national identity in which a sense of common culture would play a major role. The question that the Pakistani intelligentsia and thought leaders confronted was whether or not the regional cultures could be recognized, accommodated and effectively employed in the development of national culture, or an Islamic culture promoted. What the national language or languages of the country would be was yet another important question that the new country had to settle. Underlying the issues of culture and identity was a deep desire to separate from India in every respect by constructing a narrative of being a very different nation. It was a central theme of the two-nation theory that was further developed after winning the struggle for Pakistan.

However, there were too many voices on the issue of identity and culture after independence, which included the recognition of the languages of the constituent regions as national languages. The Bengali-speaking population in East Pakistan was more in number than all the linguistic groups, including the Punjabi-speaking majority in West Pakistan. But Bengali was very specific to this part, and alien to the West Pakistanis, and thus couldn't be the national language of the country. The leaders thought of common civilizational bonds among the constituent regions of the country as the sources of constructing national identity and national culture. To pursue the theme of separation further, they began to focus on Islamic civilization, the seven hundred years' worth of Muslim rule in India, Islam as a common religion, and Urdu as the language for the role it had played in Muslim identity and nationalism in undivided India.[10] The choice of Urdu as the national language and the continued emphasis on the two-nation theory in a climate of regional demands for identity, often pejoratively rejected as 'provincialism', provoked sharp reaction and turmoil in East Pakistan, when Jinnah, the founder of the country, announced it at the University of Dhaka.[11] The Bengali population in united Pakistan had the numerical majority. It would have been illogical, and against the spirit of democracy, to not recognize the Bengali language, so it was added as a second language. Urdu was spoken by the educated classes and understood even by ordinary people in every part of West Pakistan. Even in East Pakistan, there was an Urdu-speaking native and migrant minority from different parts of India. It was a medium of instruction in Balochistan, KP, Punjab, and parts of Sindh, and it was the language of the literati, culture, poetry, and religious and political discourses.

Never was the politics of culture independent of identity construction of the new state of Pakistan, as an Islamic, distinctive, and separate state, different from everything that defined India. In the first decade, we see a great emphasis on Muslim nationalism, and a projection of Muslim culture. There are pertinent questions regarding what this culture was: How could this be distinguished from Indian culture? Was it Islam, and therefore, universal, or geographic and confined to the culture of the regions that came to constitute Pakistan? Was it the culture of the Muslim conquerors of India—the Arabs, Turks, Persians, Afghans, and Moghuls—or of their subjects—the Muslim converts from Hinduism? Could there be a unified, singular Muslim culture to be attributed to Pakistan, or would it be a composite culture of the regions? What about the civilizational heritage of the Indus regions—Mohenjo-Daro, Harappa and Buddhist Gandhara inheritance? These have been difficult questions that Pakistanis have confronted over the decades, without finding a single answer. The view of what Pakistani culture is, can be, or ought to be, is generally a subject of individual intellectual, social, and political orientation. What is important to note is pluralism, both in the civilizational heritage of Pakistan and in the contemporary landscape of cultures, languages, religions, and ethnicities. Within them are just other layers of castes, sub-tribes, dialects, and regional variants of music, dance, arts, architecture, folklore, festivals, and customs.

Cultivating a national culture out of this diversity and pluralistic civilizational heritage was a challenge for the first generation of political leaders. Having won independence on the basis of Muslim nationalism and Islamic identity of the peoples constituting the new state, it was quite logical for them to promote commonness of religion. Islam was widely understood as civilizational bonding among Muslims of different ethnicities, regions, and linguistic groups. In this sense, they projected Islam as the unifying force. Ishtiaq Husain

Qureshi, a historian and prominent exponent of Muslim nationalism argued that, 'The homogeneity of all Islamic people is a most striking feature of the influence of Islam; a common idealism has not only affected their outlook on life, it has fashioned its very pattern.'[12] On this account, the 'uniformity of all Muslim people is far more striking than their diversity'.[13] This remains a common belief and political idea among religious parties and groups not only in Pakistan but also in other parts of the Muslim world. Islam being a common faith and universal among believers, creates a common community, the ummah, civilization, and core values, beliefs, attitudes, and practices that constitute Islamic culture.

In projecting Islam as the basis of Pakistani culture, the early ideologues of Pakistan had to address two contradictions. First was the question of ethnic and regional diversity. People in each region spoke different dialects and languages and had a strong sense of historical and ethnic identities that the demand for Pakistan and the independence movement overshadowed during the course of the struggle. An undeniable cultural fact of Pakistan is that the Muslims of different regions have diverse cultural streams. A Pashtun or Baloch Muslim has Pashtun or Baloch culture much like the Iranian, Arabs, Turks, and Afghan Muslims have their individual cultures; even within their national cultures, one may find sub-cultures of ethnic groups.

The second contradiction relates to the Muslim culture within the vast, more ancient, Indian or Hindu civilization. How much was, or is, the Muslim culture Muslim and how much it has been influenced by Hinduism is an important question that Islamic cultural puritans have to answer. Interestingly, the ideologues of Pakistani culture as Muslim culture, like Ishtiaq Husain Qureshi, concede the point that Muslim interaction with Hindus and Hinduism for centuries has produced a 'definite entity', the Indo-Muslim culture.[14] Never has there been a pure Islamic culture beyond common beliefs and common religious practices in diverse regions of Pakistan or anywhere else in the larger Muslim world. Every Muslim region, country or state, and regions within the states, have secular cultural institutions, traditions, and ways of life that generally conform to religious fundamentals but in many ways do not happen to be seeking authenticity from it that comes mainly from history and tradition. In the case of Muslim culture in India, Qureshi attempts to resolve this contradiction by suggesting that 'the core of this culture was Islam, and its outer fringe faded into the surrounding world of Hinduism. Its domain can be compared to a series of concentric circles, its intensity decreasing with the increase from the centre'.[15] The regional cultures of Pakistan have similar relationships with the centre of the Islamic belief system. How large is the Islamic cultural sphere and how narrow or wide are the regional variants is a very subjective question, and the answer can be equally subjective, depending on the personal preferences that, even within the same region, may be different for reasons of religiosity or secularity.

Emphasis on the Islamic culture of Pakistan, while ignoring other layers—ethnic diversity and local languages—of the constituent regions was a conscious and wilful effort to promote unity, solidarity and Muslim nationalism in the face of the challenges of diversity, divisions and political disarray. Those arguing the point that Islam was the central element of Pakistani culture were cognizant of the fact that without the religious bonds, the country would appear to be too diverse to build a unified nation and strong state, as distinct and separate from India. Islam was thus an ideological and cultural glue to hold all the regions together. This policy ignored two very significant streams of Pakistani culture: the influence of pre-Islamic ancient civilizations and the religions of the Indus areas, which is also known as 'ancient' Pakistan in the heritage of Mohenjo-Daro, Harappa, and Taxila. Sir Robert Eric Mortimer Wheeler, in fact, who discovered the Buddhist city at Taxila, thought it represented five thousand years of archaeological heritage of the new country. In archaeological rhetoric, he declared the country as 'five thousand years' old.[16] The Islamic culturists, in their zeal for cultivating an Islamic image of the state, made only footnoted references to the civilizational heritage of the Indus regions. This should have been the starting point for building a geographical and historical account of Pakistan as far as West Pakistan, the Pakistan of today, was concerned. The challenge of East Pakistan, now Bangladesh, was that it was very distinct and distant from the other part. The Pakistani nationalist discourse, therefore, fell back on the commonality of the faith.

There was another reason for turning a blind eye to the Indus heritage: the fanciful idea of relating the creation of Pakistan to the advent of Islam by Arab invaders. This fascination has continued through popular narratives and also by the Islamist historiography over the decades.[17] The regions that now constitute Pakistan were part of the Islamic Empire that began with the Arab invasion of Sindh. Since then, some regions were part of one or another Islamic empire in the making of which the Afghans, Persians, Turks, and then Moghuls played a great role.[18] Being a part of the Islamic Empire, the regions did acquire a distinctive demographic character as a majority on the outer Western fringe of the subcontinent, but it was no different in cultural diversity from the Muslims in the minority provinces of undivided India. How people lived their lives and what heritage they left for posterity in the Indus region was no way in conflict with the new ideal of Pakistan. Rather, it should have been regarded as a common heritage and should have figured in the national identity discourse. Unfortunately, it was not 'Islamic' and therefore did not fit into the institutional and intellectual frame of the early years of Pakistan.

The Islamic culturalists, who happened to be immigrants from India at the time of partition, intentionally overlooked the regional variants of cultures and languages. Perhaps they were not familiar enough with the regional histories, strong sense of local identities, powerful social structures embedded in caste, tribe, and feudalism and rich cultural traditions of art, music, folklore, and architecture. The ideal and the vision of Pakistan, as unique, new and to be constructed as a common Muslim homeland, pushed the regional cultures to the margins of imagination, as if they didn't exist. They were superficially discarded as 'inferior' and irrelevant to the construction of Pakistani identity and national culture. It was also the question of power, influence, and dominance of the Muslim immigrant nationalist intellectuals over the cultural narrative. Jameel Jalibi, rightly, laments the fact that the Muslim immigrant from India 'had within [him/her]self a sense of cultural superiority and forgot that such sense was a negative factor vis-à-vis the native population'.[19] But Jalibi himself commits the same error by implying that there was no Pakistan national culture to 'absorb the incoming population'.[20] However, he asserts that the culture of the immigrants and the local cultures could interact to evolve into a national culture of Pakistan.[21] Jalibi believes that a cultural synthesis of various regional cultural streams embedded in the values and traditions of Islam, Muslim civilization, and its creative energies by combining spiritual and material progress is possible and even desirable.[22] This syncretic argument is not unique to Pakistan. All non-Arab countries have evolved a national culture that has local elements embedded in the Islamic faith. It was not easy in a Pakistan still in search of an identity, possible meanings of its being and its destiny. The question the country faced, and continues to do so, is which local elements to emphasize and what will be the place of Islam in the mix of cultural streams.

In the early years, there also emerged a strong stream of Islamic literature with plots, heroes, battles, victories, and a glorification of Islamic empires and rulers. Nasim Hijazi was the most prominent of them. His presentation of selective episodes of Islamic history glorifying the Arabs, Turks and others in graphic heroic details became best sellers, and remain so today. Others, not as well known, followed the same tradition with two effects. First, the Muslims in Pakistan were imagined to be part of the Islamic imperial tradition of the past, and a consequence of its extension to the subcontinent. Second, it defined the cultural and historical alignment of Pakistan with the Islamic world, away from the Indian cultural and civilizational influences. The Muslim nationalist ideologues, literary figures, and cultural propagandists dominated the cultural politics of Pakistan in the first decade, pushing out all other narratives of the secular, regionalists, and progressive writers and intellectuals. They remained on the margins and thus insignificant, and survived amidst narrow bands of adherents and followers.

Authoritarianism, Modernity, and Culture

Pakistan is the imagination of the Muslim modernists of the late nineteenth century who became possessed with the idea of Muslim empowerment through the British educational system in colonial India and through political participation in the affairs of the new imperial state. The decline of the Muslim rule and its disintegration in the subcontinent was a constant reminder of great loss among the Muslim reformers, both religious as well as secular. Their dual reformism of religious thought and secular, political affairs were embedded in the realization that they were heirs of a great Islamic civilization. The modernists of both kinds were also optimistic about the revival of Muslim power; however, one wanted this revival by embracing the new forms of learning, while the other wanted to go back to the Islamic roots and fundamentals of Islam. This dual track of Muslim revival and identity has been one of the defining features of the politics of Pakistan.

Never is any culture fixed in time; it is a dynamic process and changes slowly with the advent of modernity—industrialization, urbanization, new technologies of production, and social changes with mass education. There is yet another aspect of modernity: political ideas, institutions, and processes embedded in liberal thoughts and ideologies. Every aspect of modernity has some influence over aspects of culture—thought process, life styles, and creative expression, from arts to writings. Just as industrialization in the West has changed many aspects of culture, modernity in Pakistan and other Muslim societies has, at least, introduced the seeds of cultural change among the more open, affluent, and educated sections of the society. Even at the popular level, the ideas of representation, rights, equality, and justice as well as a responsible and responsive government have gained deeper roots. What we can learn from the experience of other countries is that material conditions of prosperity and development change the ways people live their lives, look at the world, and imagine themselves and their society. In other words, cultural change happens with the material and ideational changes in society.

Modernity, colonial or postcolonial, has been a consequence of planned economic and social change. However, it appears to be relative, not definite, and never has it been consistent or uniform across the regions or in different spheres of national life. Like many postcolonial states, Pakistan has pursued economic development through the agency of the state as one of the primary goals. This has been motivated both by the political necessity of nation-building as well as to secure and strengthen the country from internal disorder and external threats. The instruments of modernity have been familiar, like development planning, industrialization, encouragement of private sector, building of infrastructure of energy and communication, and investing in social development projects.

Pakistan's record of economic development is mixed; it has had periods of high growth rate and then periods of stagnation and an economic downturn. Cumulatively, Pakistan's economy has grown at the average annual rate of 5% between 1947–2014.[23] The record of military governments in economic performance is comparatively better than that of the civilian regimes.[24] Political disorder, instability and chaotic economic conditions were some of the pull-factors that prompted the military to step in.[25] Therefore, the military governments had to perform better to ensure stability and growth for reasons of popular acceptance and legitimacy, as they lacked political and constitutional justification of their takeovers. The military governments projected their self-image as the 'guardian' of the state, devoted to strengthening, unifying, and developing Pakistan by getting rid of 'corrupt' and 'inefficient' politicians. Ayub Khan, the first military dictator (1958–69), taking over the country in the age when the role of the militaries in modernization and state-building was considered crucial, emerged as a reformer in the popular imagination.[26] The military-driven modernity, particularly during the Ayub regime, changed the focus of cultural politics from traditional Islam and Islamic identity to modernity, reformism, and progressive social change. In his scheme of things, a combination of economic development, political restructuring, and reformist legislation, like women's rights would create a modernist, progressive, and developmental identity of Pakistan.[27] He was critical of the traditional ulema who, in his view, had a limited vision of Islam as a set of rituals. He wanted Islam to be re-interpreted in the light of the modern age, as its essence was universal, for all times and to be harnessed for the good of state and society.[28]

The social and political conversation during the 'decade of development' changed from Islam as the marker of national identity and national culture to economic development, education, rights of women, family planning, and achieving prosperity. It was an official ideology of progressivism without the freedoms of democracy or liberal political thought. That has been a uniform template of modernity under the military regimes, with the difference of Zia ul-Haq that we will discuss later in the chapter. The authoritarianism of Ayub Khan was pervasive, from patronization of reformist religious interpretation to aligning the writers, intellectuals, and publicists with the 'reformism' of the military regime. Ambiguous as Ayub Khan was on many issues, he wanted to promote a secular national culture with economic development as its core value. He grossly ignored ethnic identities, cultural pluralism of the country, and the requirements of federal and democratic politics to hold the society and the country together. He acted according to a misconceived belief that modernity would take care of diversity and cultural pluralism, and in the process, would produce uniformity. Perhaps that could be possible, but then it would require deeper, wider and consistent modernity, over a long period of time.

After a decade in power, there seemed to be a realization within the military regime to explore the subject of national culture—what it was and what it could be and what was the best way to approach the national culture issue. It constituted a Standing Committee on National Culture in 1968 that was headed by the renowned poet and progressive thinker, Faiz Ahmad Faiz, with other prominent persons on it, to deliberate on the subject of national culture. The report of the Committee, known as the Faiz Committee Report on Culture, is the most solid work on the problem of national culture.[29] Before the Ayub government could review or open the report for a national debate, it ran into political troubles owing to mass agitation, and the General lost power within a year.

There were serious contradictions in the approach of Ayub Khan to the national culture issue. Having absolute control over the media and strict censorship rules in place, he suffocated freedom of thought and creativity, and stifled dissent. No national culture regardless of its roots and nature is possible without freedom of expression, fundamental rights, and pluralism. Ayub's approach to national culture was consistent with the colonial tradition rooted in hubris— that those in power knew what was good for the people, the nation, and the state. Like colonial modernity, authoritarian modernity introduced distortions and prevented a natural flow and development of national culture. Had it had time to consider and implement the recommendations of the Faiz Report, perhaps the official view of national culture might have changed. It was the next government, the first democratic government of the PPP, which brought the report back to life and began to recast Pakistan's national culture in the light of the recommendation of the report.

Composite National Culture

It seems that the regime type, at least in the case of Pakistan because of contestation over the national vision and identity of the country, has been a variable in fashioning politics of culture. In investigating cultural politics, it is also important to note that the state has assumed responsibility of the primary agency to shape culture, leading, influencing and even conflicting with the independent, private, and individualistic influences over what is and what ought to be the Pakistani culture. The first two regimes vacillated between Islam, and the two-nation theory, and modernity and ambiguous secularity. In both cases, there appears to be deliberate neglect of regional streams of culture, local identities, native languages, and ethnic identities. Until the end of the Ayub regime, we get a sense of cultural politics indirectly through various national policies like education, curriculum design, and economic development, as well as from the general politics of identity construction through state- and nation-building.

With the inauguration of the first democratic regime of the PPP (1971–77), we get a new vision of 'new Pakistan' which articulated a new cultural policy that had a different focus from the past, on the cultures, identities, and heritage of the constituent regions. The new people's government recognized ethnic pluralism and cultural diversity. While the provinces have a majority ethnic identity, they all have minority ethnic groups that speak different languages and have sub-identities and cultures of their own. One of the most remarkable social facts of Pakistan is that the cultural boundaries among the provinces are diffused, and the regions have interspersed linguistic and cultural groups within them. It is because of historical continuities and multifaceted interdependencies that have developed over the centuries under various empires. Even under local kingdoms, the borders among communities remained open and widely porous for migration, commerce, and ethnic intermingling. Pakistani cities and provinces, at large, represent mixed ethnicities and languages—a diversity within diversity or dynamic cultural pluralism. In the first quarter of a century of existence, this aspect of Pakistani culture became overshadowed by the political construction of cultural commonality of Islam and the requirement of a national language, Urdu being the convenient choice.

Under the new regime, the idiom of political dialogue changed from authenticity to questioning. The democratic movement against Ayub Khan had started with the questioning of development, democracy, distribution of rewards, equality, equity, and even security. Interestingly, Ayub's relative success in modernization created a space for critical thinking among the new generation, the youth that had the benefit of college education. The decade of the sixties was a critical decade of youth rebellion that explored different ideological alternatives, debated change, revolutions, Islam, and democracy. The anti-Ayub movement was initiated, created, and led by the college going young men and women—not by the political class as it is commonly believed.[30] They effectively exploited the youth awakening and general resentment against the political establishment, and used them for the movement demanding democracy. Bhutto did better than others, and had a much deeper impact on the youth than any other leader or political party.[31] Since the new regime had come into power as a political consequence of a popular democratic movement and rose out of a sense of empowerment of common people, it wanted its politics of 'new Pakistan' to reflect their ethos, values, and attitudes.

Bhutto was a master of populist politics, a true man of the masses, and a great communicator. He enthralled the crowd by his rhetoric, promises, and radical reforms of society. Never in history, had anybody exploited the myth of the common man as well as Bhutto. Bhutto had, perhaps, learnt this art from how other leaders, in Europe and the United States, had done. In his popular conversation and public demeanour, he adopted popular culture—the culture of the people. Actually, he gave respect and recognition to popular culture; no other leader in Pakistan's history had done this before. He spoke in their idiom, presented himself as an idol, a hero, and as a man of courage and vision working hard to defeat the forces of evil represented by the upper classes. This was a reflection of popular imagination of a 'hero' depicted in the Punjabi cinema of that age.

Bhutto changed from Western dress to donning the dress of the common man—shalwar kameez. He popularized shalwar kameez as the 'awami libas' (people's dress). The middle class and the upper class elites also began to change their dressing style. There was now a recognition of the national dress, which has become popular in every part of the country. Beyond populist politics, Bhutto launched too many initiatives to establish new institutions, from higher education—including a progressive, forward-looking education policy—to cultural institutions. He even persuaded Faiz Ahmad Faiz, the author of the Faiz Culture Report, to head the National Council of the Arts and implement the ideas he had articulated about Pakistan's national culture.[32]

Faiz's task, in writing the report was to 'ascertain whether as a nation, we have a cultural identity or not'.[33] His underlying finding is that 'our popular culture is in [actuality] the very basis of our national culture. The structure of the national culture can be erected on these foundations'.[34] Faiz theorizes culture as 'the whole way of life of a specific human group or society' including 'ideological and material elements', values and social practices. Faiz's conceptualization of culture is a departure from the essentialist view of Pakistani culture as purely Islamic. He brings into the culture debate and politics, the issues of history, heritage, society, humans, geography, knowledge, and issues of change and transformation. He argues:

> Since every culture relates to a specific human society and since every human society lives in time and space, every culture must be both historical and territorial, although its ideological components may include extra-territorial and supra-temporal elements. For instance, Muslim societies, in spite of racial, linguistic, and other differences, have many cultural traits in common.[35]

Based on elements of history and territory, there is another departure in the conceptualization of culture that Faiz makes from the conventional idea of Pakistani culture as Indo-Islamic . In his view, the areas that now comprise Pakistan have been on the periphery of the centre of Muslim empires in India. In the heartland of India, the Muslim high culture flourished through Arabic, Persian, and Urdu, and also through the Muslim production of knowledge and interacting, mixing and assimilating with the Indian civilization. There it acquired a distinctive feature of Indo-Islamic identity that comprised the inner core of Islam, tempered by the concentric layers of local cultures with a heavy imprint of the Indian social customs. Muslim culture in India expressed itself through arts, music, literary traditions, architecture, and the development of the Urdu language, which S.M. Ikram terms as 'a result of Hindu-Muslim collaboration, and a symbol, indeed a powerful instrument, of Hindu-Muslim unity'.[36] As the competitive quests for identity, struggle for power and recognition, and Muslim nationalism gained strength, the status of Urdu changed from non-communal language to becoming associated with the Muslim identity. Deplorably, even a leader with the stature of Mahatma Gandhi thought of Urdu as a Muslim language. He said, 'Urdu was developed by the Muslim Kings. It is for the Muslims to develop it, if they so desire,'[37] It seems that the Muslim leaders demanding a separate state of Pakistan considered Urdu as one of their remarkable identity markers. After partition, the country embraced Urdu as a national language. It has flourished in the periphery of the former centre of the Muslim empires, the regions of the Indus, as a lingua franca. The regional languages and their literary traditions have influenced the idiom, diction, and styles of Urdu prose, fiction, poetry, and literature.

The anthropological, linguistic, social, territorial, and historical features of the regions of Pakistan have historically occupied a unique position. Geographical contiguity with Central and West Asia has transformed the culture and social institutions of this region as an extension of the Muslim empires for one and a half millennium. The cultural streams of the Muslim empires have been as varied and distinctive, however, as the regions of the empire builders. It was not just the Islamic faith—common among all of them—but also the wide range of their customs, languages, traditions, aesthetic tastes in poetry, literature, and architecture that influenced the present-day regions of Pakistan. Their influences went much deeper into the Indian heartland, as the culture of the rulers developed around the centres of power: the courts. The impact of their culture over the present-day regions of Pakistan was no less strong, stable, and transformative. This is evident from the Muslim majority character of the regions, and sub-cultures and traditions bearing striking similarity to the adjacent Muslim countries of Afghanistan, Iran, Central Asia, and the Arab lands.

Throughout history, the regions of Pakistan have been on yet another periphery—that of mainland India. There may be a question of a stable and clearly discernible centre of India, which kept shifting from one empire builder to another, whether Hindu, Muslim, or British, but in every case, the regions of Pakistan, with a deepening Muslim character from seventh century onward, found themselves on the geographic and political margins. The local dynamics of power and power relationships with the larger empires weighed-in heavily in favour of semi-autonomous local rulers. We see this trend growing greater with the fragmentation of the Moghul Empire. When the centre was not able to hold itself together and was weak, the rulers on the periphery of India carved out their own pre-states or kingdoms. The British power recognized them, and entered into diplomatic and political relations with tribes and states of Balochistan, Sindh, Bahawalpur, and the Punjab, which included KP. There is an oft-debated question: was it the expansionist logic of the imperial rule in India or the defence of the Indian Empire against the Russian designs in Afghanistan—the outer periphery of defence or the buffer—that led the British to annex the states that now constitute Pakistan? Perhaps, neither of the two motives was exclusive. At the end, the result was the same: annexation and extension of imperial rule over the regions of present-day Pakistan.[38] Coming late into the empire, these regions found themselves on the periphery, and integrated into the colonial economy, politics, and modernity quite late. The impact of colonial modernity—whether positive or culturally subversive—was weaker in this part than in the heartland of India.

The geographical character as a periphery of the Moghul empire, and then of the British Raj, protected regional cultures, languages, and customs and traditions, like other geographic peripheries of any other empires. Even Urdu, a language of central India and an identity marker of Muslim nationalism, had a much weaker presence in the constituent regions of Pakistan.[39] The local cultures—folklore, local music, poetry in native languages, festivals and theatre, and other art forms, were significantly indigenous. Urdu, and before it Persian, were the languages of the elites, not of the common man, but even elites used these languages as a vehicle of literary and political conversation, not as the languages of daily or market communication.

Before Urdu was adopted as the national language of Pakistan, the regions were multi-lingual, a melting pot of cultures, tongues and diversity, and had been in a slow process of assimilation for centuries. However, with the winning of sovereignty and territorial unity as a new state and nation, the process of national culture and consciousness began to grow faster. State and its culture policies, but mainly the ideology and vision of a particular regime in power, played a main role in determining the tenor and spirit of cultural politics. The Bhutto regime brought the regional cultures back into the national mainstream. No other government had done it, except paying lip-service to regional languages and cultures. On his part, it was a genuine and sincere effort to think of national culture as inclusive of the regional cultures. Bhutto's politics and policies changed the narrative of national culture as pluralistic, diverse, and multi-ethnic. Before Bhutto, this perspective existed in the periphery; he brought it to the centre.

Zia Regime and Islamization Politics

The military and civilian regimes have been dialectically opposites of each other on every issue fundamental to the character of the state and society. They have essentially diverged in ethos, values, vision, ideology, constitutionalism, democracy, and state-society relations. The military regimes have trashed the constitutions, disfigured it to suit the personal interests of the dictators, and made all state institutions subservient to their will. In their defence is the invoked emergency argument—state decline, on account of bad politics, bad politicians, and bad governance. They projected their image as reformists, protectors, guardians, and patriots who responded to the calling of the motherland to save it from 'rapacious' politicians.

Their reformism reoriented the state from a constitutional-democratic framework to dictatorship with the military establishment at its back. Like every dictator, they personalized and centralized power, and with that, they changed the direction of politics to create a favourable political climate for their survival.

Zia ul-Haq, the leader of the third martial law of the country (1977–88), worked with the same template, as did the other three, but he took a different direction. He adopted the agenda of political Islam, calling it the ideology of Pakistan, and presented himself as the 'defender' of the faith. After reneging on his promise of holding elections within ninety days that he made to the nation at the time of takeover, he began introducing Islamization.[40] He was able to garner the support of the religious parties and conservative religious constituency that had been on the forefront of agitation against Zulfikar Ali Bhutto. He used state patronage to bring the anti-PPP social and political coalition under his control. Unabashedly, he hijacked the agenda of Nizam-i-Mustafa (Islamic system) of the religious parties that were at the forefront of the anti-Bhutto agitation launched by the PNA in 1977. He interpreted the creation of Pakistan as a struggle for founding an Islamic state.[41]

The state patronage of political Islam coincided with the uprising in Afghanistan and the formation of the Mujahedeen movement against the communist regime in Kabul. The Soviet intervention in Afghanistan generated the second wave of the Cold War that also brought a conservative Republican President, Ronald Reagan, into the White House. The military regime in Pakistan supported the Afghan Mujahedeen and allowed the religious parties to play a vital role in the Afghan Jihad. The United States, sensing an opportunity to bleed the Soviet Union, extended support and patronage to Zia ul-Haq for its larger strategic purpose of pulling the 'evil empire' down. In short, domestic, regional, and international developments during the decade of Zia (1977–88) pushed Pakistan into a new culture of religious puritanism, Jihad, and selective implementation of Islamic laws.[42] The cultural idiom during this period changed from free-wheeling cultural pluralism to religious dogmatism, conformity, authenticity, and obscurantism. Zia pushed the society into a climate of intolerance of diversity and suppression of progressive thoughts and ideals.

The regime promoted fundamentalist Islamic culture and identity. The state-controlled media and intellectuals promoted Islamic values and a conservative vision of the society. The official orientation of the state under Zia was toward the Wahhabi brand of Islam, inspired by Saudi Arabia and the Gulf states. They were critical supporters of Jihad in Afghanistan through the agency of Pakistan and have played a critical role in expanding the network of a Wahhabi-inspired madrassa network in Pakistan. There was a wilful attempt to marginalize the Indo-Islamic culture, popular Islam, the Persian influence, and regional cultures of the country.

The imposition of fundamentalist culture and values in the ideological image of Islamic orthodoxy appeared to be divorced from the traditional spirit and natural diversity of the Pakistani society. The undemocratic and divisive character of the regime provoked multiple streams of passive, and sometimes active, resistance. Since political means of resistance were few and suppressed, it was expressed through the idiom of poetry in Urdu and the regional languages.[43] The progressive writers, poets, and intellectuals contributed to a new genre of literature of resistance.[44] Women, often seen as oppressed and passive, organized open and persistent resistance under the Women Action Forum to protest against inequality and discrimination under the Islamic laws imposed by the Zia regime.[45] Similarly, ethnic Sindhis rose up against the regime in the rural areas of Sindh for the restoration of democracy. Never had rural Sindh seen such a massive uprising against Zia or any other regime.[46]

Zia's eleven year dictatorship produced a counter-culture of questioning, critical thinking, and challenging of the social and political forces aligned with him, including the intellectual thought and ideological foundations of his dictatorship. The anti-Zia counter-culture has endured many political changes over the past twenty-nine years. The dominant theme of the counter-culture is resistance against military regimes. The literature of resistance, which is an old tradition of intelligentsia dating back to opposition to the colonial rule, supports democracy and fundamental rights. It uses the language of emancipation of individual, people, and the nation.[47] The ideal appears to be a just, fair, and good society where the poor get their rights and the society is free of oppression, control, and illegitimate rule by the military. The general tenor of resistance is progressive change, reform, and giving voice to the subaltern. It exposes brutality and contradictions of the Zia regime, and attributes the current challenges faced by the society—extremism, sectarianism, terrorism, Jihadism, drugs, and Kalashnikov culture—to the Zia rule and his policies. On the other hand, there is a celebration of martyrs of democracy, of heroes that were tortured, humiliated, thrown out of jobs, and some given lashes on the back for expressing themselves as being against the imposition of military rule.

Democratic Pluralism

In large part, it was the mythology of resistance along with a long and hard struggle for the restoration of democracy and the ideal of constitutional politics that the harshest of the military rule got buried with General Zia in August 1988. In a way, it was the revenge of history that Benazir Bhutto, daughter of the prime minister Z.A. Bhutto (whom Zia had deposed and hanged) succeeded him. Although it was an incomplete and partial transfer of power to a civilian leader and still under the dense shadow of the legacies of military rule, Benazir attempted to revive the image of her father and the ideology of her party. However, she was cautious, restrained, and recognized the institutional limits on her power. In her first term (1988–90), she adopted a strategy of political survival, and attempted to rebuild the popular base of her party that had been the target of Zia's persecution.

In her second term in office (1993–96), Benazir began to resurrect the vision of her party. It was a hard task to make it relevant to the vastly changed national, political, and social climate under the influence of jihad in Afghanistan and state-driven Islamization in the country. In a bold fashion, her government authored a new cultural policy, only the second documented one in Pakistan's history, to revive the popular culture which, it argued, had suffered as a result of the imposition of 'totalitarian regimes in Pakistan which deny the wider participation of the people in shaping their social, cultural, and political institutions'.[48] It lists the sufferings of the country under the military rule as follows: 'The culture of tolerance was substituted with the culture of hatred, the legacy of mystical liberalism was allowed to be consumed by sectarian fanaticism, the people [sic] resolve to live together was poisoned with uncertainty and confusion, the spirit of Muslim culture was bartered for the culture of religious indoctrination, and the historical experience of Pakistani nation was tarnished with the blood of Clio.'[49]

This critique by the PPP of the military regime, and particularly of the Zia era, represents a growing consensus in the country on two points. First, the military regimes have cumulatively damaged the political institutions, democracy, national harmony, and preservation and promotion of true national culture that is rooted in the histories, identities, and languages of the people of Pakistan. Second, the Zia era was a disaster not only for destroying democracy and its natural flowering but also for sowing the seeds of religious extremism, polarization, and promoting a Jihadist culture. With all the flaws that democratic parties have—dynastic rule, corruption, and weak governing capacity—they are connected with the people and regions they represent. They believe and act according to unarticulated principles of democratic pluralism, which is a pragmatic requirement of their politics more than an ideology, as it gives each group and party the freedom to pursue its political agenda. Every form of genuine democratic politics promoted pluralism by recognizing the rights of others, while authoritarianism constrains pluralism because of its strategic need for centrality, dominance of a single leader or party, and artificial means of national unity—which is often an assertion of centralized authority.

With each democratic transition, after the end of military rule, the political parties have struggled to revive democratic pluralism. Some of the legacies, particularly relating to the selective enforcement of Islamic law, religious polarization, sectarianism, and militancy have been quite enduring and troublesome. Even on developing policies to deal with these troubling issues, they have moved with consensus, dialogue, and general understanding with a spirit of accommodation.[50] No cultural plurality is likely to emerge or sustain itself in the absence of political pluralism—the two are intertwined, as they reinforce and support development of each other. Since the third democratic transition in 2008, the political climate for dissent, debate, and difference has vastly improved. Comparatively, even under military regimes, Pakistan has remained relatively a far freer society than any comparable Muslim or developing, third world, state could be. The free spirit of its society has blossomed with rich colours of ethnic diversity and expressions of regional particularism in arts, culture, and indeed, diverging views of power and politics under the democratic regimes. The immature Pakistani nationalists may view cultural and political pluralism as a 'threat' to national unity, as they have often done, driven by narrow views of nation, state, and nationalism. But in our view, cultural diversity and pluralism present a rich heritage of Pakistan that needs to be protected, projected, and used in the narrative of Pakistani nationhood. An undeniable historical fact is that it is the people with the strength of their cultures and values who define a national culture; it is not the state or political authority at the top that can do it. If it does, as it has been done in Pakistan, it would only subvert a natural development of culture.

Uxi Mufti, the founding director of the Lok Virsa (Folklore Institute) and a prominent exponent of diversity and celebration of regional and local cultures, argues that, 'Pakistan is a living museum. Pakistan's culture is what the people are. You cannot enforce one culture.' Another important point he raises about the defining character of Pakistani culture, which he believes is an oral tradition, is that the 'blind men' in power have seldom seen or appreciated it.[51] This is one of the powerful views of Pakistani culture that others might view quite differently. The essential dichotomy is between those who wish to promote a national culture, above and out of the context of the cultures of the people of all the regions that form Pakistan using the symbolism of Islam, Islamic history, and the myth of Pakistan's ideology, and those who see the project of a singular national culture as subversive, unnatural, and ahistorical. They would rather like to see cultures of Pakistan—each unique in its own historical and sociological context—as authentic, equal in worth, and an essential part of the heritage of Pakistan.

The Role of Cultural Institutions

Pakistan has multiple cultural institutions that provide a forum for artists, poets, performing arts, and celebration of regional and national culture. The most important one is the Pakistan National Council of the Arts (PNCA) with the stated objective of fostering 'a clear sense of purpose in national identity and cohesion based on belief and tradition.'[52] This vision is self-contradictory, but it gives a good idea of what cultural politics the central authorities of Pakistan have been pursuing. Beliefs and traditions are two very separate and distinctive spheres of life, unless one makes a bold claim and assumes that tradition is shaped by belief system alone. As it is evident from the cultural history of the subcontinent, and other regions, local cultural traditions have survived mass conversions to new religions. Also, the issue of cohesion and national identity might be elusive goals if one enforces a hegemonic view of national culture, as all nationalists tend to do. This might amount to marginalisation and suffocation of historical, traditional, and people-centred cultures. There is now a broader recognition among the intellectual and political classes that regional cultures form the cluster that represent shades of Pakistani culture. This realization has grown more with the end of the Zia era and the restoration of democracy. It is interesting to note that all the formal cultural institutions that exist today and promote many art-forms were established during the first democratic government of Pakistan, in 1971–77. We see a clear interest among the democratic political parties in promoting local cultures that draws them closer to the people.

The Pakistan National Council of the Arts (PNCA) is the premier institution that was established in 1973. It promotes all arts and cultural forms through training, and grooming to holding exhibitions and performing events in various cities of the country. Besides PNCA, each province has cultural, literary, and linguistic academies that promote regional cultures, including the production of literature in regional languages, organizing annual festivals, and patronizing the artists and promoting their works.[53] Every region and ethnic group has a culture day that serves as an occasion for celebrating culture as well as showcasing the regional culture to the rest of the country and the world. Every province and region of Pakistan has cultural institutions on the patterns of PNCA and the National Academy of Letters. The latter funds literary regional organizations and also provides a national forum for the promotion and recognition of regional literatures, writers, and their welfare.[54] The performance of regional institutions varies from province to province. There is an extensive infrastructure of official cultural institutions in place but it remains underutilized because of bureaucratic inertia and political patronage in the appointment to institutional heads.

Two national institutions, Radio Pakistan (1947) and Pakistan Television (1964) have played a critical role in the promotion of Urdu and creation of a national consciousness among the people of different regions. They are the most effective tools in the hands of the elites at the centre, to not only propagate their policies, but also determine the national discourses on culture, politics, security, and national security. At least for fifty years, these two institutions have had complete monopoly over electronically transmitted mass communication. They were the only 'reliable' means of information, news, and entertainment for people. Their outreach has been remarkably national in scope, particularly that of Radio Pakistan with its stations and relaying facilities throughout the country. Both have been leaders and trendsetters in news and entertainment, particularly in the promotion of drama and music of all regions of the country.[55] While the emergence of hundreds of commercial radio and television stations owned and run by private entrepreneurs have broken their monopoly, the two still remain popular among the conservative sections of the society because of family-oriented nature of the programmes they run. The media has expanded rapidly, and is undergoing a revolutionary transformation with mobile radio and television platforms and direct satellites-to-home broadcasting. With the society opening up to the world, the cultural influences may not necessarily remain confined to the national cultural streams.[56] At the end, the Pakistani culture will be what the people make of it, how they live their lives, and whether or not they preserve their heritage and take pride in it. The national culture and social values in an age of globalization are subject to some change in which the dialectical forces of tradition, modernity, and new modes of living and thinking will have a significant bearing on producing 'creative' cultural pluralism.[57]

The big question is how traditional institutions that have sustained multiple streams of Pakistani culture over the centuries, and still continue to do so, are going to remain unaffected, or even rendered untenable, in the face of national and global media that is approaching individuals, households, communities, and the common social and cultural spaces. So far, the institutions of shrines—thousands of these—in every part of the country have sustained and recreated the rich colours of Pakistani culture through annual festivals, called *urs* (commemoration of the death of saints). People, regardless of faith, ethnicity or region, throng to these festivals and celebrate their cultures. It would be misleading to believe that *urs* is exclusively a religious rite, as might be the case for religious devotees, but for the ordinary folk, it is the glamour of a rich culture that attracts them.[58] The festivals generally known as *melas*, also held throughout the country, are not necessarily around the shrines; they have historical roots in the local communities, like Shandur Polo *mela* in Gilgit-Baltistan and Sibi *mela* in Balochistan. The *melas* might be local community affairs or regional and national in scope, but all of them have some common strands of popular culture. Regional and local theatre groups, music, dance, poetic sessions, drama, and display of animals, horse racing, variety of foods, and local sports competitions are common themes. The *melas* have strong folk roots, histories, and are owned by the people in which men, women, and children participate.[59]

There is a new form of festivals that have become popular among the urban, literate and the emerging middle-classes of Pakistan—the literature festivals. These are also reflective of growing modernity, globalisation, and the expansion of media from print to electronic. Ameena Saiyid and Asif Farrukhi, for example, founded the Karachi Literature Festival (KLF) in 2010 under the auspices of the Oxford

University Press (OUP), which has grown from modest attendance of 5,000 persons in the inaugural one, to 200,000 in 2017.[60] Building on the success of the KLF, the OUP launched the Islamabad Literature Festival (ILF) in 2013 and the Children Literature Festivals. The festivals bring together noted scholars, academicians, writers, artists, poets, performers, and civil society activists together. They serve as occasions to interact with national and international authors, the launching of books, and keynote speeches by the high achievers in any of the major fields of arts and humanities. Besides, they connect the public, the youth in particular, from colleges and universities, with the most significant literary works, and offer a forum for engaging on issues of national importance among the experts. The success of KLF has inspired others to found similar festivals in Lahore, Hyderabad, and in other cities of the country. The literature festivals and their growing popularity represents a modern cultural form of Pakistan. However, one cannot escape the impression of class-orientation, as the dialogue, celebration of arts and literary works and general intellectual engagement on cultural, political, and social issues represent tastes, cultural sensitivities, and literary pursuits of the urban, middle class sections of the elites. The festivals may grow more popular roots with more use of the Urdu language and accessibility to the general public through the electronic media.

Pakistani theatre groups and musical conferences at regional and national levels are much closer to the culture and heritage of the people of Pakistan. Their role in entertaining common people and sustaining folk and classical music in Pakistan is well-recognized. Hayat Ahmad Khan founded the Pakistan Music Conference in 1959 with the objective of promoting classical music. The Conference has been an annual affair since then, held regularly. It also organizes monthly events with specific focus on a particular form of music or dance. It can be credited with introducing a large number of famous Pakistani singers in all musical genres and dancers from classical to modern.[61] All the big names, the maestros of classical music, have performed at the PMC. There are similar conferences regularly organized in Karachi, Islamabad, and regional ones in other places.

Theatre is one of the common strands of arts and culture shared by the rural, common folks, and the urban literate populations of Pakistan. In recent decades, the theatre has become increasingly popular for reasons of commercial viability on account of expanding the middle class and the local, social relevance of the entertainment it provides. This is one of the traditional cultural institutions that has remained alive and close to the people of all classes. In recent decades, in addition to preserving arts and culture of the society, theatre has acquired a social and political dimension with a message of peace, harmony and tolerance, human rights and gender equality.[62] Not even the rise of electronic media and the popularity of soap operas and drama serials, one of the major evening entertainments of Pakistani society, have eclipsed stage theatre, performing live before the audience.[63] Many of the old traditions and institutions, like *chopal, thara, dera, autaak* and *baithak* (different vernacular names for gatherings of a local community) forms of social interactions have survived modernity.[64] The content of social conversation has changed from generally local, mundane issues to national politics, religion, and conflicts.

Culture is one of the defining elements of national identity, as it attempts to answer a fundamental question: who and what we are. Culture is shaped by history, traditions, customs, forms of learning, heritage, economy, and politics, and more importantly, by the cultural lives of the diverse regions of the country. In view of such a mixture of influences of so many constituent regions, Pakistani culture must be conceived as diverse and inclusive of multiple art traditions, folk heritage, and native languages. While Islam is the foundation, and the 'cornerstone' of Pakistani culture, we must not use it 'to stamp out or downplay all other influences'.[65]

Notes

1. Stephen J. Whitfield, *The Culture of the Cold War* (Baltimore, London W: The Johns Hopkins University Press, 1996); Andrew N. Rubin, *Archives of Authority: Empire, Culture and the Cold War* (Princeton, London: Princeton University Press, 2012).

2. Edward W. Said, *Culture and Imperialism: Theories of Imperialism from Adam Smith to Lenin* (New York: Alfred A. Knopf, 1993).

3. Rosamund Billington, 'Culture and Imperialism' *Culture and Society* (London: Palgrave Macmillan, 1991), 64–80.

4. A. L. Basham, *The Wonder that was India* (3rd edn. London: Sidgwick & Jackson, 1967).

5. Thomas Babington Macaulay, Baron (1800–1859), *Miscellaneous Writings and Speeches*, 4. <http://www.gutenberg.org/etext/2170>.

6. Suresh Ghosh, 'Bentinck, Macaulay and the Introduction of English Education in India' *History of Education* 24 (1995), 17.

7. 'In one point I fully agree with the gentlemen to whose general views I am opposed. I feel with them that it is impossible for us, with our limited means, to attempt to educate the body of the people. We must at present do our best to form a class who may be interpreters between us and the millions whom we govern—a class of persons Indian in blood and color, but English in tastes, in opinions, in morals, and in intellect. To that class we may leave it to refine the vernacular dialects of the country, to enrich those dialects with terms of science borrowed from the Western nomenclature, and to render them by degrees fit vehicles for conveying knowledge to the great mass of the population.' Macaulay's 'Minute on Education,' Feb. 2, 1835 can be seen at Columbia University, New York Website. <http://www.columbia.edu/itc/mealac/pritchett/00generallinks/macaulay/txt_minute_education_1835.html.> Accessed March 13, 2017.

8. Lawrence E. Harrison and Samuel P. Huntington, eds, *Culture Matters* (New York: Basic Books, 2000). All chapters touch on this subject.

9. Samuel P. Huntington, 'Cultures Count' in Ibid., xiv.

10. Dildar Ali Farman Fatehpuri, *History of Pakistan Movement and Language Controversy* (Karachi: Karachi University Press, 2001),140–217.

11. Javed Iqbal, 'The Separation of East-Pakistan: Analyzing the Causes and Fixing the Responsibility' *Pakistan Journal of History and Culture* 29/2 (2008).

12. Ishtiaq Husain Qureshi, *The Pakistani Way of Life* (Karachi: Royal Book Company, 1988), 5.

13. Ibid.

14. Ibid., 11.

15. Ibid.

16. Robert Eric Mortimer Wheeler, *Five Thousand Years of Pakistan: An Archaeological Outline* (Karachi: Royal Book Company, 1992).

17. Farhan Ahmed Shah, 'Of Textbooks, Extremism and Mohammed bin Qasim' *Daily Times,* (January 11, 2014); Nadeem F. Paracha, 'The First Pakistani?' *Dawn,* (April 12, 2015).

18. On this debate, see: Dr Syed Abdullah, *Culture Ka Masla* [Discourse on Culture], (Lahore: Sange-e-Meel Publications, 2001), 57–70.

19. Jameel Jalibi, *Pakistan: The Identity of Culture*, (Karachi: Royal Book, 1984), 90.

20. Ibid., 87.

21. Ibid.

22. Ibid., 131–4, 196.

23. Rashid Amjad, 'The Challenges of a Resilient Economy' in Isthtiaq Ahmad and Adnan Rafiq, eds. *Pakistan's Democratic Transition: Change and Persistence* (London and New York: Routledge, 2017), 193.

24. The military-led governments have performed better. See: Ibid., 193–5.

25. Eric A. Nordlinger, *Soldiers in Politics: Military Coups and Governments* (Englewood Cliffs, NJ: Prentice-Hall, 1977).

26. John Asher Johnson, *Role of the Military in Underdeveloped Countries*, (Princeton: Princeton University Press, 2015); Henry Bienen, 'Armed Forces and National Modernization: Continuing the Debate', *Comparative Politics* 16, no. 1 (1983): 1–16; Ashley J. Tellis and Michael Wills, *Military Modernization in an Era of Uncertainty* (Seattle: National Bureau of Asian Research, 2005).

27. Mohammad Ayub Khan, *Friends, Not Masters: A Political Autobiography*, (New York: Oxford University Press, 1967).

28. Muhammad Qasim Zaman, 'Islamic Modernism and the Sharia in Pakistan' *Occasional Papers*, 8, (Yale Law School Legal Scholarship Repository, Yale Law School, 2014), 9–14.

29. Ahmad Salim and Humaira Ishfaq, eds. *Faiz, Folk Heritage and Problems of Culture* (Islamabad and Lahore: Lok Virsa and Sang-e-Meel Publications, 2013), 24–30.

30. Justen Bellingham, 'The 1968–9 Pakistan Revolution: A Students' and Workers' Popular Uprising' *Marxist Left Review* 12 (Winter 2016). Accessed 13 March 2017. <http://marxistleftreview.org/index.php/no-12-winter-2016/132-the-1968-9-pakistan-revolution-a-students-and-workers-popular-uprising>.

31. Faisal Sayani, 'Bhutto and the NSF (National Students Federation)' *The Friday Times,* (January 27, 2017).

32. Ahmad Salim, *Faiz, Folk Heritage and Problems of Culture*, op.cit.

33. Ibid., 25.
34. Ibid., 26.
35. Ibid., 38.
36. S.M. Ikram, 'Introduction' *The Cultural Heritage of Pakistan* S.M. Ikram and Percival Spear eds. (Karachi: Oxford University Press, 1955), ii.
37. S.M. Ikram refers to a session of Hindi Sahitya Sammelan at Nagpur in 1940. Ibid.
38. Richard Isaac Bruce, *The Forward Policy and its Results: Or Thirty-Five Years' Work Amongst the Tribes on our North-Western Frontier of India* (Whitefish, MT: Kessinger Publishing, LLC, 2010); Andrew J. Major, *Return to Empire: Punjab under the Sikhs and British in the Mid-Nineteenth Century*, (New Delhi: Sterling Publishers Private Limited, 1996).
39. Tariq Rahman, *Language and Politics in Pakistan* (Karachi: Oxford University Press, 1996).
40. Charles H. Kennedy, 'Islamization and Legal Reform in Pakistan, 1979–1989' *Pacific Affairs* 63/1 (1990), 62–77; Shahid Javed Burki, 'Pakistan under Zia, 1977–1988' *Asian Survey* 28/10 (1988), 1082–1100; John L. Esposito, 'Islamization: Religion and Politics in Pakistan' *The Muslim World* 72/3–4 (1982),197–223.
41. Here is one of the statements of Zia ul-Haq: 'Pakistan which was created in the name of Islam will continue to survive only if it sticks to Islam. That is why I consider the introduction of [an] Islamic system as an essential prerequisite for the country.' Ian Talbot, *Pakistan: A Modern History* (New York: St. Martin's Press, 1998), 251.
42. Charles H. Kennedy, 'Islamization and Legal Reform in Pakistan, 1979–1989' *Pacific Affairs* 63/1 (1990), 62–77.
43. Rashid Amjad, ed. *Mazahamati Adab, Urdu* (Islamabad: Pakistan Academy of Literature, 1995).
44. Hafizur Rehman, ed. *Resistance Literature* (Islamabad: Pakistan Academy of Letters, 2010).
45. Shahnaz Rouse, 'Women's Movement in Pakistan: State, Class, Gender' in Kamala Visweswaran ed. *Perspectives on Modern South Asia: A Reader in Culture, History, and Representation*, (Malden, Massachusetts and Oxford: Wiley-Blackwell, 2011), 321–7; Farhat Haq, 'Women, Islam and the State in Pakistan' *The Muslim World* 86/2 (1996), 158–75; Shehrbano Zia, 'The Reinvention of Feminism in Pakistan' *Feminist Review* 91/1 (2009), 29–46.
46. Mumtaz Ahmad, 'The Crescent and the Sword: Islam, the Military, and Political Legitimacy in Pakistan, 1977–1985' *The Middle East Journal* 10/1 (1996),

372–86; Tariq Ali, 'Movement for the Restoration of Democracy in Pakistan' *India International Centre Quarterly* 11/1 (March 1984), 57–69.

47. Hafizur Rehman, op.cit.

48. *The Cultural Policy of Pakistan* (Islamabad: National Commission on History & Culture, Ministry of Culture, Sports & Tourism, Government of Pakistan, 1995), 11.

49. Ibid.

50. The examples are: Charter of Democracy, National Action Plan against terrorism and terrorist groups, military courts—though under some influence from the security establishment—and recognizing the right of the majority party to rule in the province or the centre.

51. Author's interview with Uxi Mufti, Islamabad, January 22, 2017.

52. <http://www.pnca.org.pk/aim-objectives-pnca>. Accessed on November 30, 2016.

53. 'Heritage: Traditional Music, Dance mark Baloch Culture Day' *The Express Tribune,* (March 3, 2013), <https://tribune.com.pk/story/515057/heritage-traditional-music-dance-mark-baloch-culture-day/> Accessed March 12, 2017..

54. See, Pakistan Academy of Letters, <http://www.pal.gov.pk> Accessed March 13, 2017.

55. Qasim A. Moini, 'Pakistani Radio's Evolutionary Journey' *Dawn* (February 13, 2017).

56. See a powerful argument on the clash between tradition, old politics, and the forces of market, globalization, and international ideas and the shaping of the new world in Benjamin R. Barber, 'Jihad vs. McWorld' *Atlantic Monthly*, (March, 1992).

57. Marc Raboy, 'Media Pluralism and the Promotion of Cultural Diversity' (written for UNESCO:, McGill University, December 10, 2007). <http://media.mcgill.ca/files/unesco_diversity.pdf> Accessed 13 March 2017.

58. Muhammad Azam Choudhary, 'Religious Practices at Sufi Shrines in the Punjab' *Pakistan Journal of History and Culture* 31/1 (2010),1–57.

59. Areeba Asad, '13 Famous Festivals of Pakistan You Must Attend' Accessed, 13 March 2017. <http://yumtoyikes.com/2016/08/09/famous-festivals-of-pakistan/>.

60. *Karachi Literature Festival.* Author's conversation with Nadia Ghani, Oxford University Press, Karachi. <http://www.karachiliteraturefestival.org/klf-programme>. Accessed 13 March 2017.

61. <https://apmc.wordpress.com> Accessed 13 March 2017.

62. *Ajoka.* <http://ajoka.org.pk> Accessed 13 March 2017.

63. See for instance, Shehzad Ghias, 'Pakistani Theatre in 2014' *The Express Tribune*, (December 25, 2014).

64. Nadeem Omar Tarar, 'Beyond Cultural Consumerism' *The Friday Times*, (July 1, 2016).

65. Maria Amir, 'What is "Against Pakistani Culture" Anyway' *Dawn*, (October 5, 2016).

Chapter VII

Conclusion

Conceptualizing identity, let alone deploying it in an environment of diversity, raises some serious academic and policy questions. There is hardly any objective way of handling identity issues, as too many identities by too many groups might be competing for recognition, as its instrumental use becomes handy for staking claims on economic and political resources. One of the major characteristics of identity is subjectivity: how a particular social group articulates its identity and what ethnic, linguistic, historical material it uses to authenticate its claim of what it is, and how it differentiates itself from others. However, out-group recognition is no less important than self-imagining as a separate group.[1] While many shape the process and the act of identity selection, the political interests of the dominant classes are the most important influences. It is their ideas of nation, nationalism, and state-building that create a path for the development and articulation of national identity. As we have discussed in the previous chapters, the national narratives of identity may not go unchallenged by other groups that wish to engage in identity politics to advance their claims on power and resources.

We have argued that identity construction as an interplay of competing narratives and political interests is a dynamic process. It is interesting that both the nationalist Pakistani elites—military, bureaucracy, and mainstream political parties—and the Islamists and regionalists use national culture as the foundation of their idea of identity. The problem is that each of these actors has a very different conception of national culture and its constituent elements. While the Pakistan nationalists have used religion, history, civilization and, more importantly, the ideas that shaped the struggle for an independent Pakistan—Islam and the Pakistan ideology—the regionalists have used ethnic culture, language, regional histories, and a sense of deprivation to counter the hegemonic sense of identity promoted through the unifying influences of the Urdu language and the commonality of Islam. For this reason, the politics of identity has been conflictive and may even remain so because of the transitional character of the society, state, and politics. The spread of new technologies of mass communication, urbanization, and economic forces are bound to reshape old values, cultural traditions, and result in creating identities among individuals. The growing social and geographic mobilization—the emergence of the new middle classes, urbanization, and immigration—may influence identity politics, perhaps along the same trajectories of Islam, Pakistani nationalism and ethnic identities.

We have argued that culture as one of the influences on national and sub-national identity construction can change. The reason is that culture is path-dependent.[2] The question is, which of the forces pave its path? It is essentially politics, with its expansive definition of economic planning, development, modernization, and a process of positive change, that keeps the constituent elements of a dependent social category—a manifestation of larger political process.[3] Fredrik Barth has argued that culture, which is generally understood as a central feature of ethnicity and nationalism, is 'an implication or result, rather than a primary and definitional characteristics of ethnic group organization'.[4] The reason is that cultures and identities can change with modernity.[5] In this respect, Ryan Basher makes an important point that 'the content of ethnic identification is determined by the economic and social function of a group'.[6] It is the scope and pace of modernity, its success or failure that would change or not change the economic and political status of a constituent social group within the state. Regarding the Punjab, which is synonymous with domination, hegemony, and ruling groups, the minority ethnic groups have used regional languages and cultures as instruments of expressing internal coherence, as well as asserting a claim over political resources— autonomy and creation of a province/provinces.

Identities in nations that are diverse in layers, horizontally— across the regions—and vertically—socially stratified—don't have single identities. By the character of the society, identities become multiple, layered, and contextualized. In multi-ethnic communities, cohabitating the same spaces, individuals may have more than one identity. Depending on the context and situation in which one finds himself or herself, shifts from one to another identity are common. Henry Hale presents a counter point on this subject by arguing that identities are not multiple but singular. He questions the multiple identity argument and constructivist-primordial views, including synthesizing attempts. By using insights from psychological literature on identity, he argues that generally people think of identity at a micro-individual level but does recognize that it is 'situational' and changes with a context.[7] In ethnically diverse regions of Pakistan, where caste, tribe, and location have historically been powerful identifiers, one finds multiple identities to be quite a common social affair that unfold depending on the place and context of social and political interaction. We notice that even though a strong sense of Pakistan's national identity has grown, it is not likely to render other identities—politically constructed or historically evolved—irrelevant in the ethnic regions. The national, ethnic, and even caste, village, and tribe based identities may continue to remain an important cultural and social influence on the political orientations of the people of different regions.

The nature of politics in its every aspect, from policies of state-building, economic development to distributive justice or absence of it, have the most powerful influence on shaping, reshaping, and shifting of identities. The distribution effects of both economic rewards and political power in socially uneven places like Pakistan has created a sense of deprivation among the minority ethnic groups. The populations of smaller provinces have increasingly come to believe that they are backwards because of the domination of the largest province Punjab over economy, politics, and state institutions. It is a powerful narrative that the ethnic nationalists have continuously used to counter greater influence of the Punjab. Intellectuals and social entrepreneurs from minority provinces have played a major role in framing and disseminating sub-national identity discourses. That has produced and sustained ethnicity and ethnic politics as a counterweight to the hegemony of the Punjab and the federal government. The ethnic narrative has forced the Punjab to make compromises on important issues—water distribution, Kalabagh Dam, 18th Amendment to the constitution and the NFC award. The political activists within political parties with strong ethnic orientations play a disproportionately greater role in shaping responses to the centre than any other competing actor.[8]

The identity construction in Pakistan reflects four contradictory trends—between Pakistani nationalism and multiple ethnic nationalisms rooted in regional diversity, between the idea of secular modernity and Islam, between democracy and military rule engendering a security state, and between a national culture and regional cultures and languages. These contradictions have produced, and have been reinforced by, divisive and conflictive national politics; thus, the quest for national identity has been neither smooth nor driven in one direction or by one social or political force. Rather, the identity politics has been contentious and rudderless, like a ship in rough seas, jolted in multiple directions, often losing its control and clear direction. In explaining conflicting views on national identity construction, we have rested this study on three important propositions. First, that identity is constructed—it is a political act of those who control power and have some vision of nation, nationalism, and identity. This, however, does not take place in a historical vacuum or without adequate cultural symbols and societal reference. Those weaving a national narrative in Pakistan have used all of them, but selectively, to suit their idea of Pakistani nationalism and identity. Our second proposition is that the dominant ruling elites play a much greater role in shaping identity and nationalism. We have taken a much broader view of ruling classes, which includes military, political and regional elites, intellectuals, writers, and opinion-makers. Finally, the essential character of the lands of the Indus—the constituent regions of Pakistan—is rich, deep, and has a colourful diversity of languages and tongues, dresses and cuisine, music and arts. Therefore, there are diversities within diversity in each province and its regions. Building a nation and constructing a singular identity would be problematic, as it has been in the case of Pakistan, for the reason that diversity has been rejected officially as divisive instead of being embraced as a historical reality and a defining feature of Pakistani nationalism. Let us now turn to the conflictive struggle or struggles for identity construction and the interplay of various social, ethnic, and political forces. The post-independence search for national identity exclusively in terms of Islam, the Urdu language, and the two-nation theory has ignored the culture of the people, their history, and in effect, the diverse and rich heritage of the regions that constitute Pakistan. The dominant groups, both the civilian and military that came to occupy the state structure, promoted and constructed Pakistani nationalism for its hegemony and political interest, turning a blind-eye to the regional languages and cultures. Our argument has been that a modern state of Pakistan is possible without seeking ethnic or cultural homogeneity of historically diverse populations. What was needed was constitutional politics and power sharing arrangements in which state should have guaranteed cultural and political rights, and in return, the constituent groups would have accepted the institutional and territorial legitimacy of the state more as stakeholders and citizens than as subjects. We have argued that Islamic symbolism and even invoking the common heritage of the Indus Valley civilization or some other common cultural forms, is insufficient and inherently weak material for nation-building; at best, they are secondary and more symbolic than substantive. They may work as a back-up force only if the political aspects of nationalism and national identity—democracy, decentralization, and devolution of power—have been accepted as primary political norms. These instruments have been either weak or rendered useless by the military interventions in politics. A nation like Pakistan, in an ethnically diverse environment, should be conceived both as a political category, as well as reflective of multiculturalism of the society. Ethnic diversity would require multiculturalism as a political framework, implying consent and consensus among the federating units on vital policy issues from building state institutions to ensuring autonomy and representation. Attempts to submerge or subordinate separate cultural identities that follow linguistic and ethnic lines in the context of Pakistan into an arbitrarily defined national identity has, in the past few decades, generated conflicts, weakening a sense of ownership of the state, and even its legitimacy among the ethnic nationalists of all types and from all regions of the country. The ethnic groups wish to preserve their languages, cultures, and identities, which they have felt have been threatened by the pursuit of one national language and one national identity on the basis of Urdu and Islam. They find themselves and their heritage on the margins of national identity construction. Their complaints are not unfounded. They rightly argue that state policies have 'killed local languages', (some studies estimate there to be thirteen local languages) by patronizing and promoting Urdu as the national language too zealously.[9] The question of national identity is intrinsically linked to the very idea of the state and nation that dominant elites wish to build. The elite preferences and nation-building are inherently two-sides of the same process. The main ruling groups of Pakistan have preferred a centralized and centralizing state- and nation-building process to manage diversity rather than placing diversity at the centre of this process. The problem was insecurity, fear of instability, and disorder. There have been other factors like geopolitics, perceptions of threat, and misreading of history that led the military and bureaucratic elites to believe that ethnicity and cultural pluralism could pose a threat to the new state of Pakistan, if given legitimacy and full expression. The idea that ethnic pluralism poses a threat to state has been a defining influence over the fear psychosis of the mainstream political and security elites. In their attempt to build a stable, secure, and unified state, they took the highway of political nationalism and ignored the many side roads of cultural nationalism(s). The difference between the two is this: the former is constructed, envisioned, and driven by a singular interest in promoting the idea of national state and identity; the other is organic, natural, historical, and close to the people, as it recognizes their culture, historicity, and heritage. Cultural nationalism could have been the basis of political nationalism; it can still be an effective instrument of national identity, as it would have given the people of different regions a stake in the nation-building process, and ownership of it. After the passage of the 18th Amendment, which has opened up greater avenues for provincial autonomy, it is also the responsibility of the regional and ethnic elites to celebrate and revive local cultures.[10] Actually, youth belonging to various ethnic groups in recent decades take pride in celebrating their cultures without the patronage of the state, and even local elites, in the educational institutions of the country and the eve of local festivals around shrines.[11] Since the first transition to democracy and establishment of the Lok Virsa Institute for Folklore and Heritage—with a mandate to 'preserve, document, and promote' heritage in Islamabad, has been active in educating, displaying, and celebrating regional arts, crafts, and cultures. The institute has kept organizing an annual national festival that brings together folk singers, dancers, artists, craftsmen and women, and regional foods, which is the rich heritage and colours of Pakistan brought alive.[12] There appears to be an increasingly reactive sub-nationalist trend in acclaiming diversity since the restoration of democracy, a proliferation of electronic media and the advent of ethnic television channels. Some might argue that ethnic sub-nationalism has always been a robust political and social force at the grassroots level, in some regions more than in others. The regional languages and cultures are organically linked to the social tradition and natural tastes of people at the popular level. They feel greater joy and fulfilment in the local music, arts, festivals, and performances. However, these streams run parallel to the state-sponsored national identity narrative and the Urdu language—that has become a genuine lingua franca of the country. Will there be a synthesis among the regional languages and cultures and the national language, Urdu, is a question that only the future generations may best be able to answer. Any such blending may evolve around the Urdu language at the centre, which, being the flexible language that it is, may increasingly adopt vocabulary and cultural expressions, and even render folk heritage through its several literary genres. It is already happening, like the production of folklore, stories, and histories in the Urdu language. The regional elites and nationalists may decry this, as they often have, terming this process a cultural hegemony, but the resistance has been weak, patchy, and irresolute. It is not just the official patronage of Urdu that has made it the national language, but also the Muslim identity politics of pre-independence era, and Urdu being the medium of instruction in Punjab, Balochistan, and KP schools and the language of the literate in every region that constitutes Pakistan.[13] In no sense ever has Urdu been a 'foreign' language to the Punjab at least, which is the largest province with over 60% of the population.[14] Rather we see the influence of Urdu growing over the regional languages—their vocabulary, cultural, and political expression.[15] There is a discernible trend of Urdu-ization of Punjab, particularly among the new middle class families and in the urban centres.[16] There are fears that if the Punjabis continue on this course, their second and third generations from now may lose the language. Inter-provincial migration to Karachi, Islamabad, and urban Punjab may further promote Urdu as the language of the urban areas. However, this is an emerging trend, which may not involve the larger question of national identity and national culture, which may continue to be defined by multiculturalism and diversity. Rather we have argued that accepting multiculturalism as the template for national identity and national culture is the solution.

Culture is what the people are, including their history, traditions, languages, and all aspects of social and political life from a celebration of joy to mourning of the dead. It is true that Islam is a common religion of the majority of the population, and as such, it does provide a civilizational bedrock on which social values, beliefs, and attitudes of the people rest. Even though religion has a foundational role in the shaping of Pakistani culture and identity, secular aspects of regional cultures that have evolved over centuries in the context of geography, language, tribal or caste traditions, and interaction among other people throughout the subcontinent, Afghanistan and the lands beyond, add variety, colours, and traits that have proved remarkably enduring. They are not necessarily in conflict with Islam or any other religion. They reflect the values, institutions, and social culture through which people interact with one another in the larger communities. Islam being the core of the culture, the people in Pakistan do not seek their Islamic authenticity through an Islamic state. Historically, social and religious movements in the subcontinent to 'reform' and 'purify' Islam from alien and non-Islamic influences have been in the private sphere, that still constitutes a powerful tradition. Parallel to this, the religious parties with a mission of Islamizing the state and society believe in the agency of the state through which they would like to see an enforcement of sharia or Islamic law.[17] The quest for Islamization through the state has proved to be divisive and conflictual because it has revived and strengthened religious and sectarian schism over what is true Islam and what is not. In recent decades, and owing to the ambiguous role of political Islam and the rise of sectarian extremism and conflict in the society have grown.[18] However, while professing an Islamist agenda, the religious parties have shown moderation, pragmatism, and have often joined larger coalitions led by mainstream secular parties.[19] The people at the grassroots level question the political instrumentality of Islam, and its appropriation by the state and its use for accessing political power.[20] They believe in separating the two spheres of politics and religion. It is evident from the declining popular support for the religious political parties. However, a strong proclivity for Islamic laws and a romantic view of the early years of Islam as a perfect Islamic state at the popular level does exist, and striving for it in the modern world through religious sermons and production of religious literature in Urdu is apparent. These are contradictions in the national life of Pakistan, which its elites find hard to resolve. National identity, nation-building, and even conceiving nationhood are political acts that are shaped by the competing interests of social groups, ethnicities, and national and regional elite networks. Therefore, advancing one form of national identity at the expense of others is equally a political behaviour determined by implicit or explicit interests of social groups, political players, and state institutions. For this reason, Pakistan's nation and state-building project over the past seventy years has faced persistent tension between regionalism, often denounced as illegitimate, and Pakistani nationalism, portrayed as the way forward to creating an Islamic, nation-state. Besides these actors, there are pressure groups, like religious parties, that have a distinctive voice on national and regional issues and have attempted to define Pakistani nationalism more in religious terms than secular grounds of convergence of interests and the founding of national solidarity on shared political objectives. There is an unstated aspect of this tension between the people of Pakistan that are generally secular and don't seek their Islamic authenticity through an Islamic state, and the statist allies as well as their allies in religious parties that have promoted the idea of an Islamic identity and an Islamic state. A third contestation on the question of national identity is reflected in the complex structure of civil-military relations. The military leaders have captured power four times, and even when not in power, have retained deeper influences over national security and critical foreign policy choices. Pakistan's transitions to democracy—three times in seventy years—have remained incomplete due to the legacy issues of military regimes, slow development of political institutions, and fragmentation of democratic forces, often done by the military regimes to consolidate their power. The civilian democratic forces, even weak and procedural, present a constitutional, participatory, and representative alternative to the autocratic and dictatorial view of nation, nation-building, and national identity. The armed forces, when in power, have tried to reorganize the political system, in which they played a central 'guiding' role by checking and monitoring the power of the elected representatives. The military rulers presented themselves as 'patriotic', 'nationalists', and nation-builders, while demonizing and denouncing the political class as 'corrupt', 'inefficient', and lacking the calibre and commitment of leadership that could not make Pakistan a 'genuine' democracy, a secure and strong state, and nation.[21] The military's diagnosis of the political crises of the country and its recipes for a secure and strong Pakistan written in Ayub Khan's model of 'development first, democracy later' have proven disastrous. All the military regimes have failed to understand and appreciate the 'genius' of the people of Pakistan. Ayub thought he did, and devised a form of controlled and guided basic democracy. The military regimes and their surrogate political allies have confused the question of national identity by linking it to national security, stability, order, and development, not realizing that democracy offers far better tools for accommodation, consensus building, and inclusiveness of regional interests.[22] It is one of the existential requirements of diversity, ethnicity, deep history of the Indus regions, and pragmatic political interests that Pakistan must use federalism and democracy as two principles of state- and nation-building. They provide the tools of empowerment and ownership of the state and its institutions among the constituent units and the people, and thus generate an organic view of national identity and security. It is a historical process which can be aided through practical principles of accommodation, compromise, and recognition of cultures, values, and heritage of the diverse people that Pakistan represents. Conceptualizing national identity out of the historical context of the Indus region or the cultural heritage of the people will not be helpful; rather, it will be counterproductive to national solidarity. The Indus is a region of millions of identities, strong and weak, old and new, changing, merging, and being redefined consistently. No single national identity construction enterprise may yield fruitful results by blacking them out or dimming their light. Rather they represent what Pakistani identity, culture, and its heritage actually is.

NOTES

1. Jimy M. Sanders, 'Ethnic Boundaries and Identity in Plural Societies' *Annual Review of Sociology* 28 (2002), 327–57.
2. Samuel P. Huntington 'Foreword: Cultures Count' in Lawrence E. Harrison and Samuel P. Huntington. Eds. *Culture Matters: How Values Shape Human Progress*, (New York: Basic Books, 2000), xv.
3. Ronald Inglehart, 'Culture and Democracy' in Ibid., 80–97.
4. Fredrik Barth, *Ethnic Groups and Boundaries: The Social Organization of Culture Difference* (Long Grove, Illinois: Waveland Press, Inc., 1969), 9–38.
5. Benjamin I. Schwartz, 'Culture, Modernity, and Nationalism—Further Reflections' *Daedalus* 122/3 (Summer 1993), 207–26.
6. Ryan Brasher, 'Ethnic Brother or Artificial Namesake? The Construction of Tajik

Identity in Afghanistan and Tajikistan' *Berkeley Journal of Sociology* 55 (2011), 102.

7. Henry E Hale, 'Explaining Ethnicity' *Comparative Political Studies* 37/4, 458–9.

8. David Rousseau and A. Maurits van der Veen, 'The Emergence of a Shared Identity: An Agent-Based Computer Simulation of Idea Diffusion' *The Journal of Conflict Resolution* 49/5 (October 2005), 686–712.

9. Author's interview with Uxi Mufti, Islamabad, January 22, 2017. There is no consensus on how many languages and tongues are spoken in Pakistan. The number ranges from 13 to 72 in different studies. Going by the names of the languages mentioned in these studies, it seems there is exaggeration and misinterpretation of languages. In many cases, it is the same language that has different names in different regions of the country. See, for instance, an essay on some of these books, by Rauf Parekh, 'World Mother Languages Day: 2017 Themes and Linguistic Atlas of Pakistan' *Dawn*, (February 2, 2017).

10. 'Sindh Brings out its Colours on '"Ajrak-Topi" Day' *Dawn*, (December 8, 2014).

11. Marian Rengel, *Pakistan: A Primary Source Cultural Guide* (New York: PowerPlus Books, 2004).

12. 'Lok Virsa to hold Lok Mela from April 1', *The Nation*, (April 1, 2016).

13. See for instance, V.V. Nagarkar, *Genesis of Pakistan* (New Delhi: Allied Publishers, 1975).

14. Nazir Ahmad Chaudhry, *Development of Urdu as Official Language in the Punjab, 1849–1974* (Lahore: Record Office, Punjab Government, 1977).

15. Author's observation of ethnic television channels.

16. Arsalan Altaf, 'Urdu-isation of Punjab' *Express Tribune*, (May 4, 2015).

17. Farooq Tanwir, 'Religious Parties and Politics in Pakistan' *International Journal of Comparative Sociology* (December 2002), 25–268.

18. Robert G. Wirsing, 'Political Islam, Pakistan and the Geopolitics of Religious Identity' 171.

19. Haroon K. Ullah, *Vying for Allah's Vote: Understanding Islamic Parties, Political Violence and Extremism in Pakistan* (Washington, DC: Georgetown University Press, 2014), See: Introduction.

20. Mazhar Abbas, 'Religious Parties' Dilemma' *The News*, (March 9, 2017).

21. See Altaf Gauhar, *Ayub Khan and Military Rule in Pakistan 1958–1969* (London: I. B. Tauris, 1992).

22. Ijaz Khan, 'Contending Identities of Pakistan and the Issue of Democratic Governance' *Peace and Democracy in South Asia* 2/1 & 2 (2006), 50–70.

Bibliography

BOOKS

Abbas, Hassan. *Pakistan's Drift into Extremism: Allah, the Army, and America's War on Terror*. (London & New York: Routledge, 2005).

Abbas, Tahir. ed. *Islamic Radicalism and Multicultural Politics: The British Experience*. (London: Routledge, 2011).

Abdullah, Syed. *Culture Ka Masla*. (Lahore: Sang-e-Meel Publications, 2001).

Abel, M. *Glimpses of Indian National Movement*. (Hyderabad: ICFAI University Press, 2005).

Abrahamian, Ervand. *Khomeinism: Essays on the Islamic Republic*. (Berkeley: University of California Press, 1993).

Adcock, C. S. *The Limits of Tolerance: Indian Secularism and the Politics of Religious Freedom*. (New York: Oxford University Press, 2014).

Afzal, M. Rafique. *A History of the All-India Muslim League, 1906–1947*. (Karachi: Oxford University Press, 2013).

———. *Pakistan: History and Politics, 1947–1971* (Karachi: Oxford University Press, 2009).

———. *Political Parties in Pakistan, 1947–58*. (Islamabad: National Institute of History and Culture, 1986).

Agrawal, M. M. *Ethnicity, Culture, and Nationalism in North-East India*. (New Delhi: Indus Publishers, 1996).

Ahmad Khan, Rais, Rasul B. Rais and Khalid Waheed, (eds). *South Asia: Military Power and Regional Politics*. (Islamabad: Islamabad Council of World Affairs, 1989).

Ahmad, Akhtaruddin. *Why Islam?* (Cairo: Islamic Inc. Publishing and Distribution, 1997).

Ahmad, Aziz and G. E. Von Grunebaum. eds. *Muslim Self-statement in India and Pakistan, 1857–1968.* (Lahore: Suhail Academy, 2004).

———. *Islamic Modernism in India and Pakistan, 1857–1964.* (London: Oxford University Press, 1967).

Ahmad, Imtiaz, Partha S. Ghosh, and Helmut Reifeld, *Pluralism and Equality: Values in Indian Society and Politics.* (New Delhi: Sage Publications, 2000).

Ahmad, Jamiluddin. *Mohammad Ali Jinnah: Founder of Pakistan.* ed. Ziauddin Ahmad. (Islamabad: Ministry of Information and Broadcasting, Government of Pakistan, 1976).

———. *Speeches and Writings of Mr. Jinnah*, Vol 1. (Lahore: Sh. Mohammad Ashraf & Sons, 1960).

Ahmad, Mumtaz. 'Madrassa Education in Pakistan and Bangladesh' in Satu P. Limaye, Mohan Malik and Robert G. Wirsing, eds. *Religious Radicalism and Security in South Asia* (Honolulu: Asia Pacific Center for Security Studies, 2004), 101–115.

Ahmad, Sayed Riaz. *Maulana Maududi and the Islamic State.* (Lahore: People's Publishing House, 1976).

Ahmad, Syed Nur. *From Martial Law to Martial Law: Politics in Punjab, 1919–1958*, ed. Craig Baxter. (Lahore: Vanguard, 1985).

Ahmed, Akbar S. *The Thistle and the Drone: How America's War on Terror Became a Global War on Tribal Islam.* (Washington, DC: Brookings Institution Press, 2013).

———. Liaquat H. Merchant and Sharif Al Mujahid, eds. *The Jinnah Anthology,* (New York: Oxford University Press, 2010).

———. *Jinnah, Pakistan and Islamic Identity: The Search for Saladin.* (London: Routledge, 1997).

Ahmed, Ishtiaq. *The Punjab Bloodied Partitioned and Cleansed: Unraveling the 1947 Tragedy through Secret British Reports and First-person Accounts.* (Karachi: Oxford University Press, 2012).

———. *Pakistan, the Garrison State: Origins, Evolution, Consequences, 1947–2011.* (Karachi: Oxford University Press, 2013).

Ahmed, Khaled. *Sectarian War: Pakistan's Sunni-Shia Violence and its link to the Middle East.* (Karachi: Oxford University Press, 2011).

Ahmed, Salahuddin. *Bangladesh: Past and Present.* (New Delhi: A.P.H. Pub., 2004).

Ahsan, Aitzaz. *The Indus Saga and the Making of Pakistan.* (Lahore: Nahr Ghar Publications, 2013).

Ajami, Fouad, James F. Hoge Jr. and Gideon Rose, eds. *How did this Happen? Terrorism and the New War.* (New York: BBS, Public Affairs, 2001).

Akbar, Malik Siraj. *The Redefined Dimensions of Baloch Nationalist Movement.* (New York: Xlibris, 2011).

Akbarzadeh, Shahram. *Routledge Handbook of Political Islam.* (Abingdon: Routledge, 2012).

Ali, Chaudhri Muhammad. *The Emergence of Pakistan.* (New York: Columbia University Press, 1988).

Alī, Choudhary Raḥmat and Khursheed Kamal Aziz. *Complete Works of Rahmat Ali.* (Islamabad: National Commission on Historical and Cultural Research, 1978).

Ali, Imran. ed. 'The Punjab and the Retardation of Nationalism' In *The Political Inheritance of Pakistan.* (New York: St. Martins Press, 1991), 29–52.

_____. *Canal Colonization in Punjab.* (Princeton: Princeton University Press, 1982).

Ali, Tariq. *Can Pakistan Survive?* (London: Pelican Books, 1983).

Ali, Shaukat. *Dimensions and Dilemmas of Islamist Movements.* (Lahore: Sang-e-Meel Publications, 1998).

Alkhuli, Muhammad Ali. *Need for Islam.* (Jordan: Dar Al-Falah Publishing, 2006).

Amin, Tahir. *Ethno-National Movements of Pakistan: Domestic and International Factors.* (Islamabad: Institute of Policy Studies, 1988).

_____. *Ethno-National Movements of Pakistan: Domestic and International Factors.* (Islamabad: Institute of Policy Studies, 1988).

Amjad, Rashid. (ed.). *Mazahamati Adab, Urdu.* (Islamabad: Pakistan Academy of Literature, 1995).

Amuzegar, Jahangir. 'Islamic Fundamentalism in Action: The Case of Iran' *Middle East Policy* 4/1–2 (1995), 22–33.

Anderson, Benedict R. O' G. *Imagined Communities: Reflections on the Origins and Spread of Nationalism.* (London: Verso, 1983).

Andrabi, Tahir. Jinshnu Das et al. *Religious School Enrolment in Pakistan: A Look at the Data.* (Washington, DC: World Bank Group, 2005).

Arif, Khalid Mahmud. *Working with Zia: Pakistan's Power Politics 1977–1988.* (Karachi: Oxford University Press, 1995).

Armajani, Jon. *Modern Islamist Movements: History, Religion, and Politics.* (Chichester: Wiley-Blackwell, 2012).

Ashmawy, Muhammad Saïd Al. *Islam and the Political Order.* (Washington: Council for Research in Values and Philosophies, 1994).

Avari, Burjor. *Islamic Civilization in South Asia: A History of Muslim Power and Presence in the Indian Subcontinent.* (London: Routledge, 2013).

Awan, Samina. *Political Islam in Colonial Punjab: Majlis -i-Ahrar 1929–49.* (Karachi: Oxford University Press, 2010).

Axmann, Martin. *Back to the Future: The Khanate of Kalat and the Genesis of Baluch Nationalism, 1915–1955.* (Oxford: Oxford University Press, 2012).

Ayaz, Babar. *What's Wrong with Pakistan?* (New Delhi: Hay House, 2013).

Ayoob, Mohammed. *The Many Faces of Political Islam: Religion and Politics in the Muslim World.* (Ann Arbor: University of Michigan Press, 2008).

Ayres, Alyssa. *Speaking like a State: Language and Nationalism in Pakistan.* (Cambridge: Cambridge University Press, 2009).

Azar, Edward E. and Chung–in Moon, eds. *National Security in the Third World: The Management of Internal and External Threat.* (College Park: Center for International Development and Conflict Management, University of Maryland, 1988).

Aziz, Kamal Khursheed. *The Making of Pakistan: A Study in Nationalism.* (Lahore: Sang-e-Meel Publication, 2002).

————. *A History of the Idea of Pakistan.* (Lahore: Vanguard, 1987).

————. *The Making of Pakistan: A Study in Nationalism.* Lahore: (Sang-e-Meel Publications, 2002).

Aziz, Zahid. *A Survey of the Lahore Ahmadiyya Movement: History, Beliefs, Aims and Work.* (Lahore: Ahmadiyya Anjuman Lahore Publications, 2008).

Aziz, Mazhar. *Military Control in Pakistan: The Parallel State.* (London: Routledge, 2008).

Ball, Nicole. *Security and Economy in the Third World.* (Princeton: Princeton University Press, 1988).

Baloch, Inayatullah. *The Problem of 'Greater Balochistan': A Study of Baluch Nationalism.* (Stuttgart: Steiner Verlag Wiesbaden, 1987).

Bandyopādhyāẏa, Śekhara. *Bengal, Rethinking History: Essays in Historiography.* (New Delhi: Manohar Publishers & Distributors, 2001).

Banerjee, Mukulika. *A Study of the Khudai Khidmatgar Movement, 1930–1947, N.W.F.P., British India.* (Oxford: Oxford University Press, 1994).

———. *The Pathan Unarmed: Opposition & Memory in the North West Frontier.* (Santa Fe: School of American Research Press, 2000).

Barnett R. Rubin. *The Fragmentation of Afghanistan: State Formation and Collapse in the International System.* (New Haven: Yale University Press, 2002).

Barry, Buzan, Ole Wæver, and Jaap de Wilde, 'Introduction' in *Security: A New Framework for Analysis,* (Boulder: Lynne Rienner, 1998).

Barth, Fredrik. *Ethnic Groups and Boundaries: The Social Organization of Culture Difference.* (Long Grove, Illinois: Waveland Press, Inc., 1969).

Basham, A. L. *The Wonder that was India* (3rd edn. London: Sidgwick & Jackson, 1967).

Bass, Gary Jonathan. *The Blood Telegram: Nixon, Kissinger, and a Forgotten Genocide.* (New York: Knopf, 2013).

Batra, Jagdish Chandra. *The Trial and Execution of Bhutto.* (Berkeley: University of California Press, 1979).

Baxter, Craig, et.al. *Pakistan under the Military: Eleven Years of Zia ul-Haq.* (Boulder: Westview Press, 1991).

Bayat, Asef. *Islam and Democracy: What Is the Real Question?* (Leiden: Amsterdam University Press, 2007).

Bean, Lee L. and A. D. Bhatti, 'Pakistan's Population in 1970s: Problems and Prospects' in J. Henry Korson, ed. *Contemporary Problems of Pakistan, edited by* (Leiden: E. J. Brill, 1974), 81–8.

Behuria, Ashok K. *State versus Nations in Pakistan: Sindhi, Baloch and Pakhtun Responses to Nation-Building.* (New Delhi: Institute for Defence Studies & Analyses, 2015).

Bell, Daniel. *The Coming of Post-Industrial Society.* (New York: Basic Books, 1973).

———. *The Cultural Contradictions of Capitalism.* (New York: Basic Books, 1976).

Bergesen, Albert J. *The Sayyid Qutb Reader: Selected Writings on Politics, Religion, and Society.* (New York: Routledge, 2008).

Berman, Sheri. *The Social Democratic Moment: Ideas and Politics in the Making of Interwar Europe.* (Cambridge: Harvard University Press, 1998).

Bhatt, Chetan. *Hindu Nationalism: Origins, Ideologies and Modern Myths.* (Oxford: Berg, 2001).

Bhutto, Zulfikar Ali. *If I Am Assassinated...* (New Delhi: Vikas, 1979).

Bienen, Henry. *The Military Intervene:; Case Studies in Political Development.* (New York: Russell Sage Foundation, 1968).

Billington, Rosamund, et. al. *Culture and Society.* (London: Palgrave Macmillan, 1991).

————. 'Culture and Imperialism' Rosamund Billington et. al. eds. in *Culture and Society.* (London: Palgrave Macmillan, 1991).

Binder, Leonard. *Religion and Politics in Pakistan.* (Berkeley: University of California Press, 1961).

Bokhari, Kamaran and Farid Senzai. *Political Islam in the Age of Globalization.* (New York: Palgrave Macmillan, 2013).

Booth, Ken ed. *New Thinking about Strategy and International Security.* (London: Harper Collins Academic, 1991).

Bosworth, C.E. *The Ghaznavids 994–1040.* (Edinburg: Edinburgh University Press, 1963).

Brass, Paul R. *Language, Religion and Politics in North India.* (Lincoln, N.E: Backinprint, 2005).

Brown, D. Mackenzie. *The Nationalist Movement: Indian Political Thought from Ranade to Bhave.* (Berkeley: University of California Press, 1961).

Bruce, Richard Isaac. *The Forward Policy and its Results or Thirty-Five Years Work Amongst the Tribes on our North-Western Frontier of India.* (Whitefish, MT: Kessinger Publishing, LLC, 2010).

Brynjar, Lia. *The Society of Muslim Brothers in Egypt: The Rise of an Islamic Mass Movement 1928–1942.* (New York: Ithaca Press, 2006).

Burke, S.M. *Jinnah. Speeches and Statements 1947–1948.* (Karachi: Oxford University Press, 2000).

Burke, S.M and Lawrence Ziring, *Pakistan's Foreign Policy: A Historical Analysis.* (Karachi: Oxford University Press, 1990).

Buzan, Barry. *People, States and Fear: The National Security Problem in International Relations.* (Brighton: Wheatsheaf, 1983).

Carr, E.H. 'The Nature of Politics' In E.H. Carr, ed. *The Twenty Years'*

Crisis 1919–1939: An Introduction to the Study of International Relations, (London: Macmillan, 1946).

Chaghatai, M. Ikram ed. *Shah Waliullah, 1703–1762: His Religious and Political Thought.* (Lahore: Sang-e-Meel Publications, 2005).

Chak, Farhan Mujahid. *Islam and Pakistan's Political Culture.* (London: Routledge, 2015).

Chalmers, Douglas A. and Scot Mainwaring. *Problems Confronting Contemporary Democracies: Essays in Honor of Alfred Stepan.* (Notre Dame: University of Notre Dame Press, 2012).

Chang, Ha-Joon. *Globalisation, Economic Development, and the Role of the State* (London: Zed Books, 2003).

Chaudhry, Nazir Ahmad. *Development of Urdu as Official Language in the Punjab, 1849–1974.* (Lahore: Record Office, Punjab Government, 1977).

Cheema, Pervaiz Iqbal. *Pakistan's Defence Policy, 1954–58.* (Basinstoke: Macmillan, 1990).

Chirot, Daniel. *How Societies Change.* (Thousand Oaks, CA: Pine Forge, 1994).

Choudhury, G.W. *Documents and Speeches on the Constitution of Pakistan.* (Dacca: Green Book House, 1967).

———. *Pakistan's Relations with India, 1947–66.* (London: Pall Mall Press, 1968).

Chowdury, Mustafa. *Pakistan: Its Politics and Bureaucracy.* (Kansas: Stosius Incorporated/Advent Books Division, 1988).

Cohen, Stephan P. ed. *The Future of Pakistan.* (Washington DC: The Brookings Institute Press, 2011).

———. *The Pakistan Army.* (Berkeley: University of California Press, 1984).

———. *The Idea of Pakistan.* (Washington, DC: Brookings Institution Press, 2004).

Coolsaet, R. *Jihadi Terrorism and the Radicalisation Challenge: European and American Experiences.* (Farnham, Surrey: Ashgate, 2011).

Cooper, John and Ronald L. Nettler. *Islam and Modernity: Muslim Intellectuals Respond.* (London: I. B. Tauris, 2009).

Crews, Robert D. and Amin Tarzi eds. *The Taliban and the Crisis of Afghanistan.* (Cambridge: Cambridge University Press, 2008).

Daalder, H. *The Role of the Military in the Emerging Countries*. (The Hague: Mouton, 1962).

Dabashi, Hamid. *Islamic Liberation Theology: Resisting the Empire*. (London: Routledge, 2008).

Dar, Saeeduddin Ahmad. *Ideology of Pakistan*. (Islamabad: National Institute of Historical and Cultural Research, 1998).

———. *Ideology of Pakistan*. (Islamabad: National Institute of Historical and Cultural Research, 1998).

Dashti, Naseer. *The Baloch and Balochistan: A Historical Account from the Beginning to the Fall of Baloch State*. (New York: Trafford Publishing, 2012).

Desai, Meghnad and Aitzaz Ahsan. *Divided by Democracy*. (New Delhi: Roli Books, 2005).

———. *Cross-Border Talks: Divided by Democracy*. (New Delhi: 2005).

Deutsch, Karl and William Foltz, (eds.), *Nation-Building*. (New York: Atherton Press, 1963).

Dobbin, Christine. *Basic Documents of Modern India and Pakistan 1835–1947*. (London: Von Nostrand Reinhold Company, 1970).

Doolin, Dennis James. *Pakistan: The 1958 Coup and Its Causes*. (Stanford: Department of Political Science, 1960).

Duncan, Graeme Campbell. *Democratic Theory and Practice*. (Cambridge: Cambridge University Press, 1983).

Eatwell, Roger and Anthony Wright, *Contemporary Political Ideologies*. (Boulder: Westview Press, 1993).

Eisenstadt, S.N. and Stein Rokkan, eds. *Building States and Nations*. (Beverly Hills: Sage Publications, 1973).

———. *Building States and Nations*. (Beverly Hills: Sage Publications, 1973).

Elethy, Yasser. *Islam, Context, Pluralism and Democracy: Classical and Modern Interpretations*. (London: Routledge, 2015).

Emerson, Rupert. *From Empire to Nations: The Rise to Self-Assertion of Asian and African Peoples*. (Cambridge: Harvard University Press, 1960).

Enayat, Hamid. *Modern Islamic Political Thought*. (Austin: University of Texas Press, 1982).

Esposito, John L, Tamara Sonn and John O. Voll. *Islam and Democracy after the Arab Spring*. (Oxford: Oxford University Press, 2016).

Esposito, John L. and Dalia Mogahed. *Who Speaks for Islam?: What a Billion Muslims Really Think.* (New York: Gallup Press, 2008).

_____. *The Islamic Threat: Myth or Reality.* (New York and Oxford: Oxford University Press, 1992).

_____. *Islam and Politics.* (Syracuse: Syracuse University Press, 1984).

Evans, Peter B, Dietrich Rueschemeyer, and Theda Skocpol, *Bringing the State Back In.* (Cambridge: Cambridge University Press, 1985).

Fair, C. Christine and Seth G. Jones. *Counterinsurgency in Pakistan.* (Santa Monica: Rand Corporation, 2010).

_____. *Fighting to the End: The Pakistan Army's Way of War.* (New York: Oxford University Press, 2014).

Faruqi, Zia ul-Hasan. *The Deoband School and the Demand for Pakistan.* (Bombay: Asia Publishing House, 1963).

Fatehpuri, Dildar Ali Farman. *History of Pakistan Movement and Language Controversy.* (Karachi: Karachi University Press, 2001).

Feit, Edward. *The Armed Bureaucrats: Military-Administrative Regimes and Political Development.* (Boston: Houghton Mifflin, 1972).

Finer, S.E. *The Man on Horseback: The Role of the Military in Politics.* (New York: Praeger, 1962).

Freeden, Michael, Lyman Tower Sargent, and Marc Stears, *The Oxford Handbook of Political Ideologies.* (Oxford: Oxford University Press, 2013).

_____. *Reassessing Political Ideologies: The Durability of Dissent.* (London: Routledge, 2001).

Friedman, George. *America's Secret War.* (New York: Doubleday, 2004).

Friedmann, Yohanan. *Prophecy Continuous: Aspects of Ahmadi Religious Thought and its Medieval Background.* (Oxford: Oxford University Press, 2003).

Fromkin, David. *A Peace to End All Peace.* (New York: Henry Holt and Company, 1989).

Fukuyama, Francis. *The End of History?* (Washington: National Affairs, 1989).

Garner, Roberta. 'Post War Perspectives' in Roberta Garner, ed. *Social Theory: Power and Identity in the Global Era* (Toronto: University of Toronto Press, 2010).

Gauhar, Altaf. *Ayub Khan and Military Rule in Pakistan 1958–1969.* (London: I. B. Tauris, 1992).

_____. *Ayub Khan: Pakistan's First Military Ruler.* (Lahore: Sang-e-Meel Publications, 1998).

Gayer, Laurent. *Karachi: Ordered Disorder and the Struggle for the City.* (New York: Oxford University Press, 2014).

Gellner, Ernest and John Breuilly. "Definitions." In Ernest Gellner. ed. *Nations and Nationalism,.* (Oxford: Basil Blackwell, 1983).

Gerges, Fawaz. *The Far Enemy: Why Jihad Went Global.* (New York: Cambridge University Press, 2005).

Ghazi, Mahmood Ahmad. *Islamic Renaissance in South Asia, 1707–1867: The Role of Shah Wali Allah and His Successors.* (Islamabad: Islamic Research Institute, International Islamic University, 2002).

Ghosh, S. K and Shri K. F. Rustamji. *Secularism in India: The Concept and Practice.* (New Delhi: A.P.H. Publications, 2001).

Gibson, Dawn-Marie. *A History of the Nation of Islam: Race, Islam, and the Quest for Freedom.* Santa Barbara: Praeger, 2012.

Gillespie, Michael Allen. *The Theological Origins of Modernity.* (Chicago: The University of Chicago Press, 2008).

Gilmartin, David. *Empire and Islam: Punjab and the Making of Pakistan.* (Berkeley: University of California Press, 1988).

Gilpin, Robert. *War and Change in World Politics* (Cambridge: Cambridge University Press, 1981).

Gohar, Ayub Khan. *Glimpses into the Corridors of Power.* (Karachi: Oxford University Press, 2007).

Goswami, Arvind. *3D: Deceit, Duplicity, Dissimulation of U.S. Foreign Policy towards India, Pakistan & Afghanistan.* (Bloomington: Author House, 2012).

Grare, Frederic. *Pakistan and the Afghan Conflict, 1979–1985.* (Karachi: Oxford University, 2003).

Greetz, Clifford, ed. *Old Societies and New States.* (New York: Free Press, 1963).

Gualtieri, Antonio R. *The Ahmadis: Community, Gender, and Politics in a Muslim Society.* (Montreal: McGill–Queen's University Press, 2004).

Gul, Sahar. *Women's Perceptions about Religious Extremism/Talibanization and Military Operation: A Case Study of Malakand Division*. (Islamabad: National Commission for the Status of Women, Government of Pakistan, July 2009).

Gutteridge, William F. *Military Institutions and Power in the New States*. (New York: Praeger, 1965).

Guzzini, Stefano. *Realism in International Relations and International Political Economy: The Continuing Story of a Death Foretold*. (London: Routledge, 1998).

Hafiz, M. Abdul and Abdur Rob Khan, *Nation-Building in Bangladesh: Retrospect and Prospect*. (Dhaka: Bangladesh Institute of International and Strategic Studies, 1986).

Haider, Ziad. *The Ideological Struggle for Pakistan*. (Stanford: Hoover Institution Press/Stanford University, 2010).

Hall, John. *International Orders* (Oxford: Polity Press, 1994), 80–120.

Hamid, Dabashi. *The Ideological Foundations of the Islamic Revolution in Iran: Theology of Discontent*. (London: Transaction Publishers, 2006).

Haq, Mahbub Ul. *The Strategy of Economic Planning: A Case Study of Pakistan*. (Karachi: Oxford University Press, 1963).

Haqqani, Husain. *Magnificent Delusions: Pakistan, the United States, and an Epic History of Misunderstanding*. (New York: Public Affairs, 2013).

———. *Pakistan between Mosque and Military*. (Lahore: Vanguard Books, 2005).

Harrison, Lawrence E. and Samuel P. Huntington eds. *Culture Matters: How Values Shape Human Progress*. (New York: Basic Books, 2000).

Harrison, Selig S. *In Afghanistan's Shadow: Baluch Nationalism and Soviet Temptations*. (New York: Carnegie Endowment of International Peace, 1981).

Hasan, Parvez. *Pakistan's Economy at the Crossroads: Past Policies and Present*. (Karachi: Oxford University Press, 1998).

Hasan, Syed Fida. *Pakistan the Promise of the Early Years: A Memoir*. (Lahore: Zeenat Publishers, 2016).

Hashmi, Bilal, 'Dragon Seed: Military in the State' in Hassan Gardezi and Jamil Rashid, eds. *Pakistan: The Roots of Dictatorship,* (London: Zed Press, 1983).

He, Baogang, Brian Galligan, and Takashi Inoguchi, *Federalism in Asia*. (Cheltenham: Edward Elgar, 2007).

Heatcote, T.A. *Balochistan, British and the Great Game: The Struggle for the Bolan Pass, Gateway to India*. (London: C. Hurst & Company, 2016).

Hefner, Robert. W. *Civil Islam: Muslims and Democratization in Indonesia*. (Princeton: Princeton University Press, 2000).

Heywood, Andrew. *Political Ideologies: An Introduction*. (New York: St. Martin's Press, 1992).

Hitti, Philip Khuri. *Islam: A Way of Life*, (Minnesota: University of Minnesota Press, 1970).

Hobsbawm, Eric J. *Nations and Nationalism since 1780: programme, myth and reality*. (Cambridge: Cambridge University Press, 1990).

Holdstedt, Melissa V. *Federalism: History and Current Issues*. (New York: Novinka Books, 2006).

Hoodbhoy, Pervez Amirali and Abdul Hameed Nayyar, 'Rewriting the History of Pakistan' In Asghar Khan. ed. *The Pakistan Experience: State & Religion*, (Lahore: Vanguard, 1985).

How It Threatens America. (New York: Free Press, 2010).

Hroub, Khaled, *Political Islam, Context versus Ideology*. (London: SOAS, 2012).

Humayun, Arif. *Connivance by Silence: How the Majority's Failure to Challenge Politically Motivated Interpretation of the Qur'an Empowered Radicals to Propagate Extremism*. (Philadelphia: Xlibris, 2010).

Hunter, Shireen and Huma Malik, *Modernization, Democracy, and Islam*. (Westport: Praeger Publishers, 2005).

Huntington, Samuel P. *The Third Wave: Democratization in the Late Twentieth Century*. (Norman and London: University of Oklahoma Press, 1991).

Huntington, Samuel P. *Political Order in Changing Societies*. (New Haven and London: Yale University Press, 1968).

Husain, Zahid. *Frontline Pakistan: The Struggle with Militant Islam*. (Lahore: Vanguard Books, 2007).

————. *The Scorpion's Tail: The Relentless Rise of Islamic Militants in Pakistan-And How it Threatens America*. (New York: Free Press, 2010).

Husain, Ed. *The Islamist: Why I Joined Radical Islam in Britain, What I saw Inside and Why I Left*. (London: Penguin, 2007).

Hussain, Asaf. *Elite Politics in an Ideological State: The Case of Pakistan.* (Montreal: Dawson University Press, 1979).

Hussain, Noor A. 'India's Regional Policy: Strategic and Security Dimensions' In Stephen Philip Cohen. ed. *The Security of South Asia,* (Urbana and Chicago: University of Illinois Press, 1987).

Hussain, Sayed Mushahid. *Pakistan's Politics: The Zia Years.* (Lahore: Progressive Publishers, 1990).

Hyder, Sajjad. *Foreign Policy of Pakistan: Reflections of an Ambassador.* (Lahore: Progressive Publishers, 1987).

Hyland, James L. *Democratic Theory: The Philosophical Foundations.* (Manchester: Manchester University Press, 1995).

Hyman, Anthony, Muhammed Ghayur, and Naresh Kaushik, *Pakistan, Zia and After.* (New Delhi: Abhinav Publications, 1989).

Ikram, S.M. 'Introduction' in S.M. Ikram and Percival Spear, eds. *The Cultural Heritage of Pakistan.* (Karachi: Oxford University Press, 1955).

Imran, Ali. *Power and Islamic Legitimacy in Pakistan.* in Anthony Reid and Michael Gilsenan, eds. *Legitimacy in Plural Asia.* (London and New York: Routledge, 2007), 117–138

Inayatullah, C. 'Democracy, Ethno-nationalism and the Emerging World Order' in Sushil Kumar. ed. *Gobachev's Reforms and International Change* (New Delhi: Lancers Books, 1993), 185–210.

Inbar, Efraim and Hillel Frisch, eds. *Islam and International Security Challenges and Responses,* (New York: Routledge, 2008), 153–68

Iqbal, Afzal. *Islamization of Pakistan.* (Lahore: Vanguard Books 1986).

———. *Select Writings and Speeches of Maulana Mohammed Ali.* (Lahore: Sheikh Muhammad Ashraf, 1963).

Iqbal, Javed. *Islam and Pakistan's Identity.* (Lahore: Iqbal Academy Pakistan and Vanguard Books, 2003).

Iqtidar, Humeira. *Secularizing Islamists? Jama'at-e-Islami and Jama'at-ud-Da'wa in Urban Pakistan.* (Chicago and London: The University of Chicago Press, 2011).

Irfani, Saroosh. 'Pakistan's Sectarian Violence: Between the Arabist Shift and Indo-Persian Culture' in Sathu Limaye, Mohan Malik & Robert Wirsing. eds. *Religious Radicalism and Security in South Asia,* (Honolulu, Hawaii: Asia-Pacific Center for Security Studies, 2004), 147–69.

Ispahani, Farahnaz. *Purifying the Land of the Pure: Pakistan's Religious Minorities.* (New Delhi: HarperCollins India, 2015).

Jackson, Robert H. *Quasi-states: Sovereignty, International Relations, and the Third World.* (Cambridge: Cambridge University Press, 1990).

Jackson, Roy. *Mawlana Maududi and Political Islam: Authority and the Islamic State.* (London: Routledge, 2011).

Jafery, Zaman. *Saraiki, Sind, Balochistan: S.S.B. and National Question.* (Multan: Melluha Publications, 1986).

Jaffrelot, Christophe, ed. *A History of Pakistan and Its Origins.* (London: Anthem Press, 2002).

———. *The Pakistan Paradox: Instability and Resilience.* Cynthia Schoch. trans. (Gurgaon, India: Random House India, 2015).

———. *Pakistan: Nationalism Without a Nation?* (New Delhi: Manohar, 2002).

Jahan, Rounaq. *Pakistan: Failure in National Integration.* (New York: Columbia University Press, 1972).

Jain, Arvind K. ed. *The Political Economy of Corruption.* (London: Routledge, 2001).

Jalal, Ayesha. *Democracy and Authoritarianism in South Asia: A Comparative and Historical Perspective.* (Cambridge, Great Britain: Cambridge University Press 1995).

———. *The State of Martial Rule.* (Lahore: Vanguard, 1991).

———. *The State of Martial Rule: The Origins of Pakistan's Political Economy of Defence.* (Cambridge: Cambridge University Press, 1990).

———. *The Struggle for Pakistan: A Muslim Homeland and Global Politics.* (Cambridge: Belknap Press of Harvard University Press, 2014).

Jalibi, Jameel. *Pakistan: The Identity of Culture.* (Karachi: Royal Book, 1984).

Jan, Tarik. ed. *Pakistan between Secularism and Islam: Ideology, Issues and Conflict.* (Islamabad: Institute of Policy Studies, 1998).

Janowitz, Morris. *The Military in the Political Development of New Nations.* (Chicago: University of Chicago Press, 1964).

———. *Military Institutions and Coercion in the Developing Nations: The Military in the Political Development of New Nations.* (Chicago: University of Chicago Press, 1988).

Janson, E. *India, Pakistan or Pakhtunistan?* (Uppsala: Act Universitatis Upsaliensis, 1981).

Jayal, Niraja Gopal. *Representing India: Ethnic Diversity and the Governance of Public Institutions.* (Hampshire: Palgrave Macmillan, 2006).

Job, Brian L. ed, *The Insecurity Dilemma: National Security of Third World States.* (Boulder & London: Lynne Rienner Publisher, 1992).

Joffé, E. G. H. *Islamist Radicalisation in Europe and the Middle East: Reassessing the Causes of Terrorism.* (London: I.B. Tauris, 2013).

Jones, Owen Bennett. *Pakistan: In the Eye of the Storm.* (New Haven, CT: Yale University Press, 2002).

Kamal, K.L. *Pakistan: The Garrison State.* (New Delhi: Intellectual Publishing House, 1982).

Kardar, Shahid. 'Polarizations in the Regions and Prospects for Integration' in S.A. Zaidi, ed. *Regional Imbalances and the National Question in Pakistan* (Lahore: Vangaurd, 1992), 335–55.

———. *The Political Economy of Pakistan.* (Lahore: Progressive Publishers, 1987).

Kaur, Kuldip. *Madrasa Education in India: A Study of its Past and Present.* (Chandigarh: Centre for Research in Rural & Industrial Development, 1990).

Kautsky, John H. 'Nationalism' in Harvey G. Kebschull. ed. *Politics in Transitional Societies,* (New York: Appleton-Century-Crofts, 1973), 231–43.

Kazi, Aftab A. *Ethnicity and Education in Nation-building in Pakistan.* (Lahore: Vanguard, 1994).

Keane, John. 'Despotism and Democracy—The Origin and Development of the Distinction between Civil Society and the State, 1750–8150' in John Keane, ed. *Civil Society and the State: New European Perspectives,* (London: Verso, 1988).

Kedourie, Elie. *Democracy and Arab Political Culture.* (London: Frank Cass, 1994).

Kennedy, Charles H. 'Rural Groups and the Stability of the Zia Regime' in Craig Baxter. ed. *Zia's Pakistan: Politics in a Frontline State,* (Boulder: Westview Press, 1985), 23–46.

_____. *Islamization in Pakistan*. (Islamabad: Institute of Policy Research, 1988).

_____. *Bureaucracy in Pakistan*. (Karachi: Oxford University Press, 1987).

_____. *Islamization of Laws and Economy: Case Studies on Pakistan*. (Islamabad: Institute of Policy Studies, 1996).

Kennedy, G. *The Military in the Third World*. (New York: Charles Scribner, 1974).

Keskin, Turgul. *The Sociology of Islam*. (Reading: Ithaca Press, 2012).

Khaldun, Ibn. *The Muqaddima*, Franz Rosenthal. trans. (New York: Pantheon Books, 1958).

Khaliquzzaman, Choudhry. *Pathway to Pakistan*. (Lahore: Brothers Publishers, 1961).

Khan, Abdul Ghaffar and P. S. Ramu, *Khudai Khidmatgar and National Movement: Momentous Speeches of Badshah Khan*. (Delhi: S.S. Publishers, 1992).

Khan, Adeel. *Politics of Identity: Ethnic Nationalism and the State in Pakistan*. (New Delhi: Sage Publishers, 2005).

Khan, Akbar. *Raiders in Kashmir*. (Islamabad: National Book Foundation, 1975).

Khan, Fazal Muqeem. *Pakistan: Crisis in Leadership*. (Islamabad: National Book Foundation, 1973).

Khan, Hussain Ahmad and Samina Choonara, *Re-thinking Punjab: The Construction of Siraiki Identity*. (Lahore: Research and Publication Centre, 2004).

Khan, Ijaz. *Pakistan's Strategic Culture and Foreign Policy Making: A Study of Pakistan's Post 9/11 Afghan Policy Change*. (New York: Nova Science Publishers, 2007).

Khan, Liaquat Ali. *Pakistan, the Heart of Asia; Speeches in the United States and Canada, May and June 1950*. (Cambridge: Harvard University Press, 1950).

Khan, M. Asghar. *We've Learnt Nothing from History: Pakistan, Politics and Military Power*. (Karachi: Oxford University Press, 2005).

Khan, Mohammad Asghar. *Generals in Politics: Pakistan 1958–1982*. (New Delhi: Vikas Publishing House, 1983).

Khan, Mohammad Ayub. *Speeches and Statements* (Karachi: n.d.).

_____, and Nadia Ghani, *Field Marshal Mohammad Ayub Khan: A Selection of Talks and Interviews, 1964–1967*. (Karachi: Oxford University Press, 2010).

_____. *Friends Not Masters*. (Karachi: Oxford University Press, 1967).

Khan, Muhammad Akram. *Millat aur Watan: A Debate between Maulana Syed Husain Ahmad Madni and Allama Sir Muhammad Iqbal*. (Multan: Idara Rosenama Shams, 1938).

_____. *An Introduction to Islamic Economics* (Islamabad: The International Institute of Islamic Thought and Institute for Policy Studies, 1994).

Khan, Rais Ahmad. 'Pakistan-United States Relations' in *Proceedings of the National Symposium*, (Islamabad: 1982).

Khan, Riaz M. *Untying the Afghan Knot: Negotiating Soviet Withdrawal*. (Durham: Duke University Press, 1991).

Khan, Sardar Shaukat Hayat. *A Nation that Lost its Soul*. (Lahore: Jang Publishers, 1995).

Khan, Sir Sayyid Ahmad. *Maqalat-i-Sir Sayyid Ahmad Khan*. (Lahore: Majlis-i-Taraqi-i-Urdu, 1991).

Khan, Abdul Ghaffar. *Khan Abdul Ghaffar Khan: A Centennial Tribute*. (New Delhi: Har-Anand Publications, 1995).

Khan, Yasmin. *The Great Partition: The Making of India and Pakistan*. (New Haven: Yale University Press, 2007).

Khulusi, S. A. *Islam Our Choice*. (Woking: Woking Muslim Mission & Literary Trust, 1961).

Kingsley, De Silva. *Internationalization of Ethnic Conflict in South Asia*. (Kandy: International Centre for Ethnic Studies, 1991).

Kingston, Rebecca. *Montesquieu and His Legacy*. (Albany: SUNY Press, 2009).

Krishna, Rajeshwari. *Khan Abdul Ghaffar Khan*. (Bangalore: Sapna Book House, 2002).

Kronstadt, K. Alan. *Pakistan-US Relations*. (Washington, DC: Congressional Research Service Library of Congress 2009).

Kugelman, Michael. *Urbanization in Pakistan: Causes and Consequences*. (Oslo: Norwegian Peace Building Resource Centre, January 2013).

Kukreja, Veena. *Military Intervention in Politics: A Case Study of Pakistan*. (New Delhi: NBO Publisher's Distributors, 1985).

Kurzman, Charles. ed. *Liberal Islam: A Sourcebook.* (Oxford: Oxford University Press, 1998).

Kux, Dennis. *The United States and Pakistan, 1947–2000: Disenchanted Allies.* (Washington: Woodrow Wilson Center Press, 2001).

Lamb, Alastair. *Kashmir: A Disputed Legacy, 1846–199.* (Hertinfordbury: Roxford Books, 1991).

Lampe, John R. and Mark Mazower, *Ideologies and National Identities: The Case of Twentieth-century Southeastern Europe.* (Budapest: Central European University Press, 2004).

Landau, Jacob M. *Pan-Islam: History and Politics.* (London: Routledge, 2016).

———. *Turkey Opts Out, while India's Muslims Get Involved: The Politics of Pan-Islam.* (Oxford: Oxford University Press, 1994).

Langah, Nukhbah Taj *Call for Siraiki Province* (Ottawa and Islamabad: Forum of Federations and Centre for Civic Education Pakistan, 2011).

LaPorte, Robert. *Power and Privilege: Influence and Decision-Making in Pakistan.* (California: University of California Press, 1975).

Lavan, Spencer. *The Ahmadiyah Movement: A History and Perspective.* (New Delhi: Manohar Book Service, 1974).

Lerner, Daniel. *The Passing of Traditional Society: Modernizing the Middle East.* (New York: Free Press, 1958).

Lieven, Anatol. *A Hard Country.* (London: Allen Lane, 2011).

Lofchie, Micheal F. ed. *State of the Nations.* (Berkeley: University of California Press, 1971).

Long, Roger D., et. al. *State and Nation-Building in Pakistan: Beyond Islam and Security.* (London: Routledge/Taylor & Francis Group, 2016).

Lovett, Verney. *A History of the Indian Nationalist Movement.* (Hove: Psychology Press, 1968).

Lumbard, Joseph E. B. ed. *Islam, Fundamentalism and the Betrayal of Tradition.* (World Wisdom, 2009).

M. Dessing, Nathal, Nadia Jeldtoft and Linda Woodhead. *Everyday Lived Islam in Europe.* (Burlington, VT: Ashgate, 2013).

M. Rafique Afzal, *Pakistan: History and Politics, 1947–1971.* (Karachi: Oxford University Press, 2001).

Macdonald, Duncan Black. *The Religious Attitude and Life in Islam: Being the*

Haskell Lectures on Comparative Religion Delivered before the University of Chicago in 1906. (Chicago: University of Chicago Press, 1909).

Machiavelli, Niccolo. *The Prince*. (Irving, TX: University of Dallas Press, 1980).

Madani, Maulana Hussain Ahmad *Composite Nationalism and Islam*. (New Delhi: Manohar Publ., 2005).

Madni, Maulana Syed Husain Ahmad. *Naqsh-i-Hayat*. (Karachi: Baitul Tauheed, 1953).

Mahajan. Sneh. *British Foreign Policy, 1874–1914: The Role of India*. (London: Routledge, 2002).

Mahmood, M. *The Constitution of Islamic Republic of Pakistan 1973*. (Lahore: Pakistan Law Research Academy, 2015).

Major, Andrew J. *Return to Empire: Punjab under the Sikhs and British in the Mid-Nineteenth Century*. (New Delhi: Sterling Publishers Private Limited, 1996).

Malik Siraj Akbar. *The Redefined Dimensions of Baloch Nationalist Movement*. (New York: Xlibris, 2011).

Malik, Anas. ed. *Pakistan: Founder's Aspirations and Today's Realities*. (Karachi: Oxford University Press, 2001).

Malik, Anas. 'Pakistan' In Neil DeVotta. ed. *An Introduction to South Asian Politics*, (New York: Routledge, 2016), 32–57.

Malik, Hafeez. *Moslem Nationalism in India and Pakistan*. (Washington, DC: Public Affairs Press, 1963).

Malik, Iftikhar H. *Religious Minorities in Pakistan*. (London: Minority Rights Group International, 2002).

Malik, Muhammad Fateh. *Punjabi Identity*. (Lahore: Sang-e-Meel Publications, 1989).

Malik, Rizwan. *The Politics of One Unit, 1955–58*. (Lahore: Pakistan Study Centre, University of the Punjab, 1988).

Malik, Sohail Jehangir. Safiya Aftab, and Nargis Sultana, *Pakistan's Economic Performance, 1947 to 1993: A Descriptive Analysis*. (Lahore: Sure Publishers, 1994).

Mann, Michael 'The Autonomous Power of the State: Its Origins, Mechanisms and Result' in Job A. Hall. ed. *States in History*, (Oxford: Basil Blackwell, 1986).

Markey, Daniel S. *No Exist from Pakistan.* (Cambridge: Cambridge University Press, 2013).

Markey, Daniel Seth. *No Exit from Pakistan: America's Tortured Relationship with Islamabad.* (New York: Cambridge University Press, 2013).

Maroney, Eric. *Religious Syncretism.* (London: SCM Press, 2006).

Marty, Martin E. and R. Scott Appleby. eds. *Accounting for Fundamentalists: The Dynamic Character of Movements.* (Chicago: University of Chicago Press, 2004).

Marx, Karl. *Foundations of the Critique of Political Economy.* (New York: Vintage Books, 1973).

Maududi, Sayyid Abul A'la. *The Islamic Law and Constitution.* (Lahore: Islamic Publications Ltd, 1980).

Maussen, Marcel, Veit-Michael Bader, and Annelies Moors, *Colonial and Postcolonial Governance of Islam: Continuities and Ruptures.* (Amsterdam: Amsterdam University Press, 2011).

Maududi, Sayed Abul A'la. *Musalman aur Maujuda Siyasi Kashmakash* [Muslims and the Present Political Struggle] Vol. II. (Pathankot: Maktaba-e-Jamaat-e-Islami, 1938).

————. *Nationalism and India.* (Pathankot: Maktaba-e-Jammat-e-Islami, 1967).

————. *The Islamic Way of Life.* (Islamabad: Islamic Dawah Centre International, 1980).

————. *The Islamic Way of Life.* Khuram Murad and Khurshid Ahmed. trans. (Leicester: Islamic Foundation, 1986).

————. *Islami Tehzib aur uske Usul'u Mabadi.* (Lahore: Islamic Publications, 1966).

————. *Jama'at-i-Islami; Tarikh, Maqsad aur La'ihah-i' Amal.* (Lahore: Islamic Publications, 1963).

————. *The Islamic State,* Translated by Khurshid Ahmed. trans. (Lahore: Islamic Publication, 1969).

————. *Tehrikh-e-Azadi-e-Hind aur Musalmans* [The Indian independence movement and Muslims] (Lahore: Islamic Publications, 1974).

————, and Khurshid Ahmad, *Political Theory of Islam.* (Lahore: Islamic Publications, 1980).

_____. *Islami Riyasat* [Islamic State] (Lahore: Islamic Publications Ltd., 1969).

_____. *Rasail-wa-Masail*. (Lahore: Islamic Publications Limited, 1967).

Mazrui, Ali A, Ramzi Bdran and Thomas Uthup, eds. *Resurgent Islam and Politics of Identity*. (Newcastle: Cambridge Scholars Publishing, 2014).

McGrath, Allen. *The Destruction of Pakistan's Democracy*. (Karachi: Oxford University Press, 1996).

Mehdi, Bazargan. *Religion and Liberty*. In *Liberal Islam, A Source Book*, Charles Kurzman. ed. (New York: Oxford University Press, 1998).

Memon, Ali Nawaz. *The Islamic Nation: Status & Future of Muslims in the New World Order*. (Beltsville: Writers' International, 1995).

Mernissi, Fatima. *Islam and Democracy: Fear of the Modern World*. (Reading, Mass: Addison-Wesley, 1992).

Metcalf, Barbara Daly. *Islamic Revival in British India: Deoband, 1860–1900*. (Karachi: Royal Book Company, 1989).

Miller, Judith. *God has Ninety–nine Names*. (New York: Touchstone, 1997).

Moaddel, Mansoor. *Islamic Modernism, Nationalism, and Fundamentalism: Episode and Discourse*. (Chicago: University of Chicago Press, 2005).

_____. and Kamran Talattof. Eds. *Contemporary Debates in Islam: An Anthology of Modernist and Fundamentalist Thought*. (New York: St. Martin's Press, 2000).

_____, and Kamran Talattof. Eds. *Modernist and Fundamentalist Debates in Islam: A Reader*. (New York: Palgrave, MacMillan, 2002).

Moghaddam, Arshin Adib. *A Critical Introduction to Khomeini*. (Cambridge: Cambridge University Press, 2014).

Moghissi, Haideh and Halleh Ghorashi. Eds. *Muslim Diaspora in the West: Negotiating Gender, Home and Belonging*. (London: Routledge, 2010).

Mommsen, Wolfgang J. 'The Varieties of the Nation-State in Modern History: Liberal, Imperialist, Fascist and Contemporary Notions of Nation and Nationality' In Michael Mann. ed. *The Rise and Decline of the Nation-State*, (Oxford: Basil Blackwell, 1990), 210–226.

Mondal, Anshuman A. *Nationalism and Postcolonial Identity: Culture and Ideology in India and Egypt*. (London and New York: Routledge Curzon, 2003).

Muhammad, Elijah. *History of the Nation of Islam*. (Atlanta: Secretarius Memps Publications, 1994).

Mujahid, Sharif al. *Quaid-i-Azam Jinnah: Studies in Interpretation*. (Karachi: Quaid-i-Azam Academy, 1981).

Munir, Justice Muhammad. *From Jinnah to Zia*. (Lahore: Vanguard Books, 1980).

Musharraf, Pervez. *In the Line of Fire: A Memoir*. (London: Simon & Schuster, 2006).

Mutalib, Hussin *Islam and Democracy: The Southeast Asian Experience*. (Singapore: Konrad-Adenauer-Stiftung Singapore, 2004).

Nagarkar. V.V. *Genesis of Pakistan*. (New Delhi: Allied Publishers, 1975).

Naqvi, M. B. *Pakistan at Knife's Edge*. (New Delhi: Lotus Collection, 2010).

Nasr, Seyyed Vali Raza. *The Vanguard of Islamic Revolution: The Jama'at-i-Islami of Pakistan*. (Berkeley: University of California Press, 1994).

———. *Maududi and the Making of Islamic Revivalism*. (New York: Oxford University Press, 1996).

———. *The Vanguard of the Islamic Revolution*. (Berkeley: University of California Press, 1994).

Nawaz, Shuja. *Crossed Swords: Pakistan, Its Army, and the Wars Within*. (Oxford: Oxford University Press, 2009).

Naz, Huma. *Bureaucratic Elites & Political Developments in Pakistan, 1947–58*.

(Islamabad: National Institute of Pakistan Studies, Quaid-i-Azam University, 1990).

Nesser, Petter. *Islamist Terrorism in Europe: A History*. (New York: Oxford University Press, 2015).

Nevitte, Neil and Charles H. Kennedy, *Ethnic Preference and Public Policy in Developing States*. (Boulder: Lynee Rienner Publishers, Inc., 1986).

Newberg, Paula R. *Judging the State: Courts and Constitutional Politics in Pakistan*. (Cambridge: Cambridge University Press, 1995).

———. 'Balancing Act: Prudence, Impunity, and Pakistan's Jurisprudence' in Paul Brass, ed. *Routledge Handbook of South Asian Politic,* (New York: Routledge, 2010), 177–91.

Niaz, Ilhan. *The Culture of Power and Governance in Pakistan*. (Karachi: Oxford University Press, 2010).

Nordlinger, Eric A. *Soldiers in Politics: Military Coups and Governments.* (Englewood Cliffs, NJ: Prentice-Hall, 1977).

Oldenburg, Philip. *India, Pakistan, and Democracy: Solving the Puzzle of Divergent Paths.* (Abingdon: Routledge, 2010).

Özcan, Azmi. *Pan-Islamism: Indian Muslims, the Ottomans and Britain, 1877–1924.* (Leiden: Brill, 1997).

Pangle, Thomas L. *Montesquieu's Philosophy of Liberalism: A Commentary on the Spirit of the Laws.* (Chicago: University of Chicago Press, 1973).

Panipati, Maulana Muhammad Ismail. *Maqalaat-i-Sir Siyyad.* (Lahore: Majlis-e-Taraqe-i-Adab, 1963).

Pateman, Carole. *Participation and Democratic Theory.* (Cambridge: Cambridge University Press, 1970).

Peers, Douglas M. and Nandini Goopta. *India and the British Empire.* (Oxford: Oxford University Press, 2012).

Persson, Magnus. *Great Britain, the United States, and the Security of the Middle East: The Formation of the Baghdad Pact.* (Lund: Lund University Press, 1998).

Peter, Frank. *Islamic Movements of Europe.* (London: Tauris, 2013).

_____, and Rafael Ortega. *Islamic Movements of Europe: Public Religion and Islamophobia in the Modern World.* (London: I. B. Tauris, 2014).

Peters, Rudolph. *Islam and Colonialism: The Doctrine of Jihad in Modern History.* (The Hague: Mouton, 1979).

Phadnis, Urmila. *Ethnicity and Nation-Building in South Asia.* (New Delhi: Sage Publications, 1989).

Phares, Walid. *The Coming Revolution: Struggle for Freedom in the Middle East.* (New York: Threshold Editions, 2010).

Pipes, Daniel. *In the Path of God: Islam and Political Power.* (New York: Basic Books, 1983).

Pisoiu, Daniela. *Islamist Radicalisation in Europe: An Occupational Change Process.* (Abingdon, Oxon: Routledge, 2012).

Qadri, Muhammad Tahir-ul. *Introduction to the Fatwa on Suicide Bombings and Terrorism.* Shaykh Abdul Aziz Dabbagh. trans. (London: Minhaj-ul-Qur'an International, 2010).

Qasmi, Ali Usman. *The Ahmadis and the Politics of Religious Exclusion in Pakistan.* (New York: Anthem Press, 2014).

———. *The Ahmadis and the Politics of Religious Exclusion in Pakistan*, (London: Anthem Press, 2015).

Qureshi, Ishtiaq Husain. *The Pakistani Way of Life*. (Karachi: Royal Book Company, 1988).

Qureshi, Ishtiaq Husain. *Perspectives of Islam and Pakistan*. (Karachi: Ma'aref, 1979).

Rabasa Angel and Cheryl Benard, *Eurojihad: Patterns of Islamist Radicalization and Terrorism in Europe*. (New York: Cambridge University Press, 2015).

Rabbani, Mian Raza. *A Biography of Pakistani Federalism: Unity in Diversity*. (Islamabad: Leo Books, 2014).

Rafiq, Adnan. 'New Politics of the Middle Class' in Ishtiaq Ahmad and Adnan Rafiq. ed. *Pakistan's Democratic Transition: Change and Persistence,* (London and New York: Routledge, 2017), 72–94.

Rahman, Fatima Z. 'Pakistan: A Conducive Setting for Islamist Violence against Ahmadis' in Jawad Syed, Edwina Pio, Tahir Kamran, and Abbas Zaidi. ed. *Faith-Based Violence and Deobandi Militancy in Pakistan*, (London: Palgrave Macmillan, 2016).

Rahman, Fazlur. *Islam*. (Chicago: University of Chicago Press, 1966).

———. *Islam and Modernity: Transformation of an Intellectual Tradition*. (Chicago: University of Chicago Press, 1982).

———. *Islamic Methodology in History*. (Karachi: Central Institute of Islamic Research, 1965).

Rahman, Tariq. *Language and Politics in Pakistan*. (Karachi: Oxford University Press, 1996).

Rais, Muhammad Amein. *The Muslim Brotherhood in Egypt: Its Rise Demise and Resurgence*. (Chicago: University Microfilms International, 2002).

Rais, Rasul Bakhsh. 'Pakistan's Strategic Culture and Deterrence Stability on the Subcontinent' In Michael Krepon, Joshua T. White, Julia Thompson, and Shane Mason. ed. *Deterrence Instability and Nuclear Weapons in South Asia,* (Washington: Stimson, 2015), 95–118.

———. *Recovering the Frontier State: War, Ethnicity and State in Afghanistan*. (Lanham: Lexington Books, 2008).

Rana, Muhammad Amir. *A to Z of Jihadi Organizations in Pakistan*. Translated by Saba Ansari. Lahore: Mashal Books, 2006.

Ranstrop, Magnus, ed. *Understanding Violent Radicalization: Terrorist and Jihadist Movements in Europe*. (London: Routledge, 2010).

Raqib, Mohammad. 'The Muslim Pashtun Movement of the North-West Frontier of India, 1930–1934' in M. Stephen. ed. *Civilian Jihads*, (New York: Palgrave Macmillan, 2009), 107–18.

Rashid, Ahmed. *Pakistan on Brink*. (London: Allen Lane, 2011).

Rashid, Amjad. 'The Challenges of *the* a Resilient Economy' In Isthtiaq Ahmad and Adnan Rafiq, ed. *Pakistan's Democratic Transition: Change and Persistence*, (London and New York: Routledge, 2017), 192–209.

Rašwān, Ḍiyā' and Muhḥammad Fāyiz. Faraḥāt, *The Spectrum of Islamist Movements*. (Berlin: H. Schiler, 2007).

Rehman, Hafizur ed. *Resistance Literature*. (Islamabad: Pakistan Academy of Letters, 2010).

Rengel, Marian. *Pakistan: A Primary Source Cultural Guide*. (New York: Power Plus Books, 2004).

Richter, Melvin. *The Political Theory of Montesquieu*. (New York: Cambridge University Press, 1977).

Riedel, Bruce. *Deadly Embrace: Pakistan, America, and the Future of the Global Jihad*. (Washington, DC: Brooking Institution Press, 2011).

Riff, M. A. *Dictionary of Modern Political Ideologies*. (New York: St. Martin's Press, 1987).

Riggs, Red W. *Ethnicity: Concepts and Terms Used in Ethnicity Research*. (Honolulu: International Social Science Council, 1985).

Ringer, Fritz. *Max Weber: An Intellectual Biography*. (Chicago: The University of Chicago Press, 2004).

Rizvi, Hasan Askari. *Military, State, and Society in Pakistan*. (New York: St. Martin's Press, 2000).

_____. *The Military and Politics in Pakistan, 1947–86*. (Lahore: Progressive Publishers, 1986).

_____. *Military and Politics in Pakistan, 1947–1997*. (Lahore: Sange-e-Meel Publications, 2000).

_____. 'Pakistan's Strategic Culture' In Michael R. Chalmers. ed. *South Asia in 2020: Future Strategic Balances and Alliances*. (Carlisle: Strategic Studies Institute, 2002), 305–28.

————. *Pakistan and the Geostrategic Environment*. New York: St. Martin's Press, 1993.

Robert Nichols, *A History of Pashtun Migration 1775–2006*. (Karachi: Oxford University Press, 2008).

Roger D. Long et al., *State and Nation-Building in Pakistan: Beyond Islam and Security*. (London: Routledge/Taylor & Francis Group, 2016).

Rome, Sultan-i-Rome. *Swat (1915–1969) from Genesis to Merger: An Analysis of Political, Administrative, Socio-political, and Economic Development*. (Karachi: Oxford University Press, 2008).

Rose, Leo E and Kamal Matinuddin, *Beyond Afghanistan: The Emerging US-Pakistan Relations*. (Berkeley: Institute of East Asian Studies, University of California, 1989).

Rouse, Shahnaz. 'Women's Movement in Pakistan: State, Class, Gender' In Kamala Visweswaran. ed. *Perspectives on Modern South Asia: A Reader in Culture, History, and Representation,* (Malden, Massachusetts and Oxford: Wiley-Blackwell, 2011), 321–7.

Roy, M. N. *Historical Role of Islam*. (Lahore: Sind Sagar Academy, 1974).

Roy, Olivier. *The Failure of Political Islam*. (Cambridge: Harvard University Press, 1994).

Roy, Samaren. *The Bengalees: Glimpses of History and Culture*. (New Delhi: Allied Publishers, 1999).

Rubin, Andrew N. *Archives of Authority: Empire, Culture and the Cold War*. (Princeton, London: Princeton University Press, 2012).

Rubin, Barry M *Guide to Islamist Movements* (Armonk: M.E. Sharpe, 2010).

Saeed, S.A. *A President without Precedent: A Brilliant Account of Ayub and His Regime*. (Lahore: Lahore Book Depot, 1960).

Said, Edward W. *Culture and Imperialism: Theories of Imperialism from Adam Smith to Lenin*. (New York: Alfred A. Knopf, 1993).

Salim Ahmad and Humaira Ishfaq, eds. *Faiz, Folk Heritage and Problems of Culture*. (Islamabad and Lahore: Lok Virsa and Sang-e-Meel Publications, 2013).

Sankhdher, M.M. *Secularism in India, Dilemmas and Challenges*. (New Delhi: Deep & Deep Publications, 1992).

Sargent, Lyman Tower *Contemporary Political Ideologies: A Comparative Analysis*. (Homewood: Dorsey Press, 1969).

Sayeed, Khalid B. *Politics in Pakistan: The Nature and Direction of Change* (New York: Praeger, 1980).

Sayeed, Khalid Bin. *Pakistan: The Formative Phase 1857–1948*. (Karachi: Oxford University Press, 2007).

Schlichte, Klaus. *The Dynamics of States: The Formation and Crises of State Domination*. (England: Ashgate, 2005).

Schofield, Victoria. *Bhutto: Trial and Execution*. (London: Cassell, 1979).

Sen, Ragini, Wolfgang Wagner, and Caroline Howarth, *Secularism and Religion in Multi-faith Societies: The Case of India*. (Cham: Springer, 2014).

Shackle, Christopher. *The Siraiki Language of Central Pakistan: A Reference Grammar*. (London: School of Oriental and African Studies, 1976).

Shafqat, Saeed. *Civil-Military Relations in Pakistan: From Zulfikar Ali Bhutto to Benazir Bhutto*. (Boulder, Colorado: Westview Press, 1997).

Shah, Aqil. *The Army and Democracy: Military Politics in Pakistan*. (Cambridge: Harvard University Press, 2014).

Shahi, Agha. *Pakistan's Security and Foreign Policy*. (Lahore: Progressive Publishers, 1988).

Shaikh, Farzana. *Community and Consensus in Islam: Muslim Representation in Colonial India, 1860–1947*. (Cambridge: Cambridge University Press, 1989).

———. *Making Sense of Pakistan*. (London: Hurst & Company, 2009).

Shapiro, Ian. *The State of Democratic Theory*. (Princeton: Princeton University Press, 2003).

Shehab, Rafi Ullah. *Fifty Years of Pakistan*. (Lahore: Maqbool Academy, 1990).

Sherman, Taylor C. *Muslim Belonging in Secular India*. (Cambridge: Cambridge University Press, 2015).

Sho, Kuwajima. *Muslims, Nationalism, and the Partition: 1946 Provincial Elections in India*. (New Delhi: Manohar, 1998).

Siddiqa, Ayesha. *Military Inc.: Inside Pakistan's Military Economy*. (Karachi: Oxford University Press, 2007).

Siddiqi, Aslam. *Pakistan Seeks Security*. (Lahore: Longmans, Green, Pakistan Branch, 1960).

Siddiqi, Farhan Haneef. *The Politics of Ethnicity in Pakistan*. (London & New York: Routledge, 2012).

Singh, Jaswant. *Jinnah: India-Partition-Independence.* (New Delhi: Rupa and Co., 2009).

Sinha, Himmat. *Babus, Brahmans & Bureaucrats: A Critique of the Administrative System in Pakistan.* (New Delhi: People's Publishing House, 1973).

Sisk, Timothy D. *Islam and Democracy: Religion, Politics, and Power in the Middle East.* (Washington, DC: United States Institute of Peace, 1992).

Sisson, Richard and Leo E. Rose, *War and Secession: Pakistan, India, and the Creation of Bangladesh.* (Berkeley: University of California Press, 1990).

Smit, Christian Reus. *The Moral Purpose of the State: Culture, Social Identity, and Institutional Rationality in International Relations.* (Princeton: Princeton University Press, 1999).

Smith, Anthony D. 'State-Making and Nation-Building' In A. Hall. ed. *States in History,* (Oxford: Basil Blackwell, 1986).

———. *The Ethnic Origin of Nations.* (Oxford: Basil Blackwell, 1988).

Smith, Donald Eugene. *India as a Secular State.* (Princeton: Princeton University Press, 1963).

Speier, Hans. *Democracy and Authoritarianism in South Asia: A Comparative and Historical Perspective.* (Lahore: Sang-e-Meel Publications, 1995).

———. 'Preface' in John J. Johnson. ed. *The Role of the Military in Underdeveloped Countries,* (Princeton: Princeton University Press, 1962), 1–7.

Speier, Hans. *The Sole Spokesman.* (Cambridge: Cambridge University Press, 1985).

———. *The State of Martial Rule: The Origins of Pakistan's Political Economy of Defence.* (Cambridge: Cambridge University Press, 1990).

Subrahmanyam, K. *Indian Security Perspectives.* (New Delhi: ABC Pub. House, 1982).

Suleri, Ziauddin Ahmad. *Pakistan's Lost Years: Being a Survey of a Decade of Politics, 1948–1958.* (Lahore: Progressive Papers, 1962).

Syed, Anwar Hussain. *Pakistan: Islam, Politics, and National Solidarity.* (New York: Praeger, 1982).

Talbot, Ian. *Pakistan, a Modern History.* (New York: St. Martin's Press, 1998).

———. *Provincial Politics and the Pakistan Movement: The Growth of Muslim*

League in North-West and North-East India, 1937–1947. (Karachi: Oxford University Press, 1988).

Tan, Tai Yong and Gyanesh Kudaisya, *The Aftermath of Partition in South Asia,* (London: Routledge, 2000).

Tellis, Ashley J. and Michael Wills. *Military Modernization in an Era of Uncertainty.* (Seattle: National Bureau of Asian Research, 2005).

The Cultural Policy of Pakistan. (Islamabad: National Commission on History & Culture, Ministry of Culture, Sports & Tourism, Government of Pakistan, 1995).

Thomas, Caroline. 'New Directions in Thinking about Security in the Third World' In Ken Booth. ed. *New Thinking about Strategy and International Security,* (London: Harper Collins Academic, 1991).

_____. 'Southern Instability, Security and Western Concepts: On an Unhappy Marriage and the Need for a Divorce' in Caroline Thomas and Paikiasothy Saravanamuttu, eds. *The State and Instability in the South,* (New York: St. Martin's Press, 1989).

_____. *In Search of Security: The Third World in International Relations.* (Boulder: Lynne Rienner, 1987).

Tilly, Charles. 'Reflection on the History of European State-Making' In Charles Tilly. ed. *The Formation of National States in Western Europe,* (Princeton: Princeton University Press, 1975).

Toor, Saadia. *The State of Islam: Culture and Cold War Politics in Pakistan.* (London: Pluto Press, 2011).

Tracy, Destutt De, et al. *A Commentary and Review of Montesquieu's Spirit of Laws.* (New York: B. Franklin, 1969).

Troll, Christian W. *Islam in the Indian Subcontinent: Muslims in Secular India.* (Tokyo: Sophia University, 1986).

Ullah, Haroon K. *Vying for Allah's Vote: Understanding Islamic Parties, Political Violence and Extremism in Pakistan.* (Washington, DC: Georgetown University Press, 2014).

Umar, Badruddin. *The Emergence of Bangladesh: Rise of Bengali Nationalism, 1958–1971.* (New York: Oxford University Press, 2006).

Umar, Sani Muhammad. *Islam and Colonialism: Intellectual Responses of Muslims of Northern Nigeria to British Colonial Rule.* (Amsterdam: Brill, 2006).

Usmani, Shabbir Ahmad. *Pakistan aur Khutbat-i-Usmani*. (Lahore: Shahid Book Depot, 1989).

Vahid, S. A. *Thoughts and Reflections of Iqbal*. (Lahore: Sh. Ashraf & Sons, 1964).

Valentine, Simon Rose. *Islam and the Ahmadiyya Jama'at: History, Belief, Practice*. (London: Hurst, 2008).

Veblen, Thorstein. 'The Predatory State' In Waldo R. Browne. ed. *Leviathan in Crisis*, (New York: The Viking Press, 1946), 25–33.

Vincent, Andrew. *Modern Political Ideologies*. (Oxford: Blackwell, 1995).

Volpi, Frédéric. *Political Islam Observed: Disciplinary Perspectives*. (New York: Columbia University Press, 2010).

————. *Political Islam: A Critical Reader*. (London: Routledge, 2011).

Vorys, Karl Von. *Political Development in Pakistan*. (Princeton: Princeton University Press, 2015).

Waltz, Kenneth. 'The Anarchic Structure of World Politics' *Theory of International Politics*. (Reading: Addison-Wesley Pub., 1979), 40–66.

Wariavwalla, Bharat K. 'Security with Status: What Motivates India's Security Policy' In W. Thomas Wander & Eric H. Arnett. eds. *The Proliferation of Advanced Weaponry: Technology, Motivations, and Responses,* (Washington, DC: AAAS, 1992), 255–68.

Waseem, Muhammad. *Politics and the State in Pakistan*. (Lahore: Progressive Publishers, 1989).

Weiss, Anita. *Interpreting Islam, Modernity and Women's Rights in Pakistan*. (New York: Palgrave Macmillan, 2014).

Wheeler, Robert Eric Mortimer. *Five Thousand Years of Pakistan: An Archaeological Outline*. (Karachi: Royal Book Company, 1992).

White, Vibert L. *Inside the Nation of Islam: A Historical and Personal Testimony by a Black Muslim*. (Gainesville: University Press of Florida, 2001).

Whitfield, Stephen J. *The Culture of the Cold War*. (Baltimore, London W: The Johns Hopkins University Press, 1996).

Wilder, Andrew R. *Pakistani Voter*. (Karachi: Oxford University Press, 1999).

Wilson, Peter H. *The Thirty Years War: Europe's Tragedy*. (Cambridge: Harvard University Press, 2009).

Wink, Andre. *Al-Hind: Making of the Indo-Islamic World*. (Leiden: Brill, 2002).

Wirsing, Robert G. 'Political Islam, Pakistan and the Geopolitics of Religious Identity' in Satu P. Limaye, Kohan Malik and Robert G. Wirsing, eds. *Religious Radicalism and Security in South Asia* (Honolulu: Asia-Pacific Center for Security Studies, 2004), 165–78.

Wolpert, Stanley A. *Shameful Flight: The Last Years of the British Empire in India*. (Oxford: Oxford University Press, 2006).

_____. *Jinnah of Pakistan*. (Karachi: Oxford University Press, 1989).

Wrigginns, Howard. *Pakistan in Transition*. (Islamabad: University of Islamabad Press, 1975).

Yeşilbursa, B. Kemal. *The Baghdad Pact: Anglo-American Defence Policies in the Middle East, 1950–1959*. (London: Frank Cass, 2005).

Yong, Tan Tai. *The Garrison State: Military, Government and Society in Colonial Punjab, 1849–1947*. (New Delhi: Sage Publications India, 2005).

Yousaf, Muhammad and Mark Adkin, *Afghanistan-the Bear Trap: The Defeat of a Superpower*, (Havertown: Casemate, 2001).

Yusuf, Moeed. *Decoding Pakistan's 'Strategic Shift' in Afghanistan*. (Stockholm: SIPRI, May 2013).

Zaheer, Hasan. *The Times and Trial of the Rawalpindi Conspiracy 1951: The First Coup Attempt in Pakistan*. (Karachi: Oxford University Press, 1998).

Zaidi, Shabbar. *Pakistan is Not a Failed State*. (Karachi: Zam Zam Publishers, 2014).

Ziring, Lawrence. *Pakistan at the Cross-Currents of History*. (One World Series. 2004).

_____. *The Ayub Khan Era: Politics in Pakistan, 1958–1969*. (Syracuse: Syracuse University Press, 1971).

JOURNALS

Abbott, Freeland. 'The Jamaat-e-Islami of Pakistan' *The Middle East Journal* 11 (Winter, 1957), 40.

Addi, Lahouari. Algeria's Army, Algeria's Agony' *Foreign Affairs* 77/4 (Aug 1998), 44–53.

Ahmad, Mumtaz. 'The Crescent and the Sword: Islam, the Military, and Political Legitimacy in Pakistan, 1977–1985' *The Middle East Journal* 10/1 (1996), 372–86.

Ahmad, Raza. 'The Endemic Crisis of Federalism in Pakistan' *The Lahore Journal of Economics* 15 (September 2010), 15–31.

Ahmar, Moonis. 'Ethnicity and State Power in Pakistan: The Karachi Crisis' *Asian Survey* 36/10 (October 1996), 136–40.

Ahmed, Feroz. 'Ethnicity and Politics: The Rise of Mohajir Separatism' *South Asia Bulletin*, 8 (1988), 33–57.

Ahmed, Naseem. 'General Musharaf's Taliban Policy 1999–2008' *The Dialogue* 5/2. (June, 2010), 96–124.

Ahmed, Zahid Shahab. 'The Role of the Pakistani Mass Media in the Lawyers' Resistance against the Musharraf Dictatorship, 2007–2009' *Pakistaniat: A Journal of Pakistan Studies* 4/3 (2012), 61–77.

Ahsan, Syed Badrul. 'Agartala Conspiracy Case and its Ramifications' *The Daily Observer* (Dhaka, June 19, 2015); *The All Pakistan Legal Decisions* 26.2 (1974), 140–60.

Akbar, Muqarab. 'Pakistan: An Islamic State or a State for Muslims? A Critical Appraisal of Islam's Role in Pakistan' *Pakistan Journal of Islamic Research*, 15 (2015), 25–38.

Akhtar, Nasreen 'Balochistan Nationalist Movement and Unrest in Pakistan' *South Asian Survey* 18/1 (2011), 121–35.

Alavi, Hamza. 'Social Forces and Ideology in the Making of Pakistan' *Economic and Political Weekly*, 37/51 (2002), 5119–124.

––––––. 'Misreading Partition Road Signs' *Economic and Political Weekly* (November 2002), 2–9.

––––––. 'Nationhood and Nationalities in Pakistan' *Economic and Political Weekly* 24/27 (July 1989), 1527–34.

––––––. 'The State in Postcolonial Societies: Pakistan and Bangladesh' *New Left Review*, 74 (January 1972), 59–81.

Ali Usman Qasmi, 'God's Kingdom on Earth? Politics of Islam in Pakistan, 1947–1969' *Modern Asian Studies* 44/6, (November 2010), 1197–1253.

Ali, Imtiaz. 'The Balochistan Problem' *Pakistan Horizon*, 58/2 (2005), 41–62.

Ali, Kamran Asdar. 'Pakistani Islamists Gamble on the General' *Middle East Research and Information Project, MER* 231 (Summer 2004), 2–7.

Ali, Tariq. 'Movement for the Restoration of Democracy in Pakistan' *India International Centre Quarterly* 11/1 (March 1984), 57–69.

Anderson, Michael R. 'Islamic Law and the Colonial Encounter in British India' *Institutions and Ideologies: A SOAS South Asia Reader* 10/3 (1993), 165–85.

Anjum, Tanvir. 'The Emergence of Muslim Rule in India: Some Historical Disconnects and Missing Links' *Islamic Studies* 46/2 (Summer 2007), 217–40.

Ansari, Sarfaraz. 'Forced Modernization and Public Policy: A Case Study of Ayub Khan Era (1958–69)' *Journal of Political Studies,* 18/1 (1970), 45–60.

Aqil Shah, 'Pakistan's "Armored" Democracy' *Contemporary South Asia* 4/3 (1995), 26–40.

Asaf, Hussain. 'Ethnicity, National Identity and Praetorianism: The Case of Pakistan' *Asian Survey* 16/10 (1976), 918–30.

Ashton, N.J. 'The Hijacking of a Pact: The Formation of the Baghdad Pact and Anglo-American Tensions in the Middle East, 1955–58', *Review of International Studies* 19/2 (1993), 123–37.

Awan, Waris, Rizwan Ullah Kokab, and Rehana Iqbal, 'Jama'at-i-Islami: Movement for Islamic Constitution and Anti-Ahmadiyah Campaign' *Asian Culture and History* 5/2 (2013), 181–210.

Ayoob, Mohammad. 'Pakistan's Political Development, 1947 to 1970: Bird's Eye View' *Economic and Political Weekly* 6/3–5 (1971),199–204.

_____. 'India as Regional Hegemon: External Opportunities and Internal Constraints' *International Journal* 66, (Summer 1991), 420–48.

_____. 'India In South Asia: The Quest for Regional Predominance' *World Policy Journal* 7/1 (Winter 1989–90), 107–33.

_____. 'The Security Problematic of the Third World' *World Politics* 43/2 (1991), 257–83.

Barber, Benjamin R. 'Jihad vs. McWorld' *The Atlantic Monthly* (March, 1992). <https://www.theatlantic.com/magazine/archive/1992/03/jihad-vs-mcworld/303882/>.

Barrier, Norman G., 'The Arya Samaj and Congress Politics in the Punjab, 1894–1908' *The Journal of Asian Studies* 26/3 (1967), 363–79.

Baxter, Craig. 'Pakistan Votes—1970' *Asian Survey* 11/3 (1971), 197–218.

Bellingham, Justen. 'The 1968–9 Pakistan Revolution: A Students' and Workers' Popular Uprising' *Marxist Left Review* 12, (Winter 2016), 67–74.

Bergen, Peter and Swati Pandey. 'The Madrassa Scapegoat' *The Washington Quarterly* 29/2 (Spring 2006), 115–25.

Bienen, Henry. 'Armed Forces and National Modernization: Continuing the Debate' *Comparative Politics* 16/1 (1983), 1–16.

Bopegamage, A. 'The Military as a Modernizing Agent in India' *Economic Development and Cultural Change* 20/1 (1971), 71–9.

Brahimi, Alia. 'The Taliban's Evolving Ideology' *Working Paper*. (London: LSE Global Governance, July, 2010).

Brasher, Ryan. 'Ethnic Brother or Artificial Namesake? The Construction of Tajik Identity in Afghanistan and Tajikistan' *Berkeley Journal of Sociology* 55, (2011), 97–120.

Bray, John. 'Pakistan at 50: A State in Decline?' *International Affairs* 73/2 (April 1997), 315–31.

Brodkin, E. I. 'United States and India and Pakistan: The Attitudes of the Fifties' *International Affairs (Royal Institute of International Affairs 1944)* 43/4 (1967), 664–77.

Bromund, Ted R. and Lisa Curtis. 'The Pakistan-Britain Terror Connection: Lessons and Warnings for the United States' *Backgrounder/2337* (November 2009), 1–18.

Burki, Shahid Javed. 'Pakistan under Zia, 1977–1988' *Asian Survey* 28/10 (1988), 1082–1100.

Chandio, Amir Ali and Shahida Amir Chandio, 'The Execution of Zulfiqar Ali Bhutto: Its Impacts on the Politics of Sindh' *The Government-Annual Research Journal of Political Science* 2/2 (2013), 1–18.

Chase, Robert S, Emily B. Hill and Paul. Kennedy. 'Pivotal States and U.S. Strategy' *Foreign Affairs* 75/1(1996), 48–9.

Chaudhri, Mohammed Ahsen 'The Principle of Regional Pacts' *Pakistan Horizon* 8/3 (1955), 428–36.

Chisti, Naheed Anjum. 'Jinnah's Balochistan: At Cross Road' *Journal of South Asian Development Studies* 2/2 (June 2013), 71–6.

_____. 'Jinnah's Balochistan: At Cross Road' *Journal of South Asian Development Studies* 2/2 (June 2013), 71–6.

Choudhary, Muhammad Azam. 'Religious Practices at Sufi Shrines in the Punjab' *Pakistan Journal of History and Culture* 31/1 (2010), 1–57.

Choudhury, G.W. 'Pakistan-India Relations' *Pakistan Horizon* 11/2 (1958), 57–64.

Cohen, Youssef, Brian R. Brown, and A.F. K. Organski, 'The Paradoxical Nature of State Making: The Violent Creation of Order' *American Political Science Review* 75/4 (1981), 901–10.

Constituent Assembly of Pakistan. *Debates* 5/2 (March 1949), 14–20.

Constituent Assembly of Pakistan. *Debates* 5/3 (March 1949), 39–43.

Copland, Ian. 'The Princely States, the Muslim League, and the Partition of India in 1947' *The International History Review* 13/1 (1991), 38–69.

Dobell, W. M. 'Ayub Khan as President of Pakistan' *Pacific Affairs* 42/3 (1969), 294–310.

Dunbar, David. 'Pakistan: The Failure of Political Negotiations' *Asian Survey* 12/5 (1972), 444–61.

Dunne, J. Paul. 'Economic Effects of Military Expenditure in Developing Countries' in N. P. Gleditsch, et al. *The Peace Dividend (Contributions to Economic Analysis, Vol.* 235 (1996), 439–63.

Ellen Lust, Ahran. 'The Decline and fall of the Arab State' *Survival: Global Politics and Strategy* 58/2 (2016), 7–34.

Erest, Dawn, 'The Formation of Pan–Arab Ideology in the Interwar years' *International Journal of Middle East Studies* 20/1 (1988), 67–91.

Esposito, John L. 'Islamization: Religion and Politics in Pakistan' *The Muslim World* 72/3–4 (1982), 197–223.

Fair, C. Christine. 'Time for Sober Realism: Renegotiating US Relations with Pakistan' *The Washington Quarterly* 32/2 (2009), 149–72.

_____, and Seth G. Jones. 'Pakistan's War Within' *Survival* 51/6 (January, 2010), 161–88.

_____, and Shuja Nawaz. 'The Changing Pakistan Army Officer Corps' *The Journal of Strategic Studies* 34/1 (2011), 63–94.

_____, Neil Malhotra and Jacob N. Shapiro. 'Democratic Values and Support for Militant Politics: Evidence from a National Survey of Pakistan' *Journal of Conflict Resolution* 58/5 (August 2014), 743–70.

Fish, Steven. 'Islam and Authoritarianism' *World Politics* 55, (October, 2002), 4–37.

Fukuyama, Francis. 'Transitions to the Rule of Law' *Journal of Democracy* 21/1 (January, 2010), 38.

Ganguly, Sumit. 'Pakistan's Never-Ending Story: Why the October Coup Was No Surprise' *Foreign Affairs* 79/2 (March/April, 2000), 3–7.

Ghiaz, Shoaib A. 'Miscarriage of Chief Justice, Media and the Struggle for Judicial Independence' *Law & Social Inquiry* 35/4 (July 2008), 985, 2010.

Ghosh, Suresh. 'Bentinck, Macaulay and the Introduction of English Education in India' *History of Education* 24, (1995), 17.

Gole, Nilufer. 'Islam in Public: New Visibilities and New Imaginaries' *Public Culture* 14/1 (2002),173–90

Graham, William A. 'Traditionalism in Islam: An Essay in Interpretation' *The Journal of Interdisciplinary History* 23/3 (1993), 495–522.

Hale, Henry E. 'Explaining Ethnicity' *Comparative Political Studies* 37/4 (May 2004), 458–9.

Hall, John A. 'Nationalism: Classified and Explained' *Daedalus* 122/3, (Summer 1993), 1–28.

Haq, Farhat. 'Rise of the MQM in Pakistan: Politics of Ethnic Mobilization' *Asian Survey,* 35/11 (1995), 990–1004.

———. 'Women, Islam and the State in Pakistan' *The Muslim World* 86/2 (1996), 158–75.

Haqqani, Husain. 'The Role of Islam in Pakistan's Future' *Washington Quarterly* 28/1 (2004), 83–96.

Henry W. Brands, 'India and Pakistan in American Strategic Planning, 1947–54: The Commonwealth as Collaborator' *The Journal of Imperial and Commonwealth History* 15/1 (1986), 41–54.

Huntington, Samuel P. 'Political Development and Political Decay' *World Politics* 17/3 (1965), 386–430.

———. 'Will more Countries be Democratic?' *Political Science Quarterly* 99/2 (Summer 1984), 193–218.

Hurst, Christopher O. 'Pakistan's Ethnic Divide' *Studies in Conflict & Terrorism* 19/2 (1996), 179–98.

Husain, Mahboob. 'Establishing Constitutional Status of Qadianies: A Study of Parliamentary Debates, 1974' *Pakistan Vision* 14/02 (2012), 76–93.

Imtiaz Ali, 'The Balochistan Problem' *Pakistan Horizon,* 58/2 (2005), 41–62.

Inglehart, Ronald. 'Culture and Democracy' in Ibid., 80–97.

Iqbal, Chawala, et. al. 'Islamization in Pakistan: An Overview' *Journal of Research Society of Pakistan* 52/1 (2015), 265–81.

Iqbal, Javed. 'The Separation of East–Pakistan: Analyzing the Causes and Fixing the Responsibility' *Pakistan Journal of History and Culture* 29/2 (2008), 53–74.

Islam, Nasir. 'Islam and National Identity: The Case of Pakistan and Bangladesh' *International Journal of Middle East Studies* 13/1 (Feb 1981), 55–72.

_____. 'Islam and National Identity: The Case of Pakistan and Bangladesh' *International Journal of Middle East Studies* 13/1 (1981), 55–72.

Jalal, Ayesha. 'Pakistan's Predicament' *Third World Quarterly,* 11/3 (July 1989): 233–38.

_____. 'Conjuring Pakistan: History as Official Imagining' *International Journal of Middle East Studies* 27/1, (1995), 73–89.

Jasse, Richard L. 'The Baghdad Pact: Cold War or Colonialism?' *Middle Eastern Studies* 27/1 (1991), 140–56.

Javaid, Umbreen. 'Movement for Bahawalpur Province' *Journal of Political Studies* 15 (2009), 41–57.

Jost, John T, Christopher M. Feeerico and Jamime L. Napier. 'Political Ideology: Its Structure, Functions, and Elective Affinities' *The Annual Review of Psychology* 60 (2009), 307–37, accessed, July 15, 2016. <https://psych.nyu.edu/jost/Political%20Ideology_Its%20structure,%20 functions,%20and%20elective%20a.pdf>

Kaldor, Mary. 'The Military in Development' *World Development* 4/6 (1976), 459–82.

Kanwal, Lubna. 'Economic Development in Pakistan: A Reflection of Social Division during 1947–1969' *Pakistan Journal of Social Sciences* 35/1 (2015), 497–507.

Karatnycky, Adrian. 'Muslim Countries and Democracy Gap' *Journal of Democracy* 13/1 (January 2002), 99–112.

Kaushik, Surendranath. 'Anti-Ahmadiya Movement in Pakistan' *South Asian Studies* 20/1 (1985), 16–40.

Kazi, Aftab A. 'Ethnic Nationalities, Education, and Problems of National Integration in Pakistan' *Asian Profile*, 16/2 (1988), 147–61.

Kennedy, Charles H. 'Islamization and Legal Reform in Pakistan, 1979–1989' *Pacific Affairs*, 63/1 (1990), 62–77.

———. 'Policies of Ethnic Preference in Pakistan' *Asian Survey* 24/6 (1984), 688–703.

———. 'The Politics of Ethnicity in Sindh' *Asian Survey* 31/10 (October, 1991), 946.

Khan, Adeel. 'Pakistan's Sindhi Ethnic Nationalism: Migration, Marginalization, and the Threat of "Indianization"' *Asian Survey* 42/2 (2002), 213–29.

Khan, Feroz Hassan. 'Rough Neighbours: Afghanistan and Pakistan' *Strategic Insights* 2/1 (January 2003), 1–20.

Khan, Ijaz. 'Contending Identities of Pakistan and the Issue of Democratic Governance' *Peace and Democracy in South Asia* 2/1 & 2 (2006), 50–70.

Khan, Mohammad Ayub. 'Pakistan Perspective' *Foreign Affairs* 38/4 (1960), 547–56.

Khan, Mahmood Amjad. 'Persecution of the Ahmadiyya Community in Pakistan: An Analysis under International Law and International Relations' *Harvard Human Rights Journal* 16/3 (2003): 217.

Khori, Karamatullah K. 'Sixty Years of Pakistan's Foreign Policy' *Pakistan Horizon* 60/2 (April, 2007), 9–12.

Knight, David B. 'Identity and Territory: Geographical Perspectives on Nationalism and Regionalism' *Annals of the Association of American Geographers* 72/4 (December, 1982), 514–31.

Kokab, Rizwan Ullah. 'Constitution Making in Pakistan and East Bengal's Demand for Provincial Autonomy (1947–58)' *Pakistan Vision* 12/2 (2011), 165.

Kramer, Martin. 'Islam vs. Democracy' *Commentary* 95/1 (1993), 35.

Krause, Keith and Michael C. Williams, 'Broadening the Agenda of Security Studies: Politics and Methods' *Mershon Review of International Studies* 40/2 (1996), 229–54.

Krueger, Alan B and Jitka Maleckova. 'Education, Poverty and Terrorism: Is there a Causal Connection' *Journal of Economic Perspectives* 17/4 (2003), 119–44.

Lapidus, Ira M. 'Islamic Revival and Modernity: The Contemporary Movements and the Historical Paradigms' *Journal of the Economic and Social History of the Orient* 40/4 (1997), 444–60.

LaPorte, Robert. 'Succession in Pakistan: Continuity and Change in a Garrison State' *Asian Survey* 9/11 (Nov 1969), 842–61.

LaPorte, Robert. 'Power and Privilege: Influence and Decision–Making in Pakistan' *Pacific Affairs* 50/4 (1977–1978), 673–79.

Lasswell, Harold D. 'The Garrison State' *The American Journal of Sociology* 46/4 (January 1941), 455–68.

Lau, Martin. 'Twenty-Five Years of Hudood Ordinances-A Review' *Washington and Lee Law Review*, 64/4, (September 2007), 1292–96.

Lavoy, Peter R. 'Pakistan's Strategic Culture: A Theoretical Excursion' *Strategic Insights* 6/10 (October 2005), 1-15.

Learner D. and R. D. Robinson, 'Sword and Ploughshares: The Turkish Army as a Modernizing Force' *World Politics* 13/1 (October 1960), 19–44.

Lebovic, James H. 'Spending Priorities and Democratic Rule in Latin America' *The Journal of Conflict Resolution* 45/4 (August, 2001), 427–52.

Lingard, Bob and Sajid Ali, 'Contextualising Education in Pakistan, a White Paper: Global/National Articulations in Education Policy' *Globalisation, Societies and Education* 7/3 (2009), 237–56.

Lisa, Curtis. 'The Reorientation of Pakistan's Foreign Policy Toward its Region' *Contemporary South Asia* 20/2 (2012), 255–69.

Majeed, Ghulshan and Rehana Saeed Hashmi, 'Baloch Resistance during Zulfiqar Ali Bhutto's Era: Causes and Consequences' *South Asian Studies* 29/1. (January–July 2014), 321–31.

Makeig, Douglas C. 'War, No–war and the Indo–Pakistan Negotiating Process' *Pacific Affairs* 60/2 (Summer 1987), 271–94.

Malik, Iftikhar H. 'Ethno-nationalism in Pakistan: A Commentary on Mohajir Qaumi Mahaz (MQM) in Sindh' *South Asia: Journal of South Asian Studies* 18/2 (1995), 49–72.

Malik, Jamal. 'Making of a Council: The Nadwatul Ulema' *Islamic Culture* 68/1, (1994), 1–40.

Maniruzzaman, Talukder. 'Crises in Political Development and the Collapse of the Ayub Regime in Pakistan' *The Journal of Developing Areas* 5/2 (1971), 221–38.

Marriott, Alan. 'Nationalism and Nationality in India and Pakistan' *Geography* 85/2 (April 2000), 173–78.

Maududi, Maulana Syed Abul A'la. 'Matalba-i-Nizam-i-Isami' *Tarjuman ul-Qur'an* 32/1 (1959), 12–18.

Mehmood, Aurangzeb. 'Islamisation of Economy in Pakistan: Past, Present and Future' *Islamic Studies* 41/4, (2002), 675–704.

Melson, Robert and Howard Wolpe. 'Modernization and Politics of Ethnic Communalism: A Theoretical Perspective' *American Political Science Review* 64/4 (December 1970), 1112–30.

Monshipouri, Mahmood and Amjad Samuel, 'Development and Democracy in Pakistan: Tenuous or Plausible Nexus?' *Asian Survey* 35/11 (1995), 973–89.

Mura, Andrea. 'A Genealogical Inquiry into Early Islamism: the Discourse of Hasan al-Banna' *Journal of Political Ideologies* 17/1 (2012), 61–85.

————. 'The Inclusive Dynamics of Islamic Universalism: From the Vantage Point of Sayyid Qutb's Critical Philosophy' *Comparative Philosophy* 5/1 (2014), 29–54.

Mushtaq, Muhammad. 'Regional Identities in Quest of Separate Provinces: A New Challenge for the Pakistani Federation' *Journal of Political Studies* 23/1 (2016), 289.

Naseem, S.M. 'Economists and Pakistan's Economic Development: Is there a Connection?' *The Pakistan Development Review* 37/4 (1998), 401–29.

Nasr, Seyyed Vali Raza. 'Democracy and Islamic Revivalism' *Political Science Quarterly* 110/2 (Summer 1995), 261–85.

————. 'The Rise of Sunni Militancy in Pakistan: The Changing Role of Islamism and the Ulama in Society and Politics' *Modern Asian Studies* 34 (2000), 139–80.

————. 'Military Rule, Islamism and Democracy in Pakistan' *The Middle East Journal* 58/2 (2004), 195–209.

Nguyen, Quynh T. and Dhushyanth Raju. 'Private School Participation in Pakistan' *The Lahore Journal of Economics* 20/1 (Summer 2015), 1–46.

Nielsen, Anja Dalgaard 'Violent Radicalization in Europe: What we Know and What we Don't Know' *Studies in Conflict and Terrorism* 33, (2010), 797–814.

Nietzsche, Marx. et. al. 'Modernization, Cultural Change, and the

Persistence of Traditional Values' *American Sociological Review* 65/1 (Feb, 2000), 19–51.

Noman, Omar. 'Pakistan and General Zia: Era and Legacy' *Third World Quarterly* 11/1 (January 1989), 50–4.

Notes: 'The Pakistani Lawyers' Movement and the Popular Currency of Judicial Power' *Harvard Law Review* 123/7 (May, 2010), 1705–26.

Parveen, Kausar. 'The Role of Opposition in Constitution Making: Debate on the Objectives Resolution' *Pakistan Vision* 11/1 (2010), 141–63.

Puri, Balraj. 'From Ideology- to Territory-Based Nation: Pakistan's Transition and Lessons for India' *Economic and Political Weekly* 37/9 (March, 2002), 834–35.

Qasmi, Ali Usman. 'God's Kingdom on Earth? Politics of Islam in Pakistan, 1947–1969' *Modern Asian Studies* 44/6 (2010), 1197–1253.

Rahman, Fazlur 'Muslim Modernism in the Indo–Pakistan Sub–continent' *Bulletin of the School of Oriental and African Studies* 21/1 (1958), 82–99.

_____. 'Islamic Modernism: Its Scope, Method and Alternatives' *International Journal of Middle East Studies* 1/4 (1970), 317–33.

Rahman, Zainab. 'State Restrictions on the Ahmadiyya Sect in Indonesia and Pakistan: Islam or Political Survival?' *Australian Journal of Political Science* 49/3 (2014), 408–22.

Rana, Amir 'Jihadi Print Media in Pakistan: An Overview', *Conflict and Peace Studies* 1/1 (2008), 1–18.

Rehman, Javaid. 'Islam, War on Terror and the Future of Muslim Minorities in the United Kingdom: Dilemmas of Multiculturalism in the Aftermath of the London Bombings' *Human Rights Quarterly* 29/4 (November, 2007), 845–66.

Rizvi, Hasan–Askari. 'The Legacy of Military Rule in Pakistan' *Survival* 31/3 (May–June 1989), 255–68.

Robert, McMahon J. 'United States Cold War Strategy in South Asia: Making a Military Commitment to Pakistan, 1947–1954' *The Journal of American History* 75/3 (1988), 812–40.

Rousseau, David and A. Maurits van der Veen, 'The Emergence of a Shared Identity: An Agent-Based Computer Simulation of Idea Diffusion' *The Journal of Conflict Resolution* 49/5 (October 2005), 686–712.

Sachedina, Abdul Aziz. 'The Role of Islam in the Public Square: Guidance or Governance?' *Islamic Democratic Discourse: Theory, Debates, and Philosophical Perspectives* 12/2 (2006),173–92.

Saeed, Sadia. 'Pakistani Nationalism and the State Marginalization of the Ahmadiyya Community in Pakistan', *Studies in Ethnicity and Nationalism* 7/3 (2007), 132–52.

Samad, Yunas. 'Pakistan or Punjabistan: Crisis of National Identity' *International Journal of Punjab Studies* 2/1 (1995), 23–42.

Sanders, M. Jimmy. 'Ethnic Boundaries and Identity in Plural Societies' *Annual Review of Sociology* 28, (2002), 327–57.

Sayeed, Khalid Bin. 'Religion and Nation-Building in Pakistan' *Middle East Journal* 17/3 (1963), 279–91.

———. 'Pakistan in 1983: Internal Stresses more Serious than External Problems' *Asian Survey* 24/2 (February 1984), 219–28.

Schmidt, John R. 'The Unravelling of Pakistan' *Survival* 51/3 (2009), 29–54.

Schwartz, Benjamin I. 'Culture, Modernity, and Nationalism—Further Reflections' *Daedalus: Reconstructing Nations and States* 122/3 (Summer, 1993), 207–26.

Shahzad, Aisha. 'Relative Deprivation in Pakistan: An Analysis of the Seraiki Movement' *Pakistan Perspective* 20/1 (2015), 69.

Shapiro, Jacob N. and C. Christine Fair. 'Understanding Support for Islamist Militancy?' *International Security* 34/3 (Winter 2009/2010), 79–118.

Siddiqi, Mazheruddin. 'General Characteristics of Muslim Modernism' *Islamic Studies* 9/1 (1970), 33–68.

———. 'Intellectual Bases of Muslim Modernism: I' *Islamic Studies* 9/2 (1970), 149–71.

Spencer, Jonathan. 'Post–Colonialism and the Political Imagination' *The Journal of the Royal Anthropological Institute* 3/1 (March, 1997), 1–19.

Stern, Jessica. 'Pakistan's Jihad Culture' *Foreign Affairs* 79/6 (2000), 115–26.

Subrahmanyam, K. 'India's Security Challenges and Responses: Evolving a Security Doctrine' *Strategic Analysis* 11/1 (April 1987), 6–15.

Syed, Anwar H. 'Political Parties and the Nationality Question in Pakistan' *Journal of South Asian and Middle Eastern Studies* 12/1 (Fall 1988), 42–75.

Tanwir, Farooq. 'Religious Parties and Politics in Pakistan' *International Journal of Comparative Sociology*, 43/3–5 (2002), 25–268.

Tarjuman ul-Qur'an, *Jamat-i-Islami Publications* 23/4 (March 1950), 175–9.

Thornton, Thomas P. 'The New Phase in US-Pakistani Relations' *Foreign Affairs* 68/3 (1989), 142–59.

Titus, Paul and Nina Swidler, 'Knights, Not Pawns: Ethnic Nationalism and Regional Dynamics in Postcolonial Balochistan' *International Journal of Middle East Studies*, 32/1 (Feb., 2000), 47–69.

Usmani, Maulana Shabbir Ahmad. 'Constituent Assembly of Pakistan', *Constitutional Debates* 5/3, (March 1949), 43–6.

Weinbaum, Marvin G. 'Civic Culture and Democracy in Pakistan' *Asian Survey* 36/7 (July 1996), 639–54.

_____. 'Pakistan and Afghanistan: The Strategic Relationship' *Asian Survey* 31/6. (1991), 496–511.

Wilcox, Wayne Ayres. 'The Pakistan Coup d'état of 1958' *Pacific Affairs* 38/2 (1965), 142–63.

_____. 'Pakistan: A Decade of Ayub' *Asian Survey* 9/2 (1969), 87–93.

Khalid B. Sayeed, 'Development Strategy under Ayub Khan' *Journal of Developing Societies* 14/2 (1979), 76–84.

Winthrop, Rebecca and Corinne Graff. 'Beyond Madrasas: Assessing the Link between Education and Militancy in Pakistan' *Working Paper 2* (June, 2010), 21–6.

Young, Dennis O. 'Overcoming the Obstacles to Establishing a Democratic State in Afghanistan' *Report* (2007), 5–6.

Zaidi, Syed Manzar Abbas. 'Madrassa Education in Pakistan: Controversies, Challenges and Prospects', *Report* 3 (March, 2013), 28.

Zakaria, Fareed. 'Islam, Democracy, and Constitutional Liberalism' *Political Science Quarterly* 119/1 (Spring, 2004), 1–20.

Zaman, Muhammad Qasim. 'Islamic Modernism and the Sharia in Pakistan' *Occasional Papers*, 8, Yale Law School Legal Scholarship Repository, Yale Law School (2014), 9–14.

Zia, Shehrbano 'The Reinvention of Feminism in Pakistan' *Feminist Review* 91/1 (2009), 29–46.

Index